MONEY DYNAMICS

How To Build Financial Independence

MONEY DYNAMICS

How To Build Financial Independence

Venita VanCaspel

President, VanCaspel & Co., Inc.
Houston, Texas

RESTON PUBLISHING COMPANY, INC.
Reston, Virginia

A Prentice-Hall Company

Library of Congress Cataloging in Publication Data

Van Caspel, Venita,
  Money dynamics.

  1. Investments.   2. Finance, Personal.
I. Title.
HG4521.V17   332'.024   74-32483
ISBN 0-87909-515-6
ISBN 0-87909-514-8 pbk.

Drawings by Jan Smulcer.

16 15 14

Printed in the United States of America.

*To my delightful husband, Jack, who is
secure enough within himself to allow
me the freedom to share with you
how to become financially secure*

Acknowledgments

So many have touched my life and helped me toward my goals that this page could not possibly cover them all. I would like to express my special thanks to Jan Smulcer, who did the drawings and contributes so much to making my life a cheery one; to Helen Fourmy, my long, faithful and excellent associate; to JoLieta Davis, whose talent smooths the ripples of my business life; and to all the other members of the Van Caspel Team of Financial Planners.

Contents

Preface

We live in a country with the highest per capita income ever known to mankind; yet of every 100 of our citizens who reach the age of 65, 95 are flat broke! Of every 100 who reach their "golden years," only 2 are financially independent, 23 must continue to work, and 75 are dependent on friends, relatives, or charity.

They lost the money game. The money game is not like any other game. You cannot choose whether you'll play. You cannot choose to sit out a hand or move to another game. For this game—the money game—is the only game in town.

Since you have no choice but to play, then the only intelligent thing to do is to learn the rules and play to win! Losing means spending 20 to 30 years of your life in angry frustration in a state of financial insecurity.

If you have no choice but to play the money game, and if it is so essential to win, why weren't you taught how to play it successfully in school?

I really don't know. There is an educational void in our country. We are spending millions of dollars teaching both our youth and our adults to earn dollars; yet we are not teaching them what to do with these dollars once they are earned. I find that they are making some tragic mistakes.

Somewhere, somehow, back in the dark pages of history, a false idea germinated and grew. This sinister concept was that "money is the root of all evil." This is not true. Money is not "the root of all evil." It is the misuse of money that brings corruption and human suffering. The right use of money provides the necessary food for your family; it helps build hospitals to aid them in regaining their health when they are ill; it helps build churches in which they may worship; it provides wood and bricks to be used in constructing a roof over their heads; and it provides fabrics to make the clothes that will protect their bodies from the cold winds of winter and the blistering heat of summer.

Upon you falls the responsibility to be a good steward of every dollar that comes your way.

I feel I should warn you now that applying the information contained in this book will not give you instant wealth. If I knew how to do that, as committed as I am to helping others become financially independent, do you really think I would be willing to sell that secret for so small a sum of money as the price of this book or to let you subscribe to my handy dandy investment advisory service?

On the other hand, what are your choices? I can see only three:

1 · Try to make it fast with only a very slight hope of success. (Look around you and unemotionally calculate your odds.)
2 · Try to make it slowly, with a rather good chance for success.
3 · Don't try at all. This is the choice that is being made by the majority of your fellow citizens.

I am convinced that if you are granted a reasonable amount of time, have the ability and willingness to earn an average wage, have the discipline to save a small portion of your earnings, and have the intelligence to apply the principles taught in this book, you can become financially independent. This desirable state does not take brilliance or luck. It requires discipline and the ability and willingness to make your dollars work for you as hard as you had to work to get them.

This book is written in first person and addressed directly to *you*. The only thing I have to offer is the observations and experiences that have been mine during my 14 years as a stockbroker and financial planner. During this career I have conducted over 100 public investment seminars, spoken to innumerable service and social clubs, and appeared as a guest on numerous television and radio talk shows. For the past six years I have been the author and moderator of a 30-minute television show called "Successful Texans," shown on a CBS affiliate station. Each week on this show I interview a Texan who has attained success under our free enterprise system. Daily, in my office, I counsel from five to six persons or couples, spending an hour and a half with each individual appointment, endeavoring to help them map a workable financial plan to fit their objectives. My aim is to help them and all with whom I come into contact to become financially independent. I feel this is my calling—my justification for having passed this way.

This book is written to make you knowledgeable about money matters—to inspire you, to give you hope, to motivate you to act. For unless you apply this knowledge I will have left you financially where I found you.

Financial planning must be personal. You are different from any other person. You were created as a unique individual and have developed in your own unique way. You have different financial objectives, different assets, a different tax bracket, and a different temperament from even your closest friend. Your financial program, therefore, must be designed for you and for you alone because you are special.

If you and I could sit down and plan your financial future, I would ask you many pertinent questions about you and your money. I would then endeavor to design a program that fits not only your financial needs but your emotional needs as well. To design a program for your financial needs is relatively simple, once I know all the facts, but mapping a course that fits your temperament and your prejudices and then communicating these ideas to you in such a way that you will understand and then act upon them is a continuous challenge.

Since you and I may never have this opportunity, I have designed this book to give you a step-by-step guide to be used in designing your own financial blueprint.

I have found that financial planning is like navigation. If you know where you are and where you want to go, navigation is not so difficult. It's when you don't know the two points that navigating the right course becomes difficult. To illustrate this logic, let's use a comparison. Assume you board a large luxury oceanliner with its mighty engines running in preparation to leave port. You go into the chart room and ask the captain to show you on his charts your present location, what his next port of call will be, your destination, and the route he is planning to take to get there, and he answers, "I really don't know." Would you be confident of his reaching his destination? Would you want to be a passenger on his ship?

If your answer is "No," use this same intelligence in plotting your own financial course. For you are the captain of your vitally important financial ship.

Enter now the chart room to plot your financial future. Here you will learn how to determine your present position, where you want to be on a certain date, and alternate courses available for arriving at your destination.

In my years of financial planning I have never met a person who planned to fail, but I have met many who failed to plan. Unfortunately, the results have been the same.

I have dedicated a large portion of my life to helping others like you to develop and successfully execute their plan for financial independence. Through the pages of this book I have endeavored to do the same for you.

To assure that you will have a solid foundation upon which to build, it will be necessary to begin the book with some tables and charts that may at first glance not seem as exciting as we both would like for them to be. But do persevere, devour them, and let them seep deeply into your subconscious mind. You'll find them invaluable benchmarks to the successful accomplishment of your predetermined worthwhile goal.

VENITA VANCASPEL

Dear
Investor

• **YOU ARE
AN INVESTOR**

My salutation to you is "Dear Investor" because you are an investor.
You are investing the wealth that comes your way either in present goods
and services or in future goods and services. You cannot choose whether
you will invest, but you can choose how you will invest. The wisdom you
bring to bear on this choice will have a greater influence on your future
standard of living than the amount of money that comes your way.

Your first decision is between today and tomorrow. Do you want to
consume all you earn today and hope for the best for tomorrow? As short-
sighted as this may seem, it is the course being taken by the vast majority
of your fellow citizens.

Why in a nation with a high per capita income and unparalleled
prosperity do 98 percent of our citizens reach age 65 without having made
adequate preparation to retire in financial dignity?

- ## FIVE REASONS
  ## SO MANY FAIL

There are many answers. From my years of counselling a vast number of people of all ages and incomes, I have found that there are five basic reasons: procrastination, failure to set a financial goal, ignorance of what money must do to accomplish that goal, failure to understand and apply our tax laws, and buying the wrong life insurance. In this chapter we will look at procrastination and ignorance, the twins of financial failure.

- ## PROCRASTINATION

Procrastination is a deadly enemy of your obligation to be able to retire in financial dignity. Sometimes we confuse goals and obligations. A larger home, a boat, travel to foreign lands—all these can be classified as goals. But preparing to retire in financial dignity is more than a goal. It is your obligation, a debt that you owe yourself. With proper financial planning and sound money management, it is a debt that you can pay, making your retirement years happy instead of haphazard, comfortable instead of dependent.

I have observed that in the early years of a life, when spending habits are formed, thoughts of retirement are so far away that they have little relationship to current spending patterns. There develops the habit of spending all that is earned on current needs with no thought of future needs, and the habit becomes reinforced with the same passing of time that brings retirement closer. Then when retirement time is so near as to be of immediate concern, it is often too late to make adequate preparation.

- ## THREE
  ## FINANCIAL PERIODS

A normal lifetime can be divided into three financial periods.

The first period is the "Learning Period," when you learn the vocation that will enable you to earn the money you need to sustain and enjoy your life and the lives of those dependent upon you. This usually lasts for the first 25 years of your life. The second period is the "Earning Period", when you pursue the vocation you learned during the first period. This lasts about 40 years, from age 25 to 65. The third period is determined by the decisions you make during the second period of your life. It will either be your "Yearning Years" or your "Golden Years."

If you are a male, you will probably spend 15 to 20 years in this third period. If you are female and make it to 65, plan your finances well for you'll probably be around for a very long time.

Let's look at each of these periods.

The Learning Period • I hope that you begin learning at birth and never cease to learn until you bid this world good-bye. However, your formal learning period will probably last for your first 25 years, depending on your choice of a vocation.

If you are considering whether a college education is a good investment for yourself, your children, or your grandchildren, the answer is Yes. It will cost between $12,000 and $35,000, depending on the choice of schools, vocation, and how many years before entering college. But the investment can yield a good return. Studies show that a college graduate earns from $250,000 to $279,000 more during his life than does a person with only a high school degree. A college education can bring more than just financial rewards. The ability to think and to plan is stimulated in college. There are fewer divorces among college graduates. It can add a greatly enlarged dimension to life.

There are many who like to believe that financial gains come to a person through luck. I personally do not believe in luck and have found that luck occurs when preparedness and opportunity get together. The more you place yourself in the path of opportunity, the "luckier" you will probably become.

There are many who remind me of the man who stood in front of a wood-burning stove and said, "Give me some heat and I'll give you some wood." That's not the nature of a wood-burning stove. The wood must come first. The same is true of preparation, so do not skimp on that important ingredient. Put adequate wood in the burner, and it will yield to you the warmth of financial security.

The Earning Period • The second period of your life is the "Earning Period."

Do you realize how much wealth will pass through your hands during the 40 years between 25 and 65? Do you just consider your income as "so much a month," and never add up the tremendous amount of wealth that is passing your way?

If you never earn more than $300 a month, one-eighth of a million dollars will pass your way. If you earn as much as $525, one-quarter of a million dollars will pass your way. If you earn as much as $1,000, one-half of a million dollars will pass your way. That's a lot of money. The problem is how to keep some of it from passing through your fingers.

The Secret of Accumulation of Wealth • Let me share with you a very simple secret for the accumulation of weath. The secret has only ten words in it and is so simple you will be tempted to discard it—but if you remember it and put it to use, it will be of great value to you for the remainder of your life. The secret is this: "A part of all I earn is mine to keep."

You are tempted to say, "Everything I earn is mine to keep." It isn't so, is it? It belongs to the baker, the butcher, the mortgage company, the church.

You must learn to pay yourself first. If not first, at least along with all the others. If you were to place in a line, in the order of their importance to you, all those whom you wanted to receive a portion of your paycheck, would you place yourself at the head of the line? Is that where you have been putting yourself? If you are like so many others, you've put yourself at the end of the line, trying to save what is left over and finding that your ability to spend up to and beyond your income is utterly amazing.

....over $300,000 will pass through your

hands during your earning years....

Monthly Income	10 Years	20 Years	30 Years	40 Years
400	48000	96000	144000	192000
500	60000	120000	180000	240000
600	72000	144000	216000	288000
800	96000	192000	288000	384000
1000	120000	240000	360000	480000
1500	180000	360000	540000	720000
2000	240000	480000	720000	800000

If you were to save one-tenth of all you earned and did this for ten years, how much money would you have? A whole year's salary at one time, of course. And that's not all, for you would put this money to work, and before long you would have much more working for you.

The Yearning or Golden Years • The third period of your life will be your retirement years. These will either be your "yearning" years or

your "golden" years, depending on the financial decisions you make
during your "earning" years.

   Will this period of your life take care of itself? The answer is NO.
The future belongs to those who prepare for it—and how tragically few
are preparing! Perhaps they have been lulled into a false sense of
security by the cozy sound of the words "Social Security." By the time
they have discovered that it should have been called "Social Insecurity,"
it is far too late.

   Social Security was never designed to give you or your fellow
countrymen financial independence. It was created to prevent mass
destitution. It was meant to give you a base upon which to build, and
it is your responsibility to build on this base.

   It may surprise you to learn that when you reach the age to qualify
for Social Security benefits, if your income from it and other sources is
insufficient for you to live in financial dignity, making it necessary for
you to continue to work, you will forfeit all or most of your Social
Security benefits each month until you reach age 72.

   Today more than 2¼ million of our citizens over 65 are caught in
this financial trap, forcing them to lose their Social Security benefits.
Most of them paid into the system their hard-earned dollars all of their
working years, but they are disqualified from receiving their benefits
because these are not enough to keep body and soul together.

   If they had made provisions outside of Social Security, they
could be receiving unlimited income from capital in the form of dividends, interest, and royalties and still receive their Social Security
checks.

   You may live a long time; yet longevity may be a mixed blessing.
You may decide how long you will work, or it may be decided for you,
but the decision of how long you will live is not in your hands.

   Present day medical science is getting so good at making us live longer that for every ten years we live, they add another four years to our life expectancy. Medical science may be adding years to your life, but it is still up to you to add some life to those years. Money is a necessity. It will not of itself bring you happiness—it will only give you options. However, I have yet to meet a person who found joy in poverty.

Have you ever considered what the difference in the eyes of the world is between an "old man" and an "elderly gentleman"? It's no other than income.

• THREE SOURCES
OF INCOME

There are three sources of income.

The first is you at work. However, there will come a time that regardless of how badly you want to work, the world will not let you. It will retire you.

The second source is your money at work. If you have made proper preparation and turned some of your past income into capital, there will come a time when you will no longer have to work for your money, but you can change places with your money and let your money work for you. I have found that income from capital is immensely more secure than income from labor.

The third source of income is charity.

Man at work, money at work, charity—which do you want to depend on at age 65?

Since "man at work" may not be an option open to you and "charity" has rarely brought happiness, apply your intelligence toward assuring yourself that there is sufficient "money at work" to retire in financial dignity.

• HOW MUCH WILL
YOU NEED PER MONTH?

How much will you need at retirement time? I do not know. Several factors will enter into this calculation. The number of years you have before you reach retirement, what inflation will have done to the cost of living by then, what standard of living you desire at that time, and what rate of return you will be receiving on your funds—all will influence the amount that will be required.

We can try to calculate how much income you will need at retirement. Let's begin with what you would need if you were retiring today; then adjust for what you feel will be the yearly rate of inflation.

Table 1 shows rates of inflation from 2½ to 12 percent and years until retirement from 10 years to 35 years.

Table 1. Additional Income Needed (in Dollars) at Retirement, with Various Inflation Rates

Years until retirement	2½%	3%	3½%	5%	8%	10%	12%
10	1.28	1.34	1.41	1.63	2.16	2.59	3.11
11	1.31	1.38	1.46	1.71	2.33	2.85	2.48
12	1.34	1.43	1.51	1.80	2.52	3.14	3.90
13	1.38	1.47	1.56	1.89	2.72	3.45	4.36
14	1.41	1.51	1.62	1.98	2.94	3.80	4.89
15	1.45	1.56	1.68	2.08	3.17	4.18	5.47
16	1.48	1.60	1.73	2.18	3.43	4.60	6.13
17	1.52	1.65	1.79	2.29	3.70	5.05	6.87
18	1.56	1.70	1.86	2.41	4.00	5.56	7.69
19	1.60	1.75	1.92	2.53	4.32	6.12	8.61
20	1.64	1.81	1.99	2.65	4.66	6.73	9.65
21	1.68	1.86	2.06	2.79	5.03	7.40	10.80
22	1.72	1.92	2.13	2.93	5.44	8.14	12.10
23	1.76	1.97	2.21	3.07	5.87	8.95	13.55
24	1.81	2.03	2.28	3.23	6.34	9.85	15.18
25	1.85	2.09	2.36	3.39	6.85	10.83	17.00
26	1.90	2.16	2.45	3.56	7.40	11.92	19.04
27	1.95	2.22	2.53	3.73	7.99	13.11	21.32
28	2.00	2.29	2.62	3.92	8.63	14.42	23.88
29	2.05	2.36	2.71	4.12	9.32	15.86	26.75
30	2.10	2.43	2.81	4.32	10.06	17.45	29.96
31	2.15	2.50	2.91	4.54	10.87	19.19	33.56
32	2.20	2.58	3.01	4.76	11.74	21.11	37.58
33	2.26	2.65	3.11	5.00	12.68	23.23	42.09
34	2.32	2.73	3.22	5.25	13.69	25.55	47.14
35	2.37	2.81	3.33	5.52	14.79	28.10	52.80

To calculate, subtract your age from 65 to give you the years until retirement, and read across to the rate of inflation you feel is safe to assume. This will give you how many additional dollars you will need when you retire.

For example, assume that you would need $1,000 per month if you were retiring today, that you are age 45, that you plan to retire in 20 years at age 65, and that you feel the government can slow inflation to 5 percent. (Unfortunately, not many economists today would agree.) Go down the left-hand column to 20 and across four columns to 2.65, your adjustment factor. Now let's adjust: $1,000 × 2.65 = $2,650. This would be the amount you would need per month in 20 years to obtain the same housing, food, and clothing as you do with $1,000 today.

Inflation will probably not accommodate you by stopping when you retire so you should plan an additional amount to cover continued inflation.

• HOW MUCH CAPITAL DOES THIS REQUIRE?

What goal should you set for yourself to have a monthly income of approximately $2,650 per month at age 65? Assume also that you will not receive a pension from your company. How much capital will it take to produce $2,650 per month?

Shall we use a 6 percent yield? If so, we will need $530,000 of capital ($2,650 × 200 = $530,000). That's a lot of capital. Before you become discouraged, remember you have 20 years before you need it, and if you decide to use a portion of your principal each month during retirement, this amount can be reduced. There is nothing sacred about principal. The sacred thing is to make you and it come out together!

Table 2 shows the monthly amount you would need to save at 6 percent compounded to reach goals of $100,000 to $500,000.

Table 2. Monthly Savings Needed at Six Percent Interest (Compounded Annually) to Attain Predetermined Amount of Capital

Age now	Years to retirement	Months to retirement	Desired amount			
			$100,000	$200,000	$300,000	$500,000
25	40	480	$ 51	$ 102	$ 153	$ 255
30	35	420	70	140	210	350
35	30	360	99	198	297	495
40	25	300	143	286	429	715
45	20	240	213	426	639	1,065
50	15	180	337	674	1,011	1,685
55	10	120	596	1,192	3,576	2,980

See how time helps in accomplishing your goal? If your goal is $200,000 and you begin saving at age 25, you can reach it by saving $102 per month. At age 40 the amount increases to $286 and at age 45 to $426 per month.

• TIME,
NOT INSTANT PUDDING

Time can be a great ally in accomplishing your financial goal. Use it to your advantage, rather than trying to make it fast, as tempting as that may be.

You will be tempted, for we live in an age of "Instants." We drink "instant coffee," eat "instant pudding," spoon "instant soup." Do not make the mistake of trying to carry this over to your money world. It takes time to accumulate a living estate. Many have difficulty accepting this fact of life. Many of our citizens have adopted an attitude of impatience, perhaps at the cost of serenity that is often characteristic of the Oriental. On the other hand, impatience to get things done deserves much of the credit for the achievements of Americans in building the wealthiest nation in the world.

Coming to grips with time is necessary because we all have been alloted just a certain amount of it. Time is a priceless commodity. A beer commercial says that "You only go around once in life, so grab all the gusto you can, even in the beer you drink." This recognizes the value of time and points up our great impatience.

Impatience can be a stimulus to getting things done. In managing your investments it can be disastrous. The enormous profits in managing lotteries and in owning legalized gambling in Las Vegas are monuments to the impatience of many who desire to get rich quickly.

Incidentally, I find that "rich," or even "comfortable," has different meanings to different people. To some I find it means $100,000, and to others it means a million dollars.

• IGNORANCE OF
WHAT MONEY MUST DO

The second reason for financial failure is the ignorance of what money must do to accomplish a financial goal.

In 1748 Benjamin Franklin wrote, "Money is of a prolific generating nature. Money can beget money, and its offspring can beget more." His was a definition and joyous explanation of the nature of money and one that can be of great value to you. Franklin's words "Money is of a prolific, generating nature" have a biblical ring to them, as well they may because it is in the Bible that we first become aware that we are required to be good stewards of money.

In Matthew 25: 14–29 we find this illustration:

> Again, the Kingdom of Heaven can be illustrated by the story of a man going into another country, who called together his servants and loaned them money to invest for him while he was gone. He gave $5,000 to one, $2,000 to another, and $1,000 to the last—dividing it in proportion to their abilities—and then left on his trip. The man who received the $5,000 began immediately to buy and sell with it and soon earned another $5,000. The man with $2,000 went right to work, too, and earned another $2,000.
>
> But the man who received the $1,000 dug a hole in the ground and hid the money for safekeeping. After a long time their master returned from his trip and called them to him to account for his money. The man to whom he had entrusted the $5,000 brought him $10,000.
>
> His master praised him for good work. "You have been faithful in handling this small amount," he told him, "so now I will give you many more responsibilities. Begin the joyous tasks I have assigned to you." Next came the man who had received the $2,000, with the report, "Sir, you gave me $2,000 to use, and I have doubled it."
>
> Good work, his master said. "You are a good and faithful servant. You have been faithful over this small amount, so now I will give you much more."
>
> Then the man with the $1,000 came and said, "Sir, I knew you were a hard man, and I was afraid you would rob me of what I earned, so I hid your money in the earth and here it is." But his master replied, "Wicked man! Lazy slave! Since you knew I would demand your profit, you should at least have put my money into the bank so I could have some interest. Take the money from this man and give it to the man with the $10,000. For the man who uses well what he is given shall be given more, and he shall have abundance. But from the man who is unfaithful, even what little responsibility he has shall be taken from him."

Let's analyze what the master considered good stewardship. He praised the two who traded with the money entrusted to them and gave them more. He severely reprimanded the one who dug a hole and buried the money saying, "You should at *least* have put the money into the bank so I could have some interest." Note, however, that this was not what he recommended. Had the servant lived in the United States during the periods when our banks paid 3 percent interest, in order for the money to have doubled, the master would have to have taken a 24-year trip. Even if he had earned up to 5 percent, it would have taken 14.4 years. By most standards that would be a very long trip.

Table 3 shows the rates paid by savings and loan associations and by banks from 1947 through 1974.

Table 3. Interest Rates (Percent) Paid by Savings and Loan Associations and by Banks

Year	Savings accounts in savings associations	Deposits in commercial banks
1947	2.3%	0.9%
1948	2.3	0.9
1949	2.4	0.9
1950	2.5	0.9
1951	2.6	1.1
1952	2.7	1.2
1953	2.8	1.2
1954	2.9	1.3
1955	2.9	1.4
1956	3.0	1.6
1957	3.3	2.1
1958	3.38	2.21
1959	3.53	2.36
1960	3.86	2.56
1961	3.90	2.71
1962	4.08	3.18
1963	4.17	3.31
1964	4.19	3.42
1965	4.23	3.69
1966	4.45	4.04
1967	4.67	4.24
1968	4.68	4.48
1969	4.80	4.87
1970	5.06	4.95
1971	5.33	4.78
1972	5.40	4.65
1973	5.50	5.12
1974	5.55	5.15

• THREE THINGS YOU CAN DO WITH A DOLLAR

There are only three things that you can do with a dollar—"spend," "lend," or "own." If you choice is to "spend," you have eliminated the other two choices. If you decide not to "spend" it now, but to spend it later for something you'd rather have at that time, then you have two choices open to you. You may "lend" it to one of the many savings institutions, placing it in what is commonly called a "guaranteed" or fixed dollar position. We'll look at all the ways this can be done in the chapter entitled "Lending Your Dollars." The third thing you can do with your dollar is to "own." You may own shares of American industry, real estate, energy, commodities, precious metals, or jewels. We will discuss the many ways you can own throughout this book.

For the present, let's take a good look at what effect time, the rate of return, and the amount of money you have put to work will have in accomplishing your financial goal.

• THE EIGHTH WONDER

The best way for you to obtain a graphic picture of this is to study compound interest tables. Compound interest tables are fascinating. In my opinion, the "Eighth Wonder of the World" is not the Astrodome, but compound interest.

You will find the following collection of tables helpful in your financial programming. Table 4 gives calculations showing $10,000 lump sum at varying rates compounded annually—end of year values. Table 5 lists the results of saving $1,200 per year at varying rates compounded annually—end of year values. Table 6 shows the lump sum required to equal $100,000 at the end of a specified period—varying rates. Finally, Table 7 shows the approximate annual investment required to equal $100,000 at the end of a specified period—varying rates.

Let's put Table 4 to use to help you program your financial independence.

$10,000 Lump Sum • Assume you have $10,000. What difference does time make?

Years	@ 5%
10	$16,288
20	26,532
30	43,219
40	70,399

Now let's look at the difference an additional 5 percent in the rate of return can make.

Years	@ 5%	@ 10%	Difference
10	$16,288	$ 25,937	$ 9,649
20	26,532	67,274	40,742
30	43,219	174,494	131,275
40	70,399	492,592	422,193

Now let's use Table 5 to help in your programming.

Table 4. $10,000 Lump Sum at Varying Rates Compounded Annually—End of Year Values

	5th Yr.	10th Yr.	15th Yr.	20th Yr.	25th Yr.	30th Yr.	35th Yr.	40th Yr.
1%	10,510	11,046	11,609	12,201	12,824	13,478	14,166	14,888
2%	11,040	12,189	13,458	14,859	16,406	18,113	19,998	22,080
3%	11,592	13,439	15,579	18,061	20,937	24,272	28,138	32,620
4%	12,166	14,802	18,009	21,911	26,658	32,433	39,460	48,010
5%	12,762	16,288	20,789	26,532	33,863	43,219	55,160	70,399
6%	13,382	17,908	23,965	32,071	42,918	57,434	76,860	102,857
7%	14,025	19,671	27,590	38,696	54,274	76,122	106,765	149,744
8%	14,693	21,589	31,721	46,609	68,484	100,626	147,853	217,245
9%	15,386	23,673	36,424	56,044	86,230	132,676	204,139	314,094
10%	16,105	25,937	41,772	67,274	108,347	174,494	281,024	492,592
11%	16,850	28,394	47,845	80,623	135,854	228,922	385,748	650,008
12%	17,623	31,058	54,735	96,462	170,000	299,599	527,996	930,509
13%	18,424	33,945	62,542	115,230	212,305	391,158	720,685	1,327,815
14%	19,254	37,072	71,379	137,434	264,619	509,501	981,001	1,888,835
15%	20,113	40,455	81,370	163,665	329,189	662,117	1,331,755	2,678,635
16%	21,003	44,114	92,655	194,607	408,742	858,498	1,803,140	3,787,211
17%	21,924	48,068	105,387	231,055	506,578	1,110,646	2,435,034	5,338,687
18%	22,877	52,338	119,737	273,930	626,686	1,433,706	3,279,972	7,503,783
19%	23,863	56,946	135,895	324,294	773,880	1,846,753	4,407,006	10,516,675
20%	24,883	61,917	154,070	383,375	953,962	2,373,763	5,906,682	14,697,715
21%	25,937	67,274	174,494	452,592	1,173,908	3,044,816	7,897,469	20,484,002
22%	27,027	73,046	197,422	533,576	1,442,101	3,897,578	10,534,018	28,470,377
23%	28,153	79,259	223,139	628,206	1,768,592	4,979,128	14,017,769	39,464,304
24%	29,316	85,944	251,956	738,641	2,165,419	6,348,199	18,610,540	54,559,126
25%	30,517	93,132	284,217	867,361	2,646,698	8,077,935	24,651,903	75,231,638

Table 5. $1,200 Per Year at Varying Rates
Compounded Annually—End of Year Values

	5th Yr.	10th Yr.	15th Yr.	20th Yr.	25th Yr.	30th Yr.	35th Yr.	40th Yr.
1%	6,182	12,680	19,509	26,686	34,231	43,359	50,492	59,250
2%	6,369	13,402	21,168	29,739	39,205	49,654	61,192	73,932
3%	6,561	14,169	22,988	33,211	45,063	58,803	74,731	93,195
4%	6,760	14,983	24,990	37,162	51,974	69,993	91,917	118,592
5%	6,962	15,848	27,188	41,662	60,135	83,713	113,803	152,208
6%	7,170	16,766	29,607	46,791	69,787	100,562	141,745	196,857
7%	7,383	17,740	32,265	52,638	81,211	121,287	177,495	256,332
8%	7,603	18,774	35,188	59,307	94,744	146,815	223,322	335,737
9%	7,827	19,872	38,403	66,918	110,788	178,290	282,150	441,950
10%	8,059	21,037	41,940	75,602	129,818	217,131	357,752	584,222
11%	8,295	22,273	45,828	85,518	152,398	265,095	454,996	774,992
12%	8,538	23,586	50,103	96,838	179,200	324,351	581,355	1,030,970
13%	8,786	24,976	54,806	112,164	211,020	397,578	741,298	1,374,583
14%	9,043	26,454	59,976	124,521	248,799	488,084	948,807	1,835,890
15%	9,304	28,018	65,660	141,372	293,654	599,948	1,216,015	2,455,144
16%	9,572	29,679	71,910	160,609	346,905	726,194	1,560,032	3,286,173
17%	9,848	31,440	78,778	182,566	410,115	909,004	2,002,792	4,400,869
18%	10,130	33,306	86,326	207,625	485,126	1,119,982	2,572,378	5,895,109
19%	10,419	35,284	94,620	236,216	574,117	1,380,464	3,304,696	7,896,595
20%	10,716	37,380	103,730	268,831	679,652	1,701,909	4,245,610	10,575,154
21%	11,019	39,601	113,736	306,021	804,759	2,098,358	5,453,622	14,156,310
22%	11,330	41,954	124,722	348,416	952,998	2,587,006	7,003,256	18,939,087
23%	11,649	44,446	136,779	396,727	1,128,558	3,188,884	8,989,333	25,319,371
24%	11,976	47,085	150,013	451,758	1,336,360	3,929,683	11,532,334	33,820,458
25%	12,310	49,879	164,530	514,417	1,582,186	4,840,641	14,666,342	45,132,982

Rev.

$100 Per Month • Assuming you can invest $100 per month, your results would be:

Years	Amount invested	@ 5%	@ 10%	Difference
10	$12,000	$ 15,848	$ 21,031	$ 5,183
20	24,000	41,662	75,602	33,940
30	36,000	83,713	217,131	133,418
40	48,000	152,208	584,222	432,014

Table 6. Approximate Annual Investment Required to Equal $100,000 at the End of a Specified Period—Varying Rates

	5 Yrs.	10 Yrs.	15 Yrs.	20 Yrs.	25 Yrs.	30 Yrs.	35 Yrs.	40 Yrs.
1%	19,380	9,464	6,151	4,497	3,506	2,768	2,378	2,026
2%	18,841	8,954	5,669	4,036	3,061	2,417	1,961	1,624
3%	18,290	8,470	5,220	3,613	2,663	2,041	1,606	1,288
4%	17,751	8,009	4,802	3,229	2,309	1,714	1,306	1,011
5%	17,236	7,572	4,414	2,880	1,966	1,433	1,054	788.39
6%	16,736	7,157	4,053	2,565	1,720	1,193	846.59	609.58
7%	16,254	6,764	3,719	2,280	1,478	989.39	676.08	468.14
8%	15,783	6,392	3,410	2,024	1,267	817.36	537.34	357.42
9%	15,332	6,039	3,125	1,793	1,083	673.06	425.31	271.52
10%	14,890	5,704	2,861	1,587	924.37	552.66	335.43	205.40
11%	14,467	5,388	2,618	1,403	787.41	452.67	263.74	154.84
12%	14,055	5,088	2,395	1,239	669.64	369.97	206.41	116.40
13%	13,658	4,805	2,190	1,070	568.67	301.83	168.00	87.29
14%	13,270	4,536	2,001	963.69	482.32	245.86	126.47	65.36
15%	12,898	4,283	1,828	848.82	408.64	200.02	98.68	48.88
16%	12,537	4,043	1,669	747.16	345.92	165.25	76.92	36.52
17%	12,185	3,817	1,523	657.30	292.60	132.02	59.92	27.27
18%	11,846	3,603	1,390	577.97	247.36	107.14	46.65	20.36
19%	11,517	3,401	1,268	508.01	209.02	86.93	36.31	15.20
20%	11,198	3,210	1,157	446.38	176.56	70.51	28.26	11.35
21%	10,802	3,030	1,056	392.13	149.11	57.19	22.00	8.48
22%	10,591	2,860	962.14	344.42	125.92	46.39	17.13	6.34
23%	10,301	2,700	877.33	302.48	106.33	37.63	13.35	4.74
24%	10,020	2,549	799.93	265.63	89.80	30.53	10.41	3.55
25%	9,749	2,406	729.35	233.27	75.84	24.79	8.18	2.66

Don't Fight the Battle Alone • Are you amazed at the difference an additional 5 percent can make in your results?

At 5 percent you contributed $48,000 in 40 years, and the savings institution contributed $104,208 from their profits from investing your money in American industry, real estate, and natural resources.

On the other hand, if you obtained 10 percent on your investment, you contributed $48,000, and you let American industry, real estate, and natural resources contribute $536,222 to your wealth, a difference of $432,014 or approximately 418 percent.

Table 7. Lump Sum Required to Equal $100,000 at the End of a Specified Period—Varying Rates

	5 Yrs.	10 Yrs.	15 Yrs.	20 Yrs.	25 Yrs.	30 Yrs.	35 Yrs.	40 Yrs.
1%	95,147	90,529	86,135	81,954	77,977	74,192	70,591	67,165
2%	90,573	82,348	74,301	67,297	60,953	55,207	50,003	45,289
3%	86,261	74,409	64,186	55,367	47,761	41,199	35,538	30,656
4%	82,193	67,556	55,526	45,639	37,512	30,832	25,341	20,829
5%	78,353	61,391	48,102	37,689	29,530	23,138	18,129	14,205
6%	74,726	55,839	41,727	31,180	23,300	17,411	13,011	9,722
7%	71,299	50,835	36,245	25,842	18,425	13,137	9,367	6,678
8%	68,058	46,319	31,524	21,455	14,602	9,938	6,763	4,603
9%	64,993	42,241	27,454	17,843	11,597	7,537	4,899	3,184
10%	62,092	38,554	23,940	14,864	9,230	5,731	3,558	2,209
11%	59,345	35,218	20,900	12,403	7,361	4,368	2,592	1,538
12%	56,743	32,197	18,270	10,367	5,882	3,340	1,894	1,075
13%	54,276	29,460	15,989	8,678	4,710	2,557	1,388	753.12
14%	51,937	26,974	14,010	7,276	3,780	1,963	1,019	529.43
15%	49,718	24,718	12,289	6,110	3,040	1,510	750.89	373.32
16%	47,611	22,683	10,792	5,139	2,447	1,165	554.59	264.05
17%	45,611	20,804	9,489	4,329	1,974	900.38	410.67	187.31
18%	43,711	19,107	8,352	3,651	1,596	697.49	304.88	133.27
19%	41,905	17,560	7,359	3,084	1,292	541.49	226.91	95.10
20%	40,188	16,151	6,491	2,610	1,048	421.27	169.30	68.04
21%	38,554	14,864	5,731	2,209	851.85	328.43	126.62	48.82
22%	37,000	13,690	5,065	1,874	693.43	256.57	94.93	35.12
23%	35,520	12,617	4,482	1,592	565.42	200.84	71.34	25.34
24%	34,112	11,635	3,969	1,354	461.80	157.52	53.72	18.33
25%	32,768	10,737	3,512	1,153	377.78	123.79	40.56	13.30

It is not necessary to fight the battle alone if you become knowledgeable so American free enterprise can be of help to you.

Let's now use Table 6. This table will give you the amount you must save to reach $100,000 at various rates of return over 5- to 40-year periods. A freeform graph that I have found helps my clients to visualize this table is shown in Figure 1.

I am quite aware that money does not compound in a straight line, but in a curve. However, I have learned that only a few people can relate to a curve, but almost everyone can relate to a straight line—hence the

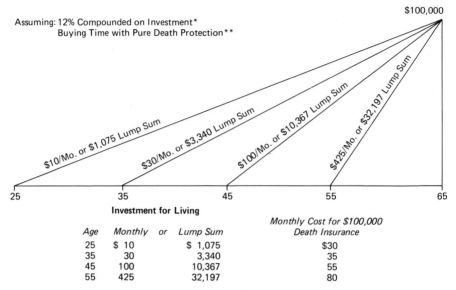

FIGURE 1.   Acquiring the $100,000 Estate by Age 65

straight lines. You will find a chart with the proper curves in the chapter on "Life Insurance—The Great National Consumer Fraud?".

To Be More Specific • Perhaps your timetable does not exactly fit into 5-year time periods, and the amounts of money you have to invest do not fit the neat blocks of $10,000 and $100 per month. There are two excellent tables that permit you to be more exact in your programming. Table 8, "One Dollar Principal Compounded Annually", gives you the sum to which one dollar of principal will accumulate at the indicated interest rates compounded annually for the given number of years. Table 9, "One Dollar Per Annum Compounded Annually", gives you the sum to which one dollar per annum, paid at the beginning of each year, will accumulate at the indicated interest rates compounded annually for the given number of years.

Assume you have 17 years before retirement, you have $14,000 you can put to work in a lump sum, and you can save $160 per month or $1920 per annum.

Using Table 8 you would go down to 17 years and across:

@ 5%	@ 10%
$14,000	$14,000
× 2.2920	× 5.0545
$32,088	$70,763

From Table 9:

@ 5%	@ 10%
$ 1,920	$ 1,920
× 27.1324	× 44.5992
$52,094	$85,630

In 17 years at 5 percent you would have $32,088 and $52,094 or $84,182. At 10 percent you would have $70,763 and $85,630 or $156,393 (exclusive of taxes).

The Rule of 72 • While I am sharing ways to program, let me give you a very simple rule that you can use without elaborate compound tables. It is the "Rule of 72." How I wish it had been taught to me at a younger age! The Rule of 72 gives the answer to the question, How long does it take $1 to become $2 at various rates of return? For example, if you obtain 1 percent on your money, it will take 72 years for $1 to become $2. If you obtain 12 percent, it will take 6 years.

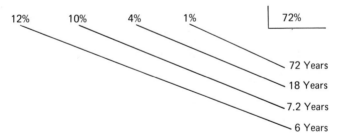

| 12% | 10% | 4% | 1% | 72% |

72 Years
18 Years
7.2 Years
6 Years

• WHICH IS
SAFER?

Is it safer to "lend" your money to a savings institution at 4 percent or to "own" at 12 percent? We will take an in-depth look at which way has truly been the "safest" long-term approach to money management.

Table 8. One Dollar Principal Compounded Annually

End of Year	2½%	3%	5%	6%	8%	10%	12%	15%
1	$ 1.0250	$ 1.0300	$ 1.0500	$ 1.0600	$ 1.0800	$ 1.1000	$ 1.1200	$ 1.1500
2	1.0506	1.0609	1.1025	1.1236	1.1664	1.2100	1.2544	1.3225
3	1.0769	1.0927	1.1576	1.1910	1.2597	1.3310	1.4049	1.5209
4	1.1038	1.1255	1.2155	1.2625	1.3605	1.4641	1.5735	1.7490
5	1.1314	1.1593	1.2763	1.3382	1.4693	1.6105	1.7623	2.0114
6	1.1597	1.1941	1.3401	1.4185	1.5869	1.7716	1.9738	2.3131
7	1.1887	1.2299	1.4071	1.5036	1.7138	1.9487	2.2107	2.6600
8	1.2184	1.2668	1.4775	1.5938	1.8509	2.1436	2.4760	3.0590
9	1.2489	1.3048	1.5513	1.6895	1.9990	2.3579	2.7731	3.5179
10	1.2801	1.3439	1.6289	1.7908	2.1589	2.5937	3.1058	4.0456
11	1.3121	1.3842	1.7103	1.8983	2.3316	2.8531	3.4785	4.6524
12	1.3449	1.4258	1.7959	2.0122	2.5182	3.1384	3.8960	5.3503
13	1.3785	1.4685	1.8856	2.1329	2.7196	3.4523	4.3635	6.1528
14	1.4130	1.5126	1.9799	2.2609	2.9372	3.7975	4.8871	7.0757
15	1.4483	1.5580	2.0789	2.3966	3.1722	4.1772	5.4736	8.1371
16	1.4845	1.6047	2.1829	2.5404	3.4259	4.5950	6.1304	9.3576
17	1.5216	1.6528	2.2920	2.6928	3.7000	5.0545	6.8660	10.7613
18	1.5597	1.7024	2.4066	2.8543	3.9960	5.5599	7.6900	12.3755
19	1.5987	1.7535	2.5270	3.0256	4.3157	6.1159	8.6128	14.2318
20	1.6386	1.8061	2.6533	3.2071	4.6610	6.7275	9.6463	16.3665
21	1.6796	1.8603	2.7860	3.3996	5.0338	7.4002	10.8038	18.8215
22	1.7216	1.9161	2.9253	3.6035	5.4365	8.1403	12.1003	21.6447
23	1.7646	1.9736	3.0715	3.8197	5.8715	8.9543	13.5523	24.8915
24	1.8087	2.0328	3.2251	4.0489	6.3412	9.8497	15.1786	28.6252
25	1.8539	2.0938	3.3864	4.2919	6.8485	10.8347	17.0001	32.9190

End of Year	2½%	3%	5%	6%	8%	10%	12%	15%
26	$ 1.9003	$ 2.1566	$ 3.5557	$ 4.5494	$ 7.3964	$ 11.9182	$ 19.0401	$ 37.8568
27	1.9478	2.2213	3.7335	4.8223	7.9881	13.1100	21.3249	43.5353
28	1.9965	2.2879	3.9201	5.1117	8.6271	14.4210	23.8839	50.0656
29	2.0464	2.3566	4.1161	5.4184	9.3173	15.8631	26.7499	57.5755
30	2.0976	2.4273	4.3219	5.7435	10.0627	17.4494	29.9599	66.2218
31	2.1500	2.5001	4.5380	6.0881	10.8677	19.1943	33.5551	76.1435
32	2.2038	2.5751	4.7649	6.4534	11.7371	21.1138	37.5817	87.5651
33	2.2589	2.6523	5.0032	6.8406	12.6760	23.2252	42.0915	100.6998
34	2.3153	2.7319	5.2533	7.2510	13.6901	25.5477	47.1425	115.8048
35	2.3732	2.8139	5.5160	7.6861	14.7853	28.1024	52.7996	133.1755
36	2.4325	2.8983	5.7918	8.1473	15.9682	30.9127	59.1356	153.1519
37	2.4933	2.9852	6.0814	8.6361	17.2456	34.0039	66.2318	176.1246
38	2.5557	3.0748	6.3855	9.1543	18.6253	37.4043	74.1797	202.5433
39	2.6196	3.1670	6.7048	9.7035	20.1153	41.1448	83.0812	232.9248
40	2.6851	3.2620	7.0400	10.2857	21.7245	45.2593	93.0510	267.8635
41	2.7522	3.3599	7.3920	10.9029	23.4625	49.7852	104.2171	308.0431
42	2.8210	3.4607	7.7616	11.5570	25.3395	54.7637	116.7231	354.2495
43	2.8915	3.5645	8.1497	12.2505	27.3666	60.2401	130.7299	407.3870
44	2.9638	3.6715	8.5572	12.9855	29.5560	66.2641	146.4175	468.4950
45	3.9379	3.7816	8.9850	13.7646	31.9204	72.8905	163.9876	538.7693
46	3.1139	3.8950	9.4343	14.5905	34.4741	80.1795	183.6661	619.5847
47	3.1917	4.0119	9.9060	15.4659	37.2320	88.1975	205.7061	712.5224
48	3.2715	4.1323	10.4013	16.3939	40.2106	97.0172	230.3908	819.4007
49	3.3533	4.2562	10.9213	17.3775	43.4274	106.7190	258.0377	942.3103
50	3.4371	4.3839	11.4674	18.4202	46.9016	117.3909	289.0022	1083.6574

Table 9. One Dollar Per Annum Compounded Annually

End of Year	3%	5%	6%	8%	10%	12%	15%
	$	$	$	$	$	$	$
1	1.0300	1.0500	1.0600	1.0800	1.1000	1.1200	1.1500
2	2.0909	2.1525	2.1836	2.2464	2.3100	2.3744	2.4725
3	3.1836	3.3101	3.3746	3.5061	3.6410	3.7793	3.9934
4	4.3091	4.5256	4.6371	4.8666	5.1051	5.3528	5.7424
5	5.4684	5.8019	5.9753	6.3359	6.7156	7.1152	7.7537
6	6.6625	7.1420	7.3938	7.9228	8.4872	9.0890	10.0668
7	7.8923	8.5491	8.8975	9.6366	10.4359	11.2297	12.7268
8	9.1591	10.0266	10.4913	11.4876	12.5795	13.7757	15.7858
9	10.4639	11.5779	12.1808	13.4866	14.3974	16.5487	19.3037
10	11.8078	13.2068	13.9716	15.6455	17.5312	19.6546	23.3493
11	13.1920	14.9171	15.8699	17.9771	20.3843	23.1331	28.0017
12	14.6178	16.7130	17.8821	20.4953	23.5227	27.0291	33.3519
13	16.0863	18.5986	20.0151	23.2149	26.9750	31.3926	39.5047
14	17.5989	20.5786	22.2760	26.1521	30.7725	36.2797	46.5804
15	19.1569	22.6575	24.6725	29.3243	34.9497	41.7533	54.7175
16	20.7616	24.8404	27.2129	32.7502	39.5447	47.8837	64.0751
17	22.4144	27.1324	29.9057	36.4502	44.5992	54.7497	74.8364
18	24.1169	29.5390	32.7600	40.4463	50.1591	62.4397	87.2118
19	25.8704	32.0660	35.7856	44.7620	56.2750	71.0524	101.4436
20	27.6765	34.7193	38.9927	49.4229	63.0025	80.6987	117.8101
21	29.5368	37.5052	42.3923	54.4568	70.4027	91.5026	136.6316
22	31.4529	40.4305	45.9958	59.8933	78.5430	103.6029	158.2764
23	33.4265	43.5020	49.8156	65.7648	87.4973	117.1552	183.1678
24	35.4593	46.7271	53.8645	72.1059	97.3471	132.3339	211.7930
25	37.5530	50.1135	58.1564	78.9544	108.1818	149.3339	244.7120

End of Year	3%	5%	6%	8%	10%	12%	15%
	$	$	$	$	$	$	$
26	39.7096	53.6691	62.7058	86.3508	120.0999	168.3740	282.5688
27	41.9309	57.4026	67.5281	94.3388	133.2099	189.6989	326.1041
28	44.2189	61.3227	72.6398	102.9659	147.6309	213.5828	376.1697
29	46.5754	65.4388	78.0582	112.2832	163.4940	240.3327	433.7451
30	49.0027	69.7608	83.8017	122.3459	180.9434	270.2926	499.9569
31	51.5028	74.2988	89.8898	133.2135	200.1378	303.8477	576.1005
32	54.0778	79.0638	96.3432	144.9506	221.2515	341.4294	663.6655
33	56.7302	84.0670	103.1838	157.6267	244.4767	383.5210	764.3654
34	59.4621	89.3203	110.4348	171.3168	270.0244	430.6635	880.1702
35	62.2759	94.8363	118.1209	186.1021	298.1268	483.4631	1013.3757
36	65.1742	100.6281	126.2681	202.0703	329.0395	542.5987	1166.4975
37	68.1594	106.7095	134.9042	219.3158	363.0434	608.8305	1342.6222
38	71.2342	113.0950	144.0585	237.9412	400.4478	683.0102	1545.1655
39	74.4013	119.7998	153.7620	258.0565	441.5926	766.0914	1778.0903
40	77.6633	126.8398	164.0477	279.7810	486.8518	859.1424	2045.9539
41	81.0232	134.2318	174.9505	303.2435	536.6370	963.3595	2353.9969
42	84.4839	141.9933	186.5076	328.5830	591.4007	1080.0826	2708.2465
43	88.0484	150.1430	198.7580	355.9496	651.6408	1210.8125	3115.6334
44	91.7199	158.7002	211.7435	385.5056	717.9048	1357.2300	3584.1285
45	95.5015	167.6852	225.5081	417.4261	790.7953	1521.2176	4122.8977
46	99.3965	177.1194	240.0986	451.9002	870.9749	1704.8838	4742.4824
47	103.4084	187.0254	255.5645	489.1322	959.1723	1910.5898	5455.0047
48	107.5406	197.4267	271.9584	529.3427	1056.1896	2140.9806	6274.4055
49	111.7969	208.3480	289.3359	572.7702	1162.9085	2399.0182	7216.7163
50	116.1808	219.8154	307.7561	619.6718	1280.2994	2688.0204	8300.3737

Suffice it to say here that if you've waited the past 18 years for $1 to become $2, you've lost the fight because inflation has more than doubled your cost of living—to say nothing of your loss through the tax bite.

At 4 percent your exercise has been similar to the little frog who was trying to hop out of the well. Every time he hopped up one foot, he slid back two. If you ignore the insidious termite called inflation, your money exercises may prove to parallel those of the little frog in the fairy tale of the frog and the princess—without the kiss of the princess to miraculously make you an affluent prince.

Application

Knowledge of any subject is of little use unless you apply it to your own particular set of circumstances. Therefore, at the end of each chapter let's apply what you have learned to help you build toward financial independence.

Which source of income do you want to depend on at age 65? How many years before you plan to retire? What would you like to have as a monthly income if you were retiring today? What inflation factor do you feel best applies to you? Now, how much will you need per month?

If you choose the guaranteed route, how much capital will this require? If you do not choose this route, what higher rate will be your minimum average objective?

⎰ 2 ⎱

The Anatomy
of
Inflation

There are four basic reasons you must learn to invest. These are:

1 · To obtain a hedge against inflation.
2 · For income.
3 · For growth of capital.
4 · For tax advantage.

In this chapter we'll take an unemotional look at inflation and the devastating path it has cut across the face of the United States, bringing havoc to many a financial plan.

Inflation is a fact of life. It is a fact you must learn to accept and to protect yourself against, or suffer the dire consequences. It has been your constant companion since the day you were born, and, from all indications, it will continue with you for the remainder of your life. This problem does not belong to the United States alone, but has been felt worldwide.

Tolstoy chronicled that every civilized nation that has ever existed has experienced its ravages.

I do not believe that history always repeats itself, but I have found that if I ignore the past, I often condemn myself to repeating the same mistakes in the future.

What has been the history of inflation in the United States?

• SINCE 1900

Let's examine the past by beginning at the turn of the century—1900. Figure 2 plots the purchasing power of our dollar from 1900 to 1974.

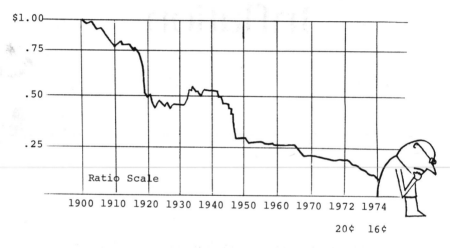

FIGURE 2. Purchasing Power of the Dollar

An even more graphic way of looking at the effect of inflation is to look at a dollar composed of quarters that you had held since 1900. You now go to the grocery store to make a purchase. How much do you think it would buy in the form of goods and services in comparison to what it bought in 1900?

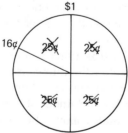

Your dollar has lost 84 percent of the only value it has—what it will buy. A dollar has no value in and of itself. Its only value is what you can exchange it for in the market place. What you want to store for the future is not so many dollars but so many pairs of shoes, tubes of lipstick, hamburgers, and so forth.

• THINK OF BREAD

In 1940 you could go to your local grocery store and buy 10 loaves of bread for $1. By 1950 you could only buy 6 loaves. By 1960 it would buy only 4 and by 1970 only 3. How many will it buy today? It is the same dollar, but it has lost the major portion of its only value.

If I can do nothing else for you in this book but to help you to convert your thinking from dollars into bread, I will have done for you an immense favor. I warn you, it is an emotional transition that only a few can make. If you can make it, you will be in the minority—but remember, it's only the minority that become financially independent.

During the years between 1940 and 1974, the dollar held its own in only two years, and then by less than 1 percent. Not even a professional gambler would accept those odds. Yet, if you are holding a dollar as a dollar today, you are betting against those odds. If you are a saver, placing your savings in a "guaranteed" savings account, you are a gambler, and if the past is any indication of the future, you are "guaranteed" to lose!

What if I were to say to you, "I want to recommend a stock for your serious consideration. I know its record has not been very good, but I have faith that it will improve. It was selling for $100 in 1933, by 1943 it had dropped to $76, by 1953 to $46, and by 1963 to $43. Today it is at $31 . . . but, don't let that discourage you. I still have faith in this stock, and I want you to invest in it." If I were to make such a "buy" recommendation to you, what would you say to me? Before you say, "You've got to be kidding!" I want you to know that this investment is recommended by most of our state and national banks, by all of our savings and loans, by all of the nation's life insurance companies that sell cash surrender value policies, by your city, and by the federal government itself. What is this investment?

It is the U.S. dollar!

• IT IS THE
U.S. DOLLAR

"Guaranteed" dollars are recommended as a good investment for you by all savings institutions and insurance companies that sell cash surrender value life insurance; yet they never want a "guaranteed" dollar for themselves. They want to "guarantee" your principal, "guarantee" your rate of return, and "guarantee" that your dollar will work for them— usually harder than it works for you. You will receive a "guarantee" that you can always get back each deflating dollar you've placed with them (excluding "your" savings account with the life insurance company). You are also guaranteed that you can never receive any more than that dollar, plus any compound interest you may have left with them, regardless of how much your money has earned for the institution to which you loaned it.

• VERBAL vs.
EMOTIONAL ACCEPTANCE

If I were to ask you the question, "Have we had inflation in the past?" your answer would be "Why, yes!" If I now ask you, "Do you think we'll have inflation in the future?" would your answer be another resounding "Yes"? Would this be your verbal answer, but not your emotional answer?

I find it very difficult for most people to emotionally accept infla- tion. Inflation is such a nonvisual thing that it's hard to realize that it is happening. However, it's getting more visual every day. Next time you go grocery shopping, dig to the back of the row of canned peaches and see if you can't find a can at a lower price than the cans in front. This may help you to become the rare person who makes this transition.

Inflation continues to nibble away at the value of your dollars. The trouble with nibbles is that over a period of time, they result in deep bites. For example, if your income was $7,500 in 1950, inflation and tax increases would require that you earn $13,900 by 1975 just to maintain your same purchasing power.

In 1939, the average family income was $1,500; 30 years later, in 1969, it was $9,500; 30 years from now, in 1999, it is estimated this will have risen to $45,500.

A 5 percent inflation is equivalent to a 5 percent cut in your gross income. Any inflation even approaching this rate is a major assault on your living standard. It is also an illness with hidden, delayed symptoms. On top of the immediate increase in the price of your necessities and luxuries alike, there is the value eaten away from your fixed savings which includes not only your bank account but also any government bonds you may own, your private pension invested in fixed securities, and, if you are banking with a life insurance company, the cash value of your life insurance policies.

It is difficult to stay ahead of rapid inflation. A married man earning $7,600 a year, for example, would need a $380-a-year raise just to keep even with the increased cost of a 5 percent inflation. Yet, that amount would put him into a higher tax bracket so that he would have to pay more in federal income taxes. State, local, and Social Security taxes will take additional bites.

If you look at the record on the rate of inflation in a year such as 1974 and find it to be 11 percent to 13 percent, depending on the indicator used, will you a few minutes later revert to talking about your savings account being a good "guaranteed" investment at 5 percent, 6 percent, or 7½ percent? If you do, I'll know that emotionally you have not accepted the fact of inflation and the reality of a negative interest. If you are in a 25 percent tax bracket and have received the average savings institution rate of return since 1964, your net gain or loss picture looks like Figure 3.

The *Encyclopaedia Britannica* states, "Important inflation can occur only with the acquiescence or active support of the government." I believe this is true. When our country attempted welfare and warfare during the Johnson administration, with no increase in taxes, unacceptable inflation was inevitable. I say "unacceptable"—yet I wonder if that is really true.

When Congress passed the Full Employment Act of 1964, it was

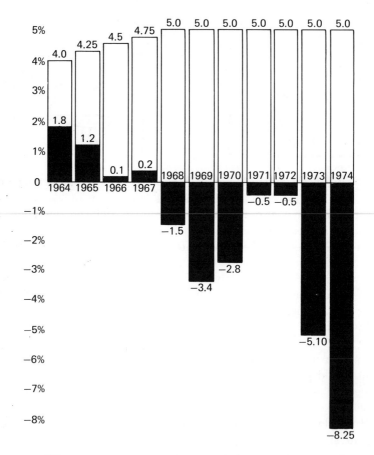

What was left after inflation and taxes (25% bracket).
Vertical bars represent savings bank interest rates.

FIGURE 3.   Inflation and Taxes—How They've Affected Your Savings

legislated that from that time forward until the Act is repealed, our country will have inflation. The Act, for all practical purposes, makes it illegal to have a depression. When unemployment reaches a certain point, the government must intervene and take measures to accelerate the economy. This means that the natural processes of supply and demand in the labor force can no longer be a stabilizing force. In fact, when we had increased unemployment in 1974, wages actually rose.

One cure for inflation is greater worker productivity. When productivity rises faster than wages, then the inflationary spiral is dampened. When the reverse is true, inflation is accelerated.

• ARE THE KNOWLEDGEABLE HURT?

Does inflation really hurt the knowledgeable investor over the long term? I believe it does not. He learns to protect himself.

Inflation brings into focus the tragic face of the hard-working, thrifty, sacrificing person who put his money into government bonds and lost—lost in purchasing power and lost the privilege of retiring in financial dignity. At least the spendthrift had the fun of spending his money until he got off of the inflation train. During his working years, raises usually matched or exceeded his increases in his cost of living. But when he got off the inflation train and it went on without him, he had no chance of keeping up with the inflationary spiral.

• STOCKS— HOW GOOD IS THE HEDGE?

Many people have looked to common stocks as an investment for the dollars they have set aside for retirement. Do common stock prices go hand in hand with inflation? The answer is often No in the short term. When inflation has been most rampant, as during the years 1970–1975, the market had some of its severest drops. The stock market was buffeted by the balance of payments deficit, by the Federal Reserve Board's playing with the money supply, by the uglies of Watergate which caused our citizens to have a bad ache in the pits of their stomachs, by the energy crisis, and by a stock brokerage fee structure that benefited the large investor, to the detriment of the small investor. This, among other things, caused him to leave the stock market—a market that must have him as an active participant in order to function properly.

When people feel badly, they sell their stocks. When they feel

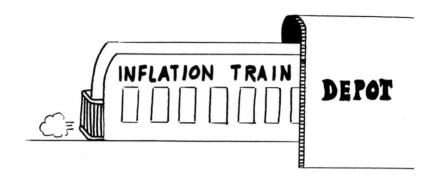

good, they buy. When more people want to sell than want to buy, the market goes down. When more want to buy than sell, the market goes up. In my many years as a stockbroker, I've never observed such widespread gloom as when the nation was in the throes of the nationally televised congressional "hearings" on Watergate. Just as the people were beginning to perk up a bit and feel the country would survive after all, along came Agnew, Cox, the tapes, the Middle Eastern war, the Arabian oil embargo, the impeachment proceedings, and, for the first time, the resignation of the President of the United States.

But ours is a resilient nation, and will go forward as it has in the past. To get a glimmer of what the future could hold, let's take a look at how the stock market has performed in the past.

One Hundred Years • In 1971 the Anchor Corporation made a comprehensive study of the stock market and its correlation to inflation covering a 100-year span. They wanted to answer three questions:

1 • Have common stocks provided an adequate hedge against rising living costs?
2 • Has income from common stocks offset rising living costs, and, if so, how adequately?
3 • How have common stock prices and dividends behaved compared to living costs during periods of inflation?

They made no assumptions, nor do I, about any possible correlation among past experience and future common stock prices, dividends, and living costs, or any recommendations as to whether an individual should invest in stocks.

The charts in Figure 4 are reprinted with their permission from *The Long View*.

How Often Have Investors Faced Inflation? • In answer to the question of how often investors have faced inflation in the past century, the Anchor Corporation found the following: Living costs rose in 61 percent of the 1-year periods, 64 percent of the 10-year periods, 72 percent of the 15-year periods, 79 percent of the 20-year periods, and 94 percent of the 30-year spans. From these graphic percentages you can see that over a 20-year span, inflation has been experienced three-quarters of the time and over 30-year spans, nearly all of the time.

How Have Stocks Behaved During Inflation? • In answer to this question, survey findings indicate that stock prices rose in 67 percent of the 1-year inflationary periods and in 9 out of 10 of the longer periods of rising cost. In the past century common stocks have increased in value in 95 percent of the 20-year periods and in all 30-year periods of rising living costs.

Have Stock Prices Increased as Much as Living Costs? • The study revealed that increases in stock prices equaled or exceeded increases in the cost of living in 72 percent of all 10-year periods, 82 percent of all 15-year periods, 90 percent of all 20-year periods, and 91 percent of all 30-year periods.

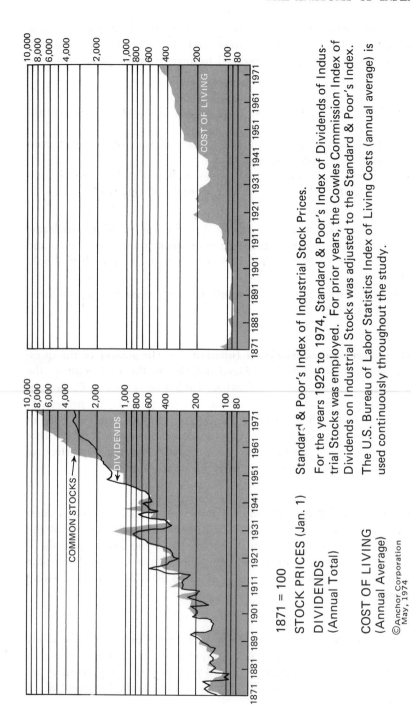

1871 = 100

STOCK PRICES (Jan. 1)   Standard & Poor's Index of Industrial Stock Prices.

DIVIDENDS   For the years 1925 to 1974, Standard & Poor's Index of Dividends of Indus-
(Annual Total)   trial Stocks was employed. For prior years, the Cowles Commission Index of
                         Dividends on Industrial Stocks was adjusted to the Standard & Poor's Index.

COST OF LIVING   The U.S. Bureau of Labor Statistics Index of Living Costs (annual average) is
(Annual Average)   used continuously throughout the study.

©Anchor Corporation
May, 1974

FIGURE 4.   Stock Prices and Dividends vs. Cost of Living

How Have Common Stock Prices Behaved During Times of Deflation?
· In 54 percent of the 1-year periods of deflation stock prices also declined in value. But they declined in only 34 percent of the 10-year periods and 13 percent of the 15-year periods.

Over long spans of deflation the investor has been more likely to profit from common stock investments than to suffer loss. Over 20-year eras of declining living costs, the investor has experienced rising stock values more than 8 times out of 10. Since 1871, common stock prices increased during both of the 30-year spans of deflation.

Moreover, when stock prices have declined during periods of deflation, the decline has generally been less than that in the cost of living.

How Have Dividends Behaved During Inflation? · Dividends increased in 73 percent of the 1-year periods, 95 percent of the 10-year periods, 89 percent of the 15-year periods, and 100 percent of the 20- and 30-year periods.

How Have Dividends Behaved During Deflation? · Dividends rose in 46 percent of the 1-year periods of deflation, decreased in 42 percent, and remained unchanged in 12 percent. Dividends rose in 66 percent of the 10-year periods of deflation, 61 percent of the 15-year periods, and 81 percent of the 20-year spans. Since 1871, dividends increased in both 30-year periods of deflation.

Inflation and Stock Prices—Short Term, Long Term · As you can readily determine from a quick look at the above data, on a day-to-day, or even on a year-to-year, basis, common stock prices do not go hand in hand, month by month, with inflation. As a matter of fact, in the short term, they often go in opposite directions. The market likes certainties. It can live with good news and can live with bad news, but it has difficulty living without knowing what the news is. Runaway inflation causes excesses and uncertainties that can adversely affect short-term market conditions. However, over the long term, in the past, a good cross-section of quality stocks has given your capital, and the income it produces, a chance to grow to offset the inroads of inflation.

· "THE SEMINAR FUND"

To help you visualize some of this past correlation, let's look at the results of a particular investment company trust, commonly called a mutual fund. I shall call it "The Seminar Fund", in that it is the one I use in my investment seminars as an example of how a fund works, not as a recommendation. It is 40 years old and was established in the depths of the depression in 1933. I consider it middle-of-the-road in its financial objective. It has a billion dollars in assets and usually contains 130 to 150 individual stocks in its portfolio. Obviously, "The Seminar Fund" is not its true name. If I stated its name, I would need to hand you a prospectus detailing costs and fees, with many scary paragraphs.

Table 10 shows an assumed investment of $10,000 over twenty 20-year periods.

In the historical past record shown here, and I do emphasize past, all distributions were reinvested and all expenses deducted (with no adjustment for personal federal income taxes, since your bracket will vary from other investors.)

In Table 10 you can see that in the past, the fund outperformed 12 percent on a lump sum investment in 16 of the 20-year periods ($10,000 @ 12 percent = $96,452.)

If you had been an investor in this fund and had cashed it in at the end of 1956, a low spot in the market, your results would have still been $63,650. This is over 9 percent compounded ($10,000 @ 9 percent = $56,072.) Therefore, if you had been so unlucky as to have been an investor during the worst 20-year period since the depths of the depression, you still did better than a so-called "guaranteed" dollar during that particular 20-year period.

A bank in 1937 was paying 1.8 percent, and a savings and loan company was paying 3.5 percent. This rate dropped to 2.2 percent in 1946 and had only risen to 3.0 percent by 1956, the end of our 20-year period.

Perhaps you have not accumulated $10,000 but do have $250 and can invest $100 per month. Table 11 lists the results of twenty 20-year periods of investing in "The Seminar Fund." If you had invested $1,200 per year for 20 years and averaged 12 percent compounded annually, your investment would have grown to $96,838. In 14 of the 20-year periods you have exceeded this amount. In 4 you would have failed to reach 12 percent. In one period, which included the depression years 1934–53, you would have averaged just under 10 percent. Your average of all the periods was $106,565, well over 12 percent.

As you see, over the long term, investing in a professionally selected, diversified portfolio of common stocks has in the past been a satisfactory hedge against the inroads of inflation and has definitely earned the right to be considered as one of the hedges you should carefully examine in your battle to protect your future purchasing power.

I personally believe that the next 15 years hold great promise be-

Table 10. Summaries of Assumed $10,000 Investment in
"The Seminar Fund"

Jan. 1–Dec. 31	Income dividends reinvested	Total investment cost	Ending value of shares
1934–53	$30,612	$40,612	$ 94,960
1935–54	27,548	37,548	118,311
1936–55	17,125	27,125	81,001
1937–56	13,644	23,644	63,650
1938–57	24,589	34,589	91,057
1939–58	21,647	31,647	103,491
1940–59	23,845	33,845	117,288
1941–60	27,101	37,101	125,444
1942–61	32,213	42,213	167,155
1943–62	30,320	40,320	124,197
1944–63	25,070	35,070	115,035
1945–64	22,350	32,350	108,569
1946–65	18,026	28,026	100,704
1947–66	20,633	30,633	104,108
1948–67	22,959	32,959	133,068
1949–68	25,937	35,937	154,719
1950–69	26,972	36,972	126,468
1951–70	25,396	35,396	108,328
1952–71	24,090	34,090	107,545
1953–72	23,894	33,894	111,248

Average of all the 20-Year Periods—$112,817.

cause by the end of 1974 65 percent of the common stocks listed on the New York Stock Exchange were selling at no more than 7 times their earnings. About 1 out of 3 stocks was selling at no more than 5 times earnings.

To put this into perspective, if you could buy all of the outstanding stock of a company that's selling at 5 times earnings, you'd be getting a 20 percent return on your investment. Even if you were to assume a decline of 25 percent, this would still mean a price–earnings ratio of only 6.7 or an earnings return of 15 percent.

• UNDERLYING VALUE IS THE KEY

Companies create wealth, and, in the past, successful investing in common stocks has resulted from becoming one of the owners of the

Table 11.   Summary of Assumed Investment of $250 and Adding $100 Per Month in "The Seminar Fund"

Jan. 1– Dec. 31	Income dividends reinvested	Total cost (including dividends reinvested)	Capital gain distributions taken in shares	Ending value of shares
1934–53	$20,580	$44,730	$21,780	$ 74,850
1935–54	19,841	43,991	22,663	101,759
1936–55	19,471	43,621	26,527	111,473
1937–56	20,439	44,589	32,106	114,505
1938–57	21,898	46,048	35,655	95,359
1939–58	21,825	45,975	35,389	123,663
1940–59	21,705	45,855	39,329	126,701
1941–60	21,480	45,630	40,463	117,815
1942–61	20,759	44,909	41,222	127,371
1943–62	19,290	43,440	38,185	94,215
1944–63	18,390	42,590	36,490	101,327
1945–64	17,690	41,840	36,970	103,693
1946–65	17,432	41,582	39,139	117,783
1947–66	17,890	42,040	42,900	108,248
1948–67	17,974	42,124	42,899	123,825
1949–68	18,151	42,301	41,308	127,516
1950–69	17,738	41,888	40,837	97,819
1951–70	17,198	41,348	37,503	86,520
1952–71	16,716	40,866	32,970	88,212
1953–72	16,020	40,170	29,928	88,655

Average—$106,565.

companies creating this wealth. Stock prices in the long term are determined by the earnings and assets of these companies.

Do not make the mistake so many investors do of taking the short-term view of the stock market when providing for your long-term goals. I find that so many predict the future by making straight line extrapolations of the latest 5- or 10-year period. When the market has gone down over a period of several years, instead of welcoming it as a buying opportunity, they sit on their hands. When the market has been going up for a period of years, they assume the opposite and eagerly jump in with the full anticipation that this happy condition will continue for the next 5 to 10 years.

Watch for times in the market when good solid values are available, and have the courage to buy at bargain prices.

Application

How can you best apply the information contained in this chapter to your own financial life? Take a moment and consider: Is inflation likely to continue? Is there such a thing as a "guaranteed," "safe," long-term investment? Has systematic investing in a diversified selected portfolio of common stocks been a good hedge against inflation? Have you mentally made the transition from dollars to bread?

3

Lending
Your
Dollars

It is your responsibility to be the steward of every dollar that comes your way. A part of each dollar should be used to feed, clothe, house, and entertain your family and yourself. A part of your dollar you should save.

In an earlier chapter you learned that there are only three things you can do with a dollar—spend, lend, or own. You will always need to have some of your funds in a "loaned" position. How much should this be? There was a time that I taught that you should keep three months expenses in cash reserves. Now I teach that you should keep as much of your funds in an idle position as it takes there to give you peace of mind. Many people need what I call "patting money" to give them that peace of mind—and peace of mind is a good investment. Determine where that level is and place those funds into a "loaned" position. In this chapter we will consider ways you may want to "lend" your money.

A very important consideration in your plan to become financially independent is the selection of the right banker. He can play a vital role in its accomplishment. Take the time and effort to select one who is knowledgeable and creative and whose bank has sufficient assets to finance any bankable project you may want to undertake. Then open your checking accounts with him.

• CHECKING ACCOUNTS

You will always need one or more checking accounts to be used for convenience and for ease of record keeping. Keep a sufficient amount on deposit to enable you to write a check whenever you choose. Feeling "poor" is not an emotionally satisfactory feeling and does not contribute to the necessary psychology of winning.

However, do not keep your balance too large. I remember one lady who came in for counseling who had $159,000 in her checking account. I asked if she had a reason for keeping this amount there and she said, "Well, I've been thinking of taking a little trip." I suppressed the desire to ask her which planet was her desired destination.

• OTHER WAYS OF "LENDING"

When you move from a checking account to other ways of "lending" your funds, you will find a wide array of choices. These are what are commonly called fixed-income instruments. As evidence of your loan to the borrower you will receive securities or instruments that represent contracts to pay back your money at a specified time and at a specified rate. These borrowers may be corporations, the federal government, or financial institutions.

Let's now examine some of the fixed-income instruments you may want to consider.

Passbook Savings Accounts • You may open a passbook savings account in any amount at either a bank or a savings and loan. Interest is earned from date of deposit to date of withdrawal or to "dividend" date. The rates are fixed by the Federal Reserve System or the Federal Home Loan Bank Board. These rates (usually slightly higher at savings institutions) have ranged in recent years from 4½ percent to 5½ percent. Deposits and withdrawals can be made at your discretion. Deposits, in most instances, are federally insured to a maximum of $40,000.

Certificates of Deposit • This is basically a deposit account opened for a minimum amount of $1,000 to $5,000. Certificates of deposit are issued by both commercial banks and savings and loan associations in maturities of from 90 days to 4 years. Interest is paid from the date of deposit to maturity at the stated rate. Interest rates are higher than those for regular savings accounts and have exceeded 7½ percent for the longer maturities. Savings and loan rates are usually one-quarter of a percent higher than those of commercial banks. These rates are fixed by law. Deposits normally can be made at any time. Withdrawals can be made prior to maturity—but with a penalty, generally a forfeiture of three months' interest and with interest earned on the amount withdrawn reduced to the passbook rate. In fact, here are examples of the penalties you could incur on a $10,000 certificate:

Type of account	Yield	Early withdrawal	Penalty	Effective yield
1 yr. certificate	6½%	11 months	$248.20	3.84%
2 yr. certificate	6½%	1 yr. 9 mos.	$354.00	4.53%
4 yr. certificate	7½%	3 yrs. 6 mos.	$931.50	4.91%

Deposits in most cases are federally insured to a maximum of $40,000.

Commercial Paper • Corporations finance much of their short-term working capital requirements by issuing commercial paper—short-term notes with a fixed maturity of from 1 to 270 days. Paper is normally issued in a minimum amount of $25,000 or as small as $10,000 at some banks for 30 days or longer, and it can be purchased on either a discount or an interest-bearing basis. The investment return is determined by the current level of short-term interest rates and, therefore, can fluctuate significantly over relatively short periods of time. The returns on commercial paper historically have been about ½ percent to 1 percent below the bank prime lending rate, except during periods in which the latter rate has not been allowed to move freely with market forces. Paper can be purchased with or without arrangements allowing prepayment of the amount initially invested plus a return at the original investment rate. Without such arrangements, paper can be sold in the short-term market at current rates, resulting in a yield greater or less than the acquisition rate.

• SAFETY

When you lend your money to a bank, it is well to follow the same procedure that a bank would—check out your borrower. How can you do this? In the case of a bank, look for the gilded seal applied to the entrance door of the bank or on the window near the door. Does it contain the letters FDIC? This means that the bank is a member of the Federal Deposit Insurance Corporation and that your account is insured up to $40,000. The Federal Deposit Insurance program insures deposits in national and most state banks, both commercial and mutual savings banks. What this means to you is that if a bank gets into financial difficulties and is closed, your savings up to $40,000 will be reimbursed by the federal government. Although the process begins soon after closure, it may take some months before you receive your money.

All national banks in the United States are required to be members of the system, and state banks may become Federal Reserve System banks by meeting stringent requirements.

All FRS banks have stringent requirements with regard to the structure of their board of directors, interlocking directorates, their relationship with security and investment companies, the payment of interest on deposits, and their relationship to branch banks. They must keep reserves in cash or on deposit with their Federal Reserve bank equivalent to a certain proportion of their various types of deposits, and they're also required to subscribe to the capital of the Federal Reserve bank of their district equal to 6 percent of their capital surplus.

There is no similar protection with savings and loan associations and credit unions, although they may operate under federal regulations with guarantees. Federal regulations do not preclude bank failure. In fact, the entire nation is familiar with the failure of the Sharpstown Bank in Houston in 1971. Sharpstown was a state bank with FDIC insurance for savings accounts up to $20,000 (which was the limit at that time). However, many people had more than that amount on deposit.

The risk can be more with some savings and loan associations. It is extremely important to learn as much as you can about an association before making a deposit. However, a superficial check may not protect you. *The National Observer* (a publication I highly recommend to you if you desire to be an informed investor) in its December 15, 1973 issue gives an account of a widow "still in shock" who deposited $42,509 in benefits from her late husband's insurance in a Norfolk, Virginia, savings and loan corporation. She never doubted the money was safe. The 57-year-old corporation was well regarded. Its officials were among the most esteemed men in the community. There were two things she did not know: The savings and loan corporation was insolvent, and its deposits were not insured. Seven days later, Virginia banking authorities closed the institution and placed it in receivership. Her money, along with that of nearly 3,500 other persons, is frozen. Unfortunately, all these people could end up with little or nothing.

Virginia's inadequacies are not unique. In Louisville, Kentucky, savings of 22,100 persons were jeopardized when two large building and loan associations failed in 1972. Their depositors are expected to recover no more than 30 percent of their money.

If you decide to use a savings and loan association, be sure to look for the gilded seal with FSLIC on the door, for this guarantees that you will have your deposit returned someday (not always on demand) up to their maximum.

In Chicago some 14,000 savers were cut off from their funds when a large savings and loan association went under in 1964. And in Maryland an estimated 50,000 depositors lost all or part of their funds when some uninsured savings and loans passed into oblivion during the 1960s.

Such misfortunes are unusual in these times of prosperity, but nothing can entirely prevent even national bank collapses. The biggest in U.S. history was in October 1972 when a national bank located in San Diego was declared insolvent. Nearly half of the $940 million on deposit was not covered by the FDIC insurance because of the $20,000 maximum. (All the deposits may still be protected under a government rescue plan.) The difficulties experienced by the Franklin National Bank of Philadelphia in 1974 are also well chronicled.

In Galveston, Texas, an old, well-respected bank was closed by the Securities and Exchange Commission in September 1972. Thanks to the affluence of some of the relatives, who paid off depositors, no one lost any money. An insurance company (a related part of this same financial empire) joined suit, suspending payment of the cash surrender value to its policyholders. These savings may also be returned in the future.

These are some of the ways you may want to consider lending money to local savings institutions. However, there is a broad range of other ways to lend money.

• GOVERNMENT
OBLIGATIONS

There are two categories of government obligations: U.S. Treasury obligations and federal agency obligations. Treasury obligations are guaranteed by the U.S. government. Agencies, unless specifically indicated, are not technically government guaranteed but are still considered to be of very high quality.

Series E Bonds • The government obligation with which you are probably the most familiar is the Series E Bonds. These bonds are issued on a discount basis. The minimum available is $25. When held to maturity, the investment return is equivalent to 6 percent compounded semi-annually. These bonds may be redeemed at any time after two months from issue at a fixed redemption value that results in a return of less than the 6 percent rate.

Series H Bonds • Series H Bonds are 10-year income bonds. They are issued at par with interest paid semiannually on a scale graduated to produce a return of 6 percent compounded semiannually when the bonds are held to maturity. The minimum amount available is $500. These bonds may be redeemed at par at the owner's option after six months from the issue date. Redemption prior to maturity results in a yield under the 6 percent rate.

If you have held Series E bonds for some years and are now in need of income, you may want to consider exchanging them for Series H Bonds. There will be no tax liability on the accumulated interest on your Series E Bonds when the exchange is made, nor will there be any until you decide to redeem the Series H Bonds. At that time a tax liability will be incurred.

Treasury Bills • Treasury bills are normally issued in maturities of 91 days, 182 days, and 1 year, and are available in a minimum amount of $10,000 directly from any of the 12 Federal Rerserve Banks or through a commercial bank or broker. Treasury bills are issued weekly on a discount basis, under competitive bidding, with the face amount payable at maturity. The investment return on bills is the difference between the cost and the face amount. Bills may be sold prior to maturity at a competitive market rate, which can result in a yield greater or smaller than the original acquisition rate. Yield on bills, like other short-term money market instruments, can fluctuate greatly, but it is generally lower than other nongovernment, short-term securities.

Treasury Notes • Notes have a fixed maturity of from 1 to 7 years and bear interest payable semiannually at fixed rates. They are available in minimum amounts of $1,000. Selected notes are auctioned competitively through the Federal Reserve System on a periodic basis. Buyers can subscribe through a commercial bank or a broker. Yields on notes are determined by the acquisition price. These notes may be sold prior to maturity at the current market rate, resulting in a yield greater or smaller than the original acquisition rate. Again, yields on Treasury notes generally are lower than their corporate counterparts because of the excellent marketability and credit rating of government securities.

Treasury Bonds • Bonds have a fixed maturity of over 7 years and are the longer counterpart of Treasury notes. Yields on Treasury bonds, because they are of longer maturity, usually are higher than those of Treasury notes.

Federal Agency Obligations • Agency obligations are issued by federal authorities such as the Federal National Mortgage Association, the Federal Home Loan Bank, the Government National Mortgage Association, and others. These instruments are varied and are tailored to meet the financing needs of the individual issuing agency. Types of issues are similar to U.S. Treasury bills, notes, and bonds. You can acquire these obligations through investment banking houses. Normally, the minimum amount available is $1,000 to $5,000. Yields are usually one-quarter to one-half of a percent higher than U.S. Treasury obligations since agencies usually are not guaranteed by the U.S. government. These issues can be sold prior to maturity at current market rates resulting in a return greater or smaller than the acquisition yield.

There is one group of securities that you may want to consider in this category. They were formally called "mortgage backed securities guaranteed by the Government National Mortgage Association" when they were first established. Since then they have received the friendlier nickname "Ginny Mae." Ginny Maes offer a number of special attractions, but their particular one is that they pay a fixed return that is often higher than you can get from a long-term bond.

Probably the main reason they aren't better known is that when the certificates first appeared in 1970, the minimum unit you could buy from most brokers was $100,000. Consequently, the buyers were banks, insurance companies, pension funds, and other institutions. Soon thereafter the minimum purchase was cut back to $25,000. Since then, one brokerage firm has created a unit trust that allows individuals to start their investment in Ginny Maes for as little as $10,000.

Ginny Mae Pass-Throughs were hatched during the credit crunch of 1969–70 when mortgage money was as tight as it has become from time to time since. The Government National Mortgage Association (GNMA), established by an act of Congress, said, in effect, to savings and loan associations, banks, and mortgage bankers, "When you have closed enough mortgages, collect them into a pool; then issue certificates, backed by the mortgages, to raise cash so you can loan out more mortgage money. We'll guarantee the pool, so investors will buy the certificates without worry." The packager of the mortgage pool then "passes through" the mortgage payments he receives to certificate holders.

Why should you buy a Ginny Mae Pass-Through instead of a

corporate bond? Well, you may like the idea of spreading a portion of your money into real estate. In this manner you can become a mortgage lender without any of the worries about collecting rent, defaults, or bookkeeping. Full payments, on time, are "backed by the full faith and credit of the United States Government," and no corporate bond can make that statement. Bonds can be called back by the issuer, some within 5 years of issuance date, and you would lose that nice high interest return you had counted on. Ginny Mae certificates usually assure you current rates for 12 years.

But perhaps most important, you are buying a mortgage, and the pool sponsor sends you a monthly check. Part of the payment represents interest and part return of your principal. (The principal portion, since it is a return of your capital, is not taxed as income.) With a bond, of course, you have to wait until it matures before your principal is returned. This feature may be of special value to you if you are retired and need a monthly check. If you do not need to use the earnings for monthly expenses, you can reinvest. The effect of monthly compounding is a return higher than that of a bond that pays the same return but sends you interest checks only twice a year.

If you are receiving, for example, 7.7 percent monthly from a Ginny Mae Pass-Through, this would be equivalent to a corporate bond paying 8.25 percent from a semiannual coupon payment.

A number of firms make a secondary market in Ginny Maes so there is no liquidity problem. There is the risk, however, that interest rates may go up. Therefore, since a prospective buyer can get a higher return if he buys a new pass-through instead of yours, your certificate will bring a lower figure than you paid for it. If the interest rate goes down, the reverse occurs and your pass-through can probably be sold for more than you paid for it.

Municipal Bonds • Municipal bonds (or notes) are issued by local governments (cities, states, and various districts and political subdivisions) instead of the federal government and its agencies. Municipals provide lower returns or yields than government bonds, primarily because of the special feature they provide: The interest paid on municipal obligations is totally exempt from federal income tax. (I will cover them in more detail in the chapter entitled "Avoiding the One-Way Trip to Washington.")

Yields on municipal issues are determined by the current level of interest rates, the credit rating of the issuer, and the tax laws.

Typically, municipal bonds are issued in a series of bonds with anywhere from 10 to 30 maturity dates. Interest is normally paid semiannually. Investors tend to buy them as they are issued and hold them until maturity. However, municipals, like other bonds, can be sold prior to maturity in the secondary dealer market at the then prevailing market rates. Such a sale may result in a return greater or less than the yield at acquisition.

• CORPORATE BONDS

Another way you may want to consider lending your money is through the purchase of corporate bonds. Corporate bonds (or notes) can be classified into a number of subcategories depending on the type of corporation issuing the bond, but from your point of view, there are essentially only two types: straight bonds and convertible bonds. Straight corporate bonds, like most governments and municipals, pay semi-annual interest to maturity, whereupon you receive the principal amount. Convertible bonds offer one additional feature: They can be exchanged, at any time you wish, for a fixed number of shares of the issuing company's common stock. Therefore, convertibles have dual characteristics—as fixed-income securities (like any other bonds) and as equity securities that may appreciate (or depreciate) in accordance with the stock price movement of the company's common stock. If a convertible bond trades at a price above that which it would as a straight bond for the same company, maturity, etc., it is usually thought of as an equity security rather than as a bond.

Corporate bonds are usually sold in minimum amounts of $1,000, although there are some $500 bonds. The yield is subject to the current level of interest rates, the maturity, and the credit standing of the issuer. Because no corporation is considered to be as creditworthy as the federal government, corporate bonds generally pay a slightly higher return—usually ½ percent to 2 percent higher—than comparable government bonds. Obviously, even when comparing one corporation to another, some are riskier and therefore have to pay more to borrow money. There were times, such as in the mid-1970s, when "junk bonds" reached yields as high as 14 percent to 16 percent. Like other bonds, corporates can be sold prior to maturity at prevailing market rates.

Many bonds permit the issuing corporation to redeem them early, usually for a price slightly higher than the maturity value. This call privilege gives the borrower an element of protection in that he can call in his bonds and issue new ones at a lower interest rate if rates have declined since the time the original bonds were issued. Actually, only bonds trading at a premium over par (indicating that interest yields are now lower than they were at time of issue) are subject to call.

You will want to become familiar with corporate bonds because they can be extremely useful in short-term financial planning. Bonds can be a safe short-term investment. If history repeats itself, they can become long-term speculations.

Bonds should be considered as a possible investment vehicle when stock market prices are historically high. When the market reaches a low price–earnings level and your financial objective is growth of capital, you should then consider selling them and moving into the stock market.

Let's assume the market is presently at a high level, and you desire to buy a bond. You will need to know about the issuer. The best source of this information is either Moody's or Standard and Poor's ratings. This will tell you their opinion of the company's ability to meet its principal and interest payments under adverse economic conditions. Two measures of this ability are the amount by which earnings exceed interest payments over a period of years and the amount of stock equity in a corporation in relation to borrowed funds.

If these rating services rate a bond in one of the top four categories, the bond is considered to be of investment-grade quality. To merit the very top rating, the speculative element is considered to be almost nonexistent. By the fifth rating, the speculative element has become quite significant, and by the seventh rating, the speculative element predominates.

Assume you have decided on an "A" rated bond and have selected a bond of the XYZ Corporation. Assume further that it is a 20-year bond bearing an $8\frac{1}{2}$ percent interest rate. You would then receive $85 per year on your $1,000 investment (if bought at par) for a period of 20 years, and at the end of the 20 years, if you still hold the bond, you would receive back your $1,000 principal. If you wanted your $1,000 prior to the twentieth year, you could sell your bond in the open market in much the same way that you would sell a stock. As with stocks, bonds on the open market are worth only what others will pay for them. In the bond market, buyers are usually willing to pay prices that closely coincide with the prevailing interest rate. If that rate were to remain at $8\frac{1}{2}$ percent, then a bond with an income of $85 a year would continue to have a market value of $1,000, and you would break even when you sold (exclusive of any commissions). But if the prevailing interest rate were to rise to $9\frac{1}{2}$ percent after one year, an income of $85 a year would no longer be worth $1,000. In order to yield $9\frac{1}{2}$ percent, the XYZ bond with $85 a year income would sell for about $913. And if the prevailing interest rate should decline, say, from $8\frac{1}{2}$ to $7\frac{1}{2}$ percent, a buyer would have to pay about $1,100 for an income of $85 a year. Or you could sell your bond for about $1,100. In other words, in this example (with an 8½ percent bond 19 years from maturity), an increase of one percentage point in the general interest rate would give you a loss of about $87, while a decrease of one percentage point in the general interest rate would give you a profit of about $100.

In capsule form, this is how all bonds work. Because they represent a fixed stream of income, their market value will fall when the general interest rate rises and rise when the interest rate falls.

Suffice it to say that although all bonds are worth $1,000 on the day they are issued and on the day of maturity, their market value wanders considerably during the interim. Because the cost of money has risen so dramatically since the mid-1960s, the market values of virtually all bonds issued prior to that time have declined to well below their $1,000 face values. This kind of market risk in the bond market is very real and exists regardless of the credit worthiness of the borrower.

Bond interest rates fluctuate for a number of reasons. Probably chief among them during the past few years has been price inflation and expectations of future inflation. As inflation rates increase, consumers and businesses are willing to increase their borrowing to buy at today's lower prices, and individuals become less willing to save at existing interest rate levels. Therefore, interest rates rise to compensate the saver for the expected erosion in the purchasing power of the dollar and to wipe out the advantage to the borrower of speeding up his purchases.

Another key factor has been the policy of the Federal Reserve to "play" with the supply of money—increasing and decreasing it in an effort to either stimulate or decelerate the economy. In the short run, an acceleration in the rate of growth of the money supply will produce lower interest rates, but over time it will also promote a higher rate of inflation that will result in higher interest rates.

Fluctuation of economic activity also has influenced interest rates. The demand for credit rises as economic activity picks up, and therefore interest rates tend to rise; the demand for credit falls as economic activity slows, and this pushes interest rates down.

• CORPORATE AND
MUNICIPAL BOND FUNDS

If you have limited funds, it will be difficult for you to buy and sell small quantities of bonds because of the spread between "bid" and "asked" in these small purchases. It is also difficult to diversify adequately. For this reason you may want to use professionally managed corporate and municipal bond funds. They offer a savings of the time and talent required to judge the merits of individual issues, their ratings, their maturities, coupon rates, a determination of how much to invest in each issue, the clipping of coupons (it's always sounded like fun, but it's really quite a nuisance), watching for called bonds, safekeeping securities, and year-end accounting.

The specialists managing the fund select the bonds to obtain a special combination of yield, proper diversification, marketability, suitability, and call protection. They will also follow the financial progress of all the issues in the fund. You will pay an initial sales charge, which is included in the offering price, plus a modest annual fee for custodial and portfolio evaluating services in the municipal and government bond funds, and a management fee of around one-half of 1 percent annually of the net asset value on the corporate bond fund.

Current market prices are readily obtainable. Prices at which each bond fund can be bought or sold are published daily.

• CREDIT UNIONS

I find many of my clients who work for corporations, the city, or our public schools use their credit union for a portion of their savings dollar. You may have a credit union available to you. It can be extremely handy for making deposits. In fact, your company may offer the service of depositing the amount you designate directly into your account. The credit union also provides a handy way to borrow.

I find, however, that many mistakenly think that they offer a less expensive way to borrow. This often is not true. Many credit unions charge 1 percent of the unpaid monthly balance, which is 12 percent per annum. Others charge three-quarters of 1 percent. This amounts to 9 percent. If you have acceptable collateral, you can usually borrow at a lower cost from your banker.

• MORTGAGES

Another way to lend money is to carry the mortgage balance on a home or other real estate you are selling. There are many who consider this quite an acceptable way to lend money. On the whole, I would not agree. The rates are frozen throughout the life of the mortgage, and the mortgage is an illiquid instrument except when sold at a considerable discount.

If you are selling a piece of property and are convinced the only way you can get the extra few thousands you desire for your property is to take a second lien for that amount, go ahead and do so. If you collect on the loan, fine. If you do not, don't worry for you could not have sold it for the full amount you desired anyway. I have done this when selling my home on two occasions and have received payment on both second liens ahead of schedule and for the full amount.

• HISTORIC RATES OF RETURN

The rate of return you will receive by "lending" your dollars through any of the above methods will vary with economic conditions. Table 12 shows yields on various fixed income instruments over the past 43 years.

Fixed income securities may be safe short-term investments and risky long-term investments. A bond purchased January 1, 1964, yielding 4.36 percent would have shown a loss of 34.1 percent (adjusted for inflation—56.0 percent) if sold ten years later.

• CASH SURRENDER VALUE

Another way that many families lend money, probably without realizing it, is by banking with life insurance companies by buying protection that contains a savings program. Of all the ways that you can "lend" money, this is perhaps the least rewarding. The policy does indicate earnings of 2½ percent to 3½ percent on the cash reserve, but if the policyholder dies, his family receives only the face amount, not the face amount plus the savings account as many seem to be led to believe by current advertising.

• ANNUITIES

Annuities are another way some choose to save for the future. What about annuities? Should you take the beautiful full-page color ads in your weekly magazines seriously and "invest" in an annuity for your happy golden years?

The best answer to this question can be found by looking at the past advertisements of insurance companies trying to entice you to buy an annuity.

Table 12.   Average Annual Yield on Selected Types of Investments, 1930–1973

Year	Savings Accounts in Savings Associations	Time & Savings Deposits in Commercial Banks	United States Government Bonds	Corporate (Aaa) Bonds
1930	5.3%	3.9%	3.3%	4.6%
1931	5.1	3.8	3.3	4.6
1932	4.1	3.4	3.7	5.0
1933	3.4	3.4	3.3	4.5
1934	3.5	3.0	3.1	4.0
1935	3.1	2.6	2.8	3.6
1936	3.2	2.0	2.6	3.2
1937	3.5	1.8	2.7	3.3
1938	3.5	1.7	2.6	3.2
1939	3.4	1.6	2.4	3.0
1940	3.3	1.3	2.2	2.8
1941	3.1	1.3	2.0	2.8
1942	3.0	1.1	2.5	2.8
1943	2.9	0.9	2.5	2.7
1944	2.8	0.9	2.5	2.7
1945	2.5	0.8	2.4	2.6
1946	2.2	0.8	2.2	2.5
1947	2.3	0.9	2.2	2.6
1948	2.3	0.9	2.4	2.8
1949	2.4	0.9	2.3	2.7
1950	2.5	0.9	2.3	2.6
1951	2.6	1.1	2.6	2.9
1952	2.7	1.2	2.7	3.0
1953	2.8	1.2	2.9	3.2
1954	2.9	1.3	2.6	2.9
1955	2.9	1.4	2.8	3.1
1956	3.0	1.6	3.1	3.4
1957	3.3	2.1	3.5	3.9
1958	3.38	2.21	3.43	3.79
1959	3.53	2.36	4.07	4.38
1960	3.86	2.56	4.01	4.41
1961	3.90	2.71	3.90	4.35
1962	4.08	3.18	3.95	4.33
1963	4.17	3.31	4.00	4.26
1964	4.19	3.42	4.15	4.40
1965	4.23	3.69	4.21	4.49
1966	4.45	4.04	4.66	5.13
1967	4.67	4.24	4.85	5.51
1968	4.68	4.48	5.25	6.18
1969	4.80	4.87	6.10	7.03
1970	5.06	4.95	6.59	8.04
1971	5.33	4.78	5.74	7.39
1972	5.40	4.65	5.63	7.21
1973	5.55	N.A.	6.30	7.44

Sources: Federal Home Loan Bank Board; United States Savings and Loan League; National Association of Mutual Savings Banks; Federal Reserve Board; Federal Deposit Insurance Corporation; Moody's Investors Service.

Go to your local library and request that they bring to you their *Life* magazines. You might start with the February 1, 1943, issue. There you will find a half-page ad with a bold headline that reads "$150 a Month as Long as You Live." The familiar logo at the bottom reads "_____ Mutual Retirement Income Plan Guarantees Your Future." The fine print does not say how much you would need to invest to retire at 60 with $150 per month, but it does hint that the smiling couple in the picture began at age 40, 20 years previous to the time it showed them in happy retirement. Now ask the librarian for the January 16, 1950, issue of *Life*. It also carried an ad by the same company headlined "How We Retired with $200 a Month." The ad shows another mature, well-dressed couple. There is a sandy beach and waving palm trees in the background. This one also does not mention the amount of investment they would have had to make over that period of time. The same logo though, "_____ Mutual Retirement Income Plan Guarantees Your Future."

Now ask for the January 15, 1951, issue of *Life*. It carried the *identical* picture as the January 16, 1950, ad, the same script, except the headline had been changed to "How We Retired with *$250* a Month." Yes, it had the same guarantee at the bottom. The January 23, 1956, *Life* magazine ran another ad by the same insurance company. This headline read "How a Man of 35 Can Retire at 55 with $300 a Month." The inflation train continues to run faster and faster, but the ad department seems to be able to keep up by increasing the ante each time.

"Retire on $150 a Month" sounded pretty good back then, so this dollar figure was commonly used in offering fixed-dollar retirement plans. But the story kept changing. The changes in these figures provide unique evidence that there is no such thing as a "guaranteed," "riskless" way to achieve financial independence.

Have you ever wondered why the annuity ads often show a man fishing? Do you think it's because he wants to eat?

• **SHOULD YOU EVER BORROW MONEY?**

Should you ever consider reversing the "lending" process and you be the recipient? Of course you should, if you can put the money to work so that your after-tax cost is less than the amount you will earn on the investment you made with the loan.

In fact, in these days of high taxes it is difficult to accumulate a large estate without borrowing money. The great financier Bernard Baruch, when asked how he made his fortune, replied, "O.P.M.—Other People's Money."

Where, when, and how should you borrow money?

If you have collateral in the form of publicly traded stocks, your least expensive source for loans in normal times will usually be your own bank. You should go to the collateral loan department (never to the consumer loan department unless you lack collateral).

Assume you want to buy an automobile. You own 100 shares of an excellent stock for which you paid $50 a share, and it is now trading at $100 with excellent growth potential for the future. Why kill the goose that is laying the golden egg, and why realize a $5,000 capital gain on which you will be required to pay federal income taxes?

Take your stock to your banker and pledge it as collateral. You will be required to leave the stock certificate with him and sign a stock power that allows him to sell the stock and keep the amount you owe to him if you do not repay or renew the loan the day it becomes due.

Collateral loans are usually made for 90 days or 180 days. You may pay on the principal in the interim, but you are not required to do so. On the date the loan becomes due you will be required to send your banker a check for the interest, and you may, if you desire, send him a letter requesting that he renew the loan. Usually this will be acceptable to your banker, for banks must lend money to earn a profit. They have already made a credit check on you and found you acceptable.

Sometimes you'll get a rookie loan officer who learned at banking school that borrowers should be reducing their principal periodically. However, after a little discussion with him as to how banks make their profit, he usually will be quite agreeable to renewing your note.

Always go boldly to borrow money—not with head bowed in an apologetic manner. If your banker had a house to rent and you were considering renting one, in what posture would you go to him? In this instance you have come to do him the "favor" of renting his money so that he can make a profit.

Your banker is always happy to rent you money if you can prove you don't need it. What is your proof that you really don't need it? Your stock certificate, of course, for you obviously could sell the stock and have the money.

Another reason for borrowing on your stock rather than cashing it in is that you are more likely to repay the bank than yourself. For example, you want to buy an automobile, but you don't have that amount in savings. Make a collateral loan to pay for the auto. Then when you finish paying the bank the loan, you will have your auto and your stock.

Build up your collateral and you'll always have the wherewithal for borrowing money that you can put to work. My personal philosophy is that every one of my dollars should be put to work 1 and $7/10$ times—since 70 percent is what my banker will usually loan to me on collateral.

Interest Deductible • Interest is deductible on your income tax return. Assume you borrow at 10 percent and are in the 30 percent tax bracket; your net cost after taxes will be 7 percent. If you are in the 50 percent bracket, net cost is only 5 percent. Can you invest this money so that your after-tax return will be greater than your after-tax cost? If so, rent the money. If not, your answer is obvious.

Savings Accounts as Collateral • I find that often a person whom I'm counseling proudly tells me he has found an inexpensive source for a loan by pledging his savings account as collateral. If you need funds and you have them in a savings account, go ahead and draw them out and use them. They are probably paying you 2 percent less than they are charging you; therefore you are 2 percent in the hole by borrowing your own money.

An exception to this would be if you are very near a dividend date. For example, assume you have a 1-year $10,000 certificate of deposit that matures December 31. You need funds on November 1. Use your certificate of deposit for collateral. You'll pay them interest at 8 percent for two months, but they'll pay you interest at 6 percent for 12 months: $10,000 @ 6 percent for 12 months equals $600. $10,000 @ 8 percent equals $800 ÷ 12 months = $66.66 × 2 months equals $133.32. Therefore, you still salvage $466.68 of your interest and have the funds you need. This $133.32 is deductible on your income tax. (But the $600 is taxable.)

If your certificate of deposit or savings account is at a bank, you can usually borrow 100 percent. If it is a savings and loan, they will usually loan 90 percent.

Servicing the Loan • You will need sufficient funds or income to pay your interest on your loan when due. There are some stock investments that have a high after-tax yield that can service your loan while you are enjoying appreciation of the stock, plus hopefully putting the funds you have borrowed to work profitably.

A particular commercial real estate investment trust (commonly called REITs and discussed more fully in another chapter) has produced for our clients an excellent return from which they could service their loans. For those who invested at $10, the dividend of $1.20 is 12 percent. For those who invested later, the yield has been 9.6 percent, with 76 percent tax sheltered.

If you have a certain type of tax-sheltered annuity, you may also choose to borrow against it rather than withdraw the funds and realize a tax liability. In this case, the loan will be obtained from the investment company that holds your annuity, and the amount you may borrow will be from 90 percent to 96 percent.

Borrowing Against Cash Value of an Insurance Policy • There are many who consider this a low-cost source of loans. In my opinion, the only time you should borrow on your cash surrender value is when your health is so poor that you cannot pass a physical for a new policy. If you can pass a physical and obtain pure protection at a lower cost, do so. When you have the new coverage, redeem the old policy. You will then have the cash you need without paying the insurance company to borrow your own money.

If your health is such that you cannot pass a physical, borrow the money from your policy and put it to work advantageously. Let's assume that you can borrow the cash surrender value for 5½ percent. Technically, at the same time, they are paying you approximately 2½ percent on the cash reserves. This is only a 3 percent spread. In addition, the interest is deductible, thereby lowering your after-tax cost.

• SUMMARY

Should you ever put your dollars in a "loaned" position? Yes, if you need a position for your investment dollars or when interest rates reach the astronomical heights they did in 1974 (12 to 13 percent on 30 day— $100,000 certificates of deposit.) But you should rarely do so on a long-term basis. As you can see from Table 12, over the past 10 years you would have suffered a loss if you had held bonds for long periods of time. Interest rates have risen, and inflation has taken its toll. You should learn to use fixed-income instruments when it is to your advantage to be out of the stock market, but do not complacently overstay.

On the other hand, should you ever do the reverse and borrow money? The answer is yes, if your return is greater than your after-tax cost and if you can sell your investment for more than you owe. Always be solvent.

Application

How can you apply the information contained in this chapter to your own financial future? Take a moment now to consider these questions: How much do you need to hold in cash reserves to give you peace of mind? Where should you keep these "loaned" dollars? How do you keep current on the best yields that will also fit your needs and time schedule? Should you take the trouble to check the assets and credit standing of a savings institution before making a deposit? How would you do this? Can you borrow money and still have peace of mind? What collateral do you have now? What steps do you plan to take to build your collateral?

{4}

How,
What, and
Where
Stocks
Are Traded

Now lets take a look at how you can "own" shares of American Industry.

- ### "PLAYING
  ### THE MARKET"

I often have people come up to me at our seminars or at social occasions and say almost smugly, "I play the market," as if the market were a game. They seem to think I should be pleased and give them a loving pat on the head. Investing is not a game. It is a very exacting art and science that requires skill, training, knowledge, and discipline. Even with these qualifications you will not always be right. This is a very dynamic and fast-moving world we live in, and it changes every minute of every day.

Successful investing is a skill you must learn yourself or hire the professionals to do it for you. You have no choice. You must save for the future. If you place your money in a fixed, "guaranteed" position, present inflation and the tax bite "guarantee" that you will have less purchasing power at the end of the year than at the beginning. You'll become like our little frog without the magic kiss.

To be successful in the stock market you will need to know how to use the mass network of facilities available to you for trading securities.

Stocks that are publicly held are classified as either listed or unlisted (commonly referred to as over-the-counter). Listed means that a stock is listed on a national or regional exchange. These represent, in dollar assets, the largest segment of the American economy. There is no asset you own that you can so readily turn into cash as a stock listed on a national exchange. It offers almost instant liquidity.

Our four largest exchanges are the New York Stock Exchange, the American Stock Exchange, the Pacific Stock Exchange, and the Mid-West Stock Exchange.

• THE BIG BOARD

The New York Stock Exchange is the oldest and largest. It began very informally near the time of the birth of our nation. Our first Secretary of the Treasury needed to set up a monetary system. To have a monetary system in this new nation, he needed to establish banks. To establish banks, he needed stockholders who were willing to invest capital. However, no one was willing to invest capital in bank stocks if there was no way to sell their shares. To make a market for these bank stocks and other issues, a group of 11 men used to meet under a buttonwood tree at the foot of a street called Wall, and trade among themselves and as agents for their clients. They eventually moved inside, and from this humble beginning grew the mighty New York Stock Exchange.

• HOW WALL STREET GOT ITS NAME

It might interest you to know how Wall Street got its name. The Dutch, who first settled Manhattan Island, were very fond of pork so they brought hogs from the Netherlands. To confine the hogs they built a wall to make a pig pen—hence the street got its name Wall Street. It's fun to note that some of our stock market history goes back to pigs and hogs. Unfortunately, we still have a few investors who get piggish. It is always good to remember an old saying, "In Wall Street, the bulls sometimes make it and the bears sometimes make it, but the hogs never do." *

* Esar, Evan. *Twenty Thousand Quips and Quotes*. New York: Doubleday, 1968.

• THE OVER-THE-COUNTER MARKET

Another vast area of the stock market is the "unlisted" market, called the over-the-counter market, that has no "counter" or meeting place. Once I had a lady become confused and ask me for an "under-the-counter" stock. After she told me the stock she had in mind, I decided she had accidentally hit on a good description.

The over-the-counter market is a vast negotiated market. In the past there has been no central market place. Various brokerage houses would "make a market" in a particular stock. This means they would inventory the stock they bought and sold. There are now over 50,000 stocks traded in the over-the-counter market, through a network of telephone and tele-type wires linking the various brokerage houses. There is a daily "pink sheet" giving "Bid" and "Asked" quotations of the market makers from the previous day reporting to the National Quotation Bureau. ("Bid" means what someone is willing to pay for the stock. "Asked" is the amount for which someone is willing to sell.) When you see a market report on a listed stock in the paper, you know that a trade actually took place at that price. In the over-the-counter market you could have a quote with no trade taking place.

There is a wide range of quality in the stocks traded in the over-the-counter market. Traditionally, bank and insurance company stocks have been traded there, even though they have substantial assets. On the opposite end are "penny stocks" (those that sell for a nominal amount per share), which also trade there.

Often a stock is traded over the counter for years, and as it grows in assets and popularity it will apply for listing on a national exchange and be accepted.

In the past, I have warned that if you are new to the market, you probably should avoid the over-the-counter market until you become more knowledgeable. With the establishment of NASDAQ the whole complexion of this market has begun to change.

• NASDAQ

In February 1971, the National Association of Security Dealers Advanced Quotations appeared on the scene, and it is in the process of making the over-the-counter market "a lady," as the expression goes. Various market makers of OTC stocks feed in the changes in their markets to Bunker-Ramo Central Control, which updates the "bid" and "asked" quotes on each issue every five minutes, showing the best "bid" and "asked" offers available.

NASDAQ has had a profound effect on the OTC market, making current markets available to all parts of the country at the same time and enabling dealers to give prompt and accurate service.

• YOUR BROKERAGE ACCOUNT

How do you use this mass network of facilities? How do you open an account with a stockbroker? It's just as easy as opening a charge account. As a matter of fact, your prospective broker will probably ask fewer questions than the department store where you applied for your last charge account. He will need to know your address, home and office telephone numbers, occupation and company for whom you work, if you are over 21, spouse's name (if married), social security number, if you are a U.S. citizen, bank reference, and how you want your stocks registered. When you make a purchase or sale, it is a firm commitment, regardless of whether the stock goes up or down. A confirmation is mailed to you showing the number of shares of stock purchased or sold, price, commission and fees, net amount due, and settlement date. Within five business days from the trade date you must pay for stocks you have bought. If you have sold a stock, you must deliver your stock certificate within the same period of time to receive payment.

How Your Order Is Executed • After your account has been opened you may place your orders by telephone with your broker and ask him to buy or sell securities for you. For example, let's assume you place an order to buy 100 shares of General Widgets "at the market." Your broker then gives the order to his company's trader. The trader immediately contacts their floor broker on the floor of the exchange who quickly walks (it's against the rules to run) to the post where General Widgets is traded. Since you want to buy, the floor broker tries to buy at the lowest price.

At the same time, there may be a farmer in Vermont who must have funds to pay for his son's college tuition. He contacts his broker, his broker contacts his floor broker, and the two of them meet at the General Widgets post. The exchange is an auction market, and bids and offer are made by outcry. That's why the floor of the exchange is so noisy and may look and sound like a madhouse. Your company's floor broker will be trying to buy for you at, say, $50 per share. The farmer's broker will be trying to sell at $50¼. Your broker finally decides he can't buy for you at $50, so $50⅛ is agreed upon. Millions of dollars worth of stock changes hands daily. However, no contracts are signed, and there is no shaking of hands. In this business your word is your bond; and when it isn't, you're no longer in this business. A record of the trade is written on a slip of paper and handed to a runner who places the slip in a pneumatic tube that carries it to the tape operator. Within approximately three minutes, if you are sitting in front of a tape in a brokerage office, you will see your trade coming across the screen, GWI 50 ⅛. This is for 100 shares. If the trade had been for 200, it would have shown GWI 2s 50 ⅛. If the trade was for 1,000 shares, it would appear GWI 1000s 50 ⅛.

Round Lot, Odd Lot · All transactions shown on the tape and reported in the financial section of your newspaper are for round lots (100-share trades or multiples of 100). This does not mean, however, that if you want to own some shares of General Widgets, you have to have $5,012.50 plus commission. For instance, if you want to buy 10 shares, you certainly may. You would give your 10-share order to the broker who would contact the odd lot broker. The odd lot broker buys in round lots on the exchange and divides it into odd lots. You pay an odd lot differential for his service. In this example, it would be an additional ⅛ of a point or $.125, because the stock is under $55 per share. If it had been over $55, you would have paid ¼ of a point or $.25. This is not a commission. It is an odd lot differential. Your commission would be in addition to the differential. As you can see, it's not enough difference to discourage you from buying in odd lots.

If you buy an odd lot on a round lot—for example, 125 shares—you pay an odd lot differential on the 25 shares if you trade on the New York Stock Exchange. If it's traded on the Pacific Stock Exchange, it trades with the round lot without the odd lot differential.

The amount you pay per share for your odd lot purchase is determined by the price of the next round lot trade after your order is received. For example, if the next round lot trade was $50⅛, you would pay $50¼.

Commissions Are Low · Stocks carry one of the lowest commission rates for the exchange of property in the United States. Remember the commission you paid when you sold your last house? Was it 6 percent to the realtor, plus all the closing costs, making your total between 10 percent and 12 percent? You can sell 100 shares of a $40 listed stock for a commission of around 1½ percent, and this will probably go lower. Quite a difference, isn't it?

· **THE LANGUAGE
   OF INVESTING**

The first information you will need to know is the different kinds of securities. There are basically three with which you'll be concerned. These are:

1 · Common stock

2 · Preferred stock

3 · Bonds or debentures

Common Stock · All corporations have common stock. If you organized a corporation for the purpose of buying a popcorn stand at the corner of Main Street and First, and sold one share of common stock to nine persons at $100 per share and one share to yourself at $100, the corporation would have capital of $1,000 and ten stockholders. In buying one of these shares you became a shareholder of the corporation. You took an equity position and will participate in the future gains or lack of gains of the corporation for as long as you hold your share.

Preferred Stock · Preferred stock is a stock on which a fixed dividend must be paid before the common shareholder is entitled to a dividend each year. The dividend is usually higher, and if it is a cumulative preferred stock, any past dividends that have been omitted must be paid before the common shareholder is entitled to a dividend. If the preferred is also convertible, it will have a conversion ratio into the common.

There is much confusion about preferred stock. I'm amazed at how the uninitiated seem to feel that "preferred" means "better." This is rarely true. Unless it's convertible, it has neither the growth potential of a common stock nor the safety of a bond. I personally believe there are better ways to invest.

Bonds or Debentures · The third type of security is a bond or debenture as we discussed previously. A corporate bond may be a mortgage bond. For example, if you were to invest in a particular railroad bond, you would hold a mortgage on specific freight cars.

A much larger area of the bond market are debentures. Your security for this type of bond is the general credit rating of the issuing corporation. For example, you may buy an American Telephone and Telegraph Debenture, 8.70 percent, due in 2002. In this instance you do not acquire a mortgage on specific telephones, but instead your security is based on the tremendous assets and credit of AT&T.

Characteristics of common stocks and bonds can be oversimplified by stating them in this manner:

Stocks

1 · Not guaranteed as to principal.

2 · Not guaranteed as to rate of return.

3 · Guaranteed to participate in the future destiny of the company.

Bonds

1 · "Guaranteed" as to principal if assets are available.

2 · "Guaranteed" as to rate of return if funds are available.

3 · Not guaranteed to grow regardless of any increase in the profits of the corporation.

Convertibles • There are those who feel that convertible bonds give the best of two worlds—offering you the third characteristic under stocks, and the first two under bonds; however, they frequently fall short on both scores.

A convertible bond is a bond that usually carries a lower interest rate than a regular corporate bond, but is convertible into common at a specified ratio. For example, if a convertible is bought at par, which in a bond is usually $1,000, and is convertible into 100 shares of common at the holder's option and the common is selling at $10, there would be no incentive to exchange, for the bond will usually carry a higher yield than the common. However, if the market price of the common should increase to $15, you would now have a bond with a value of $1,500. If, on the other hand, the common goes below $10, you still have your bond with its higher yield acting as a cushion under the bond.

How have they performed? Not well enough for any gold stars. The size and quality of the convertible market has left much to be desired. In severe market declines they have suffered along with their common neighbors.

Our emphasis in this book will be on common stocks since they offer you the greatest potential for gain (or loss). There are a vast array of stocks, so which ones will be best for you? To shed some light on this subject you will need to know the relationships among earnings, dividends and yields and what they mean to you.

• BE AN
INFORMED INVESTOR

The adage of "investigate before you invest" should be heeded. There is a wealth of information available to you on all listed stocks and a large number of over-the-counter securities.

Standard and Poor Reports are excellent sources of information.

Study these. Learn to analyze financial statements. An excellent booklet entitled "Understanding a Financial Statement" that should be of help to you can be obtained from the New York Stock Exchange.

The Wall Street Journal, Barrons, Forbes and *Financial Trends* will bring you much needed information. As you study and invest, you will begin to get a feel for the market and hopefully develop some "gut" feelings that will enable you to profit from owning your share of American industry.

Application

What course of study and action will you now take to become better informed about how to invest in American industry? Which financial publications will you make available to yourself for regular study? Do bonds or common stocks best fit your needs? What steps do you plan to take to select the right planner to best fit your financial objectives and your temperament?

$$\left\{ 5 \right\}$$

How
To Select
Stocks
for Income

- **KNOWING THE RATIOS**

Let's assume that we are studying two well-managed companies, X and Y. They both manufacture an excellent product for which there has been an increasing demand. For ease of comparison, assume the stock of both companies sells for $10 per share and that both earn $1 per share.

Stock X pays a 50¢ dividend, and stock Y pays a 10¢ dividend. What is the yield of each and what is the price–earnings ratio?

Stock	Market price	Earnings per share	Dividend	Yield	Price–Earnings ratio
X	$10	$1	50¢	5%	10:1
Y	$10	$1	10¢	1%	10:1

Yield is the relationship of the dividend to the market price. Therefore, a 50¢ yield on a $10 stock would be 5 percent per annum. A 10¢ dividend would then be a 1 percent yield.

The *price–earnings ratio*, often referred to as the P/E, is the relationship of the market price to the earnings. It indicates how much the investing public is willing to pay for $1 of earnings. In both stocks the amount is $10, making the P/E ratio 10:1.

Which Stock is Best? • Which stock is best for you, X or Y? When I ask this question in the seminars, the majority choose stock X. The savings institution's advertising campaigns have made them very income conscious.

Did you answer X or Y? The correct answer for you depends on your financial objective. Do you need income now, or do you need income later? If you need it now, you should choose stock X; if you need it later, you should choose stock Y. If the company pays out 50¢ to you and you are in a 30 percent tax bracket, you lose 15¢ to Washington. If you are in a 50 percent bracket, you lose 25¢. If your need is for income later, then you very well may come out better if the company plows back the 90¢ into enlarged plants and facilities, with the hope that some day stock Y will grow in value to perhaps $15 per share. Sometimes it's better to get your eyes off the extra 4 percent income and on to the 50 percent potential in capital gains.

There is often another factor to be considered, and that is your temperament. There is a triangle in finance as there may be in romance. Let's look at the financial triangle and see where you should place yourself for your mental comfort and for the best correlation with your financial objectives.

Triangle of Finance • At the top of the triangle I have placed "Growth," at the left "Income," and at the right "Stability." (I used to call this corner "Safety," but with our present rate of inflation, you may be "stable" without being "safe," so I have changed it to "Stability.") By stability, I mean a guarantee of the same number of dollars at a future date, not the return of the same purchasing power.

As you can see, the farther you move toward Growth, the farther you move from Stability and Income. You may be young enough to invest for Growth, but when you move in that direction, you could have increased volatility. This may disturb your peace of mind, and peace of mind is a good investment, too. If you were my client, I would try to determine your peace of mind level because regardless of how well the investment fits your financial objective, if you are uncom-

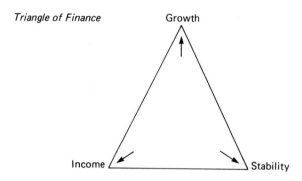

Triangle of Finance

Growth

Income

Stability

fortable with it, it's not right for you and you may abandon it before it has had time to achieve the desired goal.

Let's examine first the chief characteristics you should look for if your desire is for income.

• HOW TO SELECT INCOME STOCKS

Income stocks are relatively easy to select as compared to growth stocks. However, there are some important keys you'll want to determine before you give your broker the buy order.

Good Dividends That Keep Increasing • You want stocks that not only pay good dividends but also have a record of increasing their dividends rather consistently. If you are dependent on your dividends for your groceries and the price of food continues to rise, you must either increase your income or reduce your intake. Most of us would probably be a lot healthier if we did the latter, but we have a tendency to reject this alternative.

Dividends That Are Earned • You should carefully determine if the corporation is earning the dividend. A few years ago many of the bank trust departments were putting shares of Sinclair Oil in trust accounts they managed for widows who needed income. Sinclair was paying a liberal dividend. Unfortunately, the trust officers did not look to see if the company was earning the amount they were paying. They were not. The day of reckoning came, as it usually does, the dividend was cut, and many a widow's account suffered capital losses.

Do not reach too far for yield and jeopardize your capital.

Often I have calls from someone who is going through a Standard and Poor's Stock Guide and who spots a stock paying a 12 percent to 14 percent yield. They'll excitedly call to buy it, assuming that no one else has been so observant as to have spotted this bonanza. Usually, the reason for the high yield is the poor evaluation the market has given to the future prospects of the company.

This is not always true. During the gloomy months of 1973 and 1974, there were some very fine Real Estate Investment Trusts that offered a solid 12 percent to 14 percent yield.

Resistance to Business Cycles • A characteristic of all good income stocks should be that they have a good measure of resistance against cyclical waves in the economy. A rather earthy description might be "stomach stocks." The consumer demand for the products produced by these companies will continue through both good and bad points in the economic cycle.

Long Dividend Record • In selecting stocks for dependable income, it is obvious you will want to choose quality issues since younger, less tested companies have not been around long enough to establish an extended dividend payment record.

Income stocks usually pay out between 65 percent to 75 percent of their net earnings in cash dividends. Once a regular dividend rate has been established, it is unlikely that it will be reduced due to poor earnings in a single year.

During times of market corrections I often have calls from less sophisticated holders of income stocks who are worried that their dividend will be cut because the market price is down. If all is well with their company, I try to calm them with the explanation that short-term market prices often have no relationship to earnings. (In the long term they usually do.) 1972–1974 were banner years for corporate profits, but it was not reflected in the market prices.

Who Decides the Amount of the Dividend? • The amount remaining after the expenses and taxes have been paid by a company is the amount available for dividends. The decision as to whether a dividend should be paid and how much it should be is made by the board of directors. The amount of the earnings, the need for retained earnings, and the past dividend record all influence the directors' decision.

Yield on Original Purchase Price • As you've learned above, the yield on a stock is the relationship of the dividend to the market price. Every shareholder is entitled to the same dividend per share. However, the market price paid by one shareholder may be different from that paid by another. If you paid $50 for a share of stock and the dividend is $2, your yield on your original investment is 4 percent ($2 divided by $50). If you paid $35, the $2 represents a return, or yield, on your original investment of slightly more than 5.7 percent.

Most yields, however, are calculated on current market price. Assuming the price per share is now $60, still with a $2 dividend, the yield would be slightly over 3.3 percent.

Looking Ahead • If you do not need income now, consider companies with slightly lower yields. Often these companies are plowing back a larger portion of their earnings into expanded facilities that should in time yield higher earnings that would allow them to pay out higher dividends. Over a 10- to 15-year period many growth stocks have actually had a larger cash pay-out than income stock. One percent on $10,000 is only $100. But let's assume the growth stock continues to grow and reaches a value of $100,000. (One percent on $100,000 is $1,000 or 10 percent on your original investment.)

A booklet you may find of help if you are interested in selecting stocks for income is one published by the New York Stock Exchange entitled "Investment Facts—Cash Dividends Every Three Months From

25 to 100 Years." The booklet points out that the widespread ownership of stocks listed on the New York Stock Exchange is due in large part to a growing awareness that surplus dollars can be put to work in investments that will reflect the ever-changing economic conditions of our country.

The ability of common stocks to mirror these developments constitutes their greatest attribute. Of course, it is also their greatest risk.

On the plus side is the fact that over the years, good common stocks often have helped their owners keep in step with living costs.

There is no such phenomenon as a "sure thing," and history carries no guarantee of the future. But the facts history has recorded may serve as a clue to the future. If so, it may be of help to look at the long-time dividend payers listed in this booklet.

The booklet lists recent prices of the stock, the dividend record, and its yield. Of these common stocks, 466 have paid a cash dividend every single quarter for 25 years, and 100 have paid a dividend for every quarter for 50 to over 100 years.

Preferred Stocks • Preferred stocks are equities senior to the common, but junior to indebtedness of the issuer. Preferred stock dividend income is 85 percent tax-exempt for corporations, which often makes them attractive corporate investments. This fact tends to raise the price of the preferred in the market place, which will generally make them less attractive to you for your individual investment program. You will normally receive a higher rate of return from a high-quality corporate bond than from a preferred stock.

• INCOME vs. GROWTH

The equities market provides a wide spectrum of alternatives with respect to rates of return. When investing in growth companies, you must pay a premium in terms of P/E relationship and, therefore, receive less in the way of current income. Growth companies have an opportunity to reinvest their earnings at higher rates than are available to you as a stockholder if the earnings were paid out to you and you had only the after-tax amount to invest. Therefore, growth companies have very low pay-out ratios.

It is too simplistic, but there is a great deal of truth in the fact that the highest yielding common stocks have low expectations of future growth and, therefore, low P/Es.

If you do not expect growth of the company, you should ask

yourself why the price is so low making the yield so high. Is the company in serious financial straits? Is the company likely to cut its dividends? Is the regulatory environment likely to be adverse so that the company may have to reduce its dividend to conserve its cash for working capital needs? What is the outlook for the industry, etc.?

It is clear that investing for income is not without risk. If you had bought steel company or copper company issues a few years ago for income, you would have had your dividends reduced and in some instances eliminated. Not only did the income go down, but the principal loss was substantial—more than 50 percent in some cases. It is also clear, however, that investing for high income can have its rewards. In the merger craze of the late 1960s, finance companies and cash-rich insurance companies, considered "income common stocks," became the targets of acquiring companies. Some of those acquired had spectacular rises in their prices, and if you sold your shares at the proper time, you could have realized substantial capital gains.

In summary, if your desire is for income:

1 · Look for companies that have a long unbroken dividend record.

2 · Don't reach too far for yield and jeopardize principal.

3 · Too high a yield can be dangerous and misleading.

4 · Favor companies producing consumer goods and services.

5 · Select sound companies that continue to increase their dividends.

During the mid-1970s the validity of investing in income stocks was praised by many and discouraged by others. Those who suggested their purchase pointed out that stocks paying good dividends held up better in market declines. Those who discouraged buying income stocks pointed out other vehicles that became available in good supply that paid a higher income with less risk in the short term. Good corporate bonds and bond funds offered 9 percent yields, and certificates of deposit in amount over $100,000 reached the 12 percent level for short periods of time.

Many top investment advisory services will not accept accounts with an "income" objective, limiting themselves to "growth" and "aggressive growth."

Income stocks are not too difficult to select after you've conscientiously done your homework. However, selecting growth stocks can be one of the greatest challenges you have ever undertaken. Let's now embark on this challenge.

Application

Take a financial and emotional inventory of yourself and ask: Do you need income now, or do you need income later? Where do you fit temperamentally on the financial triangle? Even if your objective is growth, are there times when income stocks are preferable? If your objective is income, have you thoroughly checked a potential stock investment to see if it measures up to the income criteria above?

$$\left\{ \; 6 \; \right\}$$

Growth Stocks— The Royal Road to Riches?

During the surging sixties the magic word on Wall Street, Main Street, Podunk Street or most any street you happened to be traveling at the time, was "Growth"! Investing in "growth" stocks was the royal highway to riches. So greatly did some "investors" become enamored of that magic word that they were willing to pay fantastic prices for new and relatively untested electronic and scientific issues. So unrealistic did they become that they actually paid as high as 70 times earnings. In some instances there were no earnings at all.

- ## GROWTH STOCKS— WHAT ARE THEY?

What are growth stocks, and why should you consider investing in them?

A growth company is usually one that is increasing its sales and earnings at a faster rate than the growth of the national population and business in general. The long-term annual growth rate of our population has been about 3 percent. In recent years large families have become taboo, and we are beginning to move toward zero population growth. The annual growth in gross national product has been around 6.6 percent in recent years. A growth company as a rule of thumb should be increasing its sales and net earnings at least as fast as the combination of the two, and preferably much faster.

Growth companies are usually producing goods and/or services in dynamic and new industries. The 1940s saw the surge of oil stocks, television shares, and pharmaceutical companies. The 1950s continued the drug stocks' popularity, with flurries in uranium, cameras, electronics, missiles and automation.

The 1960s saw leisure time industries, baby products, electronics continued, with computer-oriented stocks keeping pace, technology related industries, life insurance companies, drugs, retail, convenience goods, soft drinks, and, most especially, the surge of the conglomerates trying to leverage their balance sheets, many times using what became known as "funny money." Ling-Temco-Vought, Gulf and Western, Textron, and International Telephone and Telegraph all brought visions of investor "sugar plums" during their heydays of mergers and acquisitions. There was a short period of time when there were jokes in the investment community of investment decisions becoming a matter of which one of the few conglomerates to choose. The tinsel began to tarnish, the craze passed, and we returned to sound investment evaluation based on realities rather than the new math of Wall Street, which seemed to say 2 plus 2 equals 5.

• THE
MID SEVENTIES

During the first part of the 1970s the market suffered a major correction. This correction was much more extensive than the widely followed Dow Jones Industrial Average revealed. The decline of the Dow, though sizable, was not bad enough to explain the awful sense of despair that gripped Wall Street during the latter part of 1973 and on through 1974 and 1975. It did not tell how hard the overall stock market was hit. The only averages that showed declines approaching the true magnitude were the superbroad unweighted ones such as the *Value Line Composite* and the *Indicator Digest* average.

The bull market of the 1960s was in the supergrowth stocks—the franchises, the computer leasers, and the like—not the staid, less volatile Dow 30. The Dow went up during those years, but the broader averages went up more rapidly and also went down more rapidly when the high flyers fell out of favor.

Why was the market plunge so severe in 1973 and 1974? There are many reasons, all interrelated and interacting. Let's look at a few of them.

Many market declines are in direct relationship to the junk some stockbrokers "peddle" on the way up. Being a broker is a volatile vocation, but it is made more so by the short memories of a large portion of its personnel. It was another case of too much sizzle and not enough steak.

The Federal Reserve Board instituted extremely restrictive money policies in an effort to slow down runaway inflation. The results of its actions could be compared to taking a man who has been accustomed to three gourmet meals a day and throwing him into solitary confinement, giving him only bread and water and then beating him with a stick. The market must have a steady flow of money to function properly. Historical studies show a direct relation between the supply of money in the economy and stock market prices.

The uglies of Watergate disillusioned the American public like nothing else had in many a decade. Their faith in their leaders was badly shaken. A sense of uneasiness and gloom settled over our nation. When people feel badly inside, they sell their stocks. When they feel good, they buy. Gut-level feelings have no correlations with earnings. Human emotion took over, and they sold and sold.

It is at times such as those that we need to read these words: ". . . even in the general moment of gloom in which this . . . is written, when many begin to wonder if declines will never halt, the appropriate abracadabra may be: 'They always did.'" *

• **HOW TO SPOT
  GROWTH STOCKS**

To become good at selecting stocks for growth you must be aware of current events—current trends, current psychology, current money markets. In fact, you must be truly current. You live in a dynamic world that changes daily. One of the most stimulating characteristics of being a financial planner is that every day is a new day in the market. Nothing remains static. There is no way you can be a truly top-notch investor by buying blue chips and throwing them in a drawer and forgetting them. This only increases your risk and lowers your opportunity for gain.

* Bernard M. Baruch, October 1932.

Be in the Right Industry • If I were to choose the most important consideration for selecting growth stocks, I would have to say that it is to be in the right industry at the right time. There is always an industry moving up, regardless of the general overall trend of the market. During the drastic declines of 1974, the oil equipment, sugar, and gold stocks steadily gained. You should endeavor to predict a trend before it happens and to move out before the trend runs out. You should try to be aware of technological changes and opinions of the buying public. It will not pay you to be right if nobody cares. Sitting with money in a stagnant "correct" situation while other stocks are moving up just doesn't take the place of making money.

Fantasy Stocks • Do not buy what I call fantasy stocks—stocks based on an idea yet to come. The idea may be great—even correct and true— but how do you know there will be adequate financing, good and honest management, marketing ability, and public acceptance of the product? (What people want and what they need are different things.) You might say, "But look at Haloid that later became Xerox." There is no way that those who bought Haloid could have known it would become one of the best-managed sales organizations that the country had seen for many a year. Too, you could have bought Xerox many times since its beginning and made just as much money with proper timing on buys and sells. If you will wait until some of the results are in, it may save you some heartaches. (Of course, you will also need to be astute enough to avoid getting on at the front of the bus while the informed are getting off at the back.)

This is different from a story stock from which good results have already been realized, but even better results are expected. The best story is the "Good Earnings Story."

Management the Key • There is no substitute for energetic, intelligent, dedicated, and enthusiastic management. They should be a stock-minded management team that is interested in increasing the market price of their stock, and this can only be sustained in the long term by increased earnings.

With good management and an average product it is possible to make money. A superior product with poor management may well yield very disappointing results. The key is good management and a superior product together.

How can you obtain this information? It is not an easy task. Resource materials and publications you may find helpful are *Standard & Poor's, Fortune, Forbes, Barrons, Financial Trends*, and *The Wall Street Journal.*

Self-Generating Earnings •   Select a company that has self-generating rising earnings and reserves with expectations for continued increases over the foreseeable future. Few companies really shine solely by acquisitions as many seemed to believe during the conglomerate era of mergers. Pre-tax earnings on assets of growth companies should be between 15 percent and 30 percent. Companies that have enjoyed such gains are Tampax, Avon, Merk, Coca Cola, Eastman Kodak, Minnesota Mining, Proctor and Gamble, IBM, Xerox, and Hewlett-Packard.

Technological Research and Development Are a Must •   A growth company must retain a large portion of its earnings for research and development that will produce a saleable product that offers excellence in quality, design, or performance, and hopefully all three.

Flair for Salesmanship •   A growth company must have a dynamic aggressive sales department. A good example of salesmanship is Revlon. They are masters at selling "hope in a jar." Their ads are so compelling that it takes restraint to read their brilliant magazine ads and not dash to the nearest cosmetic counter.

• INVESTOR OR
SPECULATOR

We've covered some of the basic characteristics you must consider in becoming an investor for growth. Should you ever speculate in the stock market? Are there categories between being an investor and being a rank speculator?

The Trader •   In even the most valid growth stock selection there is a time to buy and a time to sell. However, there is another area of the stock market that I would classify between the growth stock investor and the rank gambler. He is the trader. I must admit that the line of demarcation does get hazy at times.

There appear to be at least three classes of people who fit this category. If you do not have ample capital, I hope you will resist the temptation to join their ranks as most out-and-out traders die broke. These three classes are:

> 1 ·   The constitutional speculators; not necessarily gamblers, but people willing to "take a chance"—to take big risks in hope of great gain.

2 · Those who truly think they can supplement their income by modest trading in and out of the market.

3 · People with large amounts of income to whom fully taxable income is unattractive, but to whom long-term capital gains taxed at only 25 percent (or perhaps 35 percent) are most alluring.

In entering the market for trading purposes, timing is all important. This must be finely tuned.

Cyclical Stocks · Most short-term speculators use the so-called "cyclical" stocks. These shares are found in those industries most sensitive to swings in the business cycle. They include the heavily capitalized industries such as steel and heavy machinery. These areas are traditionally strongest in periods of prosperity and at a low ebb in times of recession. The trick is to buy cyclical stocks in the early stages of a business upturn and sell them as closely as possible to the crest. This is not easy.

Popular Favorites · Another trading technique is to move along with the popular stocks of the moment. You can make as much money, short term, on what others think a stock is worth, as on what it is really worth. In the long term we always return to basics.

Following the fashions in finance is hazardous. However, if, by using good logic, you are convinced that a new industry is about to boom, then cautious selections of a stock in that industry may prove rewarding. The trick is to buy early and then, when everyone is clamoring for shares in that industry, sell! Almost invariably the stock market darlings, at the height of their popularity, will sell above sensible valuations.

Special Situations · Another area of speculation is the area of special situations. This can cover a great many areas—mergers, sudden increase in the price of a valuable asset, a new mineral find, a new venture, and so on. Your success will greatly depend on your getting accurate information ahead of the pack. Is the product or service in the mainstream of a rapidly growing demand? Is the demand likely to last? If it is a new venture, determine if it is well capitalized. At least half of all new ventures fold because they run out of capital before they can get into full-fledged operation.

Who will be managing the company? Innovators may have a highly functional idea or patent, but they'll fail because they do not know how to run a business. Creative design people often are very poor at manufacturing techniques, cost control, merchandising, financing, and record keeping. Check to see if those who will run the business are personally solvent and have adequate practical or technical background. The key man may be a fantastic salesman and a poor production man, or vice versa. He may know sales promotion but have no idea about cost controls.

The third thing to consider in a new company is superiority of product or service. New products should be advanced, unusual, and ahead of the field.

Finally, can you afford to lose everything you put into the new company and not miss the money?

On the record, the chances of a new company growing from zero to great substance are very slim. But if this kind of speculation adds zest to your life and you can afford it, happy hunting!

• RIGHT STOCK ACTION

I'm not a chartist. I know very few chartists who have the discipline to act upon the signals the charts give.

Don't Be Greedy • One characteristic I have observed about the timing of all good traders is that they never try to squeeze out the last point in a stock. When the great financier Bernard Baruch was questioned on how he made so much money in the stock market, he answered, "I always sold too soon." He always tried to leave a little in it for the next buyer.

Cut Losses Quickly • In trading it is absolutely necessary to cut your losses quickly. If you've made an error in judgment, don't wait around to find out just how wrong you really were. You can't afford an ego trip. If a 10 percent drop occurs, seriously consider getting out.

Some of my clients act as if the stock knew they owned it or what they paid for it. The stock doesn't even know that your cousin, once removed, works for the company.

Don't think about an impending dividend, or that you have a loss in the stock, or that you just bought it. Also, don't hesitate to buy it back, even at a higher price, if you made a mistake in selling. Above all, don't fall in love with a stock—don't marry it. Be objective. Be flexible. Don't be guilty of prejudices in stock. We all have them occasionally, but the sooner you recognize them and shed stocks that hinder your investment judgment, the better investor you'll become.

Tax considerations should be the furthest from your mind. You are only trying to use $1 to make $2, not trying to do tax planning while in front of a stock board watching the "horses" run.

Don't Cry • Two other cardinal rules are "Don't cry" and "Don't look back." Lick your wounds and charge forward.

• A PROFITABLE PORTFOLIO

There are three basics to choosing and keeping a profitable portfolio of stocks. They are diversification, proper selection, and constant supervision. Let's examine the first, diversification. Diversification means spreading the risk. The old adage of not putting all your eggs in one basket has considerable merit in assembling a good investment portfolio.

Diversification • Don't put all your faith in only one company for it may disappoint you. You may be well informed on sales figures, competitive situations, or whatever, but always be prepared for a disaster. Going for broke on a winner could make you rich, but no one knows which stock will be the big winner. If you buy a diversified group of fundamentally sound stocks with good earnings, the chances are that in a good market you will catch at least some of the big winners. Most big money in a diversified portfolio comes from one or two big winners.

Don't be deceived into thinking 10 oil stocks is diversification; it is not. You should have a portfolio covering a wider range of industries. For example, you may have some stocks in the soft drink industry, the retail area, drugs, home furnishings, electrical equipment, brewing, agricultural machinery, gold mining, and others.

When managing your own portfolio, you may find it extremely helpful to limit yourself to 10 stocks, regardless of the amount of money you have to invest. I'm surprised to find that investors think they can only own 100 shares of each company's stock. If the capital you have available for investing is sufficiently large, perhaps you should consider owning 1,000 shares of each stock.

Moving to Strength • Don't overdiversify. You cannot be truly current on more than 10 stocks at a time. If you limit your holdings to 10 stocks and a stock comes to your attention that you feel you should buy, what will this force you to do? To eliminate one. So you go down through your list and sell the one that is doing the poorest job for you. Now, won't you? I wish this were true of all my clients. Many go through and pick out

their winner to sell and smugly say, "You'll never go broke taking a profit."
They are keeping their losers and selling their winners. That's not the
way to up-grade a portfolio. Sell the poorest performer. This allows you
the possibility of continuously moving to a position of strength.

Timing Is the Key • There is a time to buy and a time to sell. The old
adage about buying low and selling high is easy to say and very hard to
do. You never know what the high or low is often until it's too late for
maximum advantage.

But how do you determine when to buy and when to sell? Let's look
at buying first.

When To Buy • Buying is easier to time than selling. There are times
I am almost convinced that any time is a good time to buy good stocks at
a reasonable price/earnings ratio.

Let me give you an example. I was counseling a young couple, and
we had selected the stock that fit their financial requirements. It was
selling at $23 and was not overpriced based on past earnings and antici-
pated growth of earnings. The husband asked if I thought it might be
possible to buy the stock at $22 by waiting a while. The market did look as
if it could make a slight correction so I agreed to call them when it
reached $22. It reached their price in about a month, and I called them
to let them know it was time to purchase. Their response was, "Oh, I'm
sorry, but we've already spent the money." A good rule for them very well
might have been "Any time is a good time to buy good stocks."

When To Sell • I have a very simple rule for judging when to sell a
stock I own. It's so simple you'll probably dismiss the whole idea. However, I've found over the years that it has helped me cut through the
tinsel and fog and to reach good decisions as to when to sell.

I do not look at what price I paid for a stock unless selling it
would cause me to incur a large capital gains tax liability. I simply ask
myself, "If I had the money this stock would bring in my hands at this
moment, would I buy this stock at this price?" If my answer is Yes, I
hold. If it is No, I sell. The only difference between my owning this
stock and having the money is a small amount of commission which I
should not let affect my judgment.

You may have great difficulty selling. Most people do. If you have
a gain, you may not be able to bear the thought of selling and paying
the capital gains tax. When you analyze the situation, there are only
two ways to avoid eventually paying it—neither of which you are going
to like. You can hold until it goes back to what you paid for it, or until
death, at which time the old cost basis is wiped out.

On the other hand, if you have a loss, you may say, "I won't sell for I just can't afford to take a loss." You already have the loss. You only have two questions now that you should ask yourself. Can you deduct the loss advantageously on your income tax, and where are you most likely to make up your losses—where you are or in another stock?

Lay your hand over the cost basis of your stocks and judge them individually on their potential over the next six months.

Don't Average Down • I am not in agreement with a large number of stockbrokers who advise their clients to average down. What is meant by averaging down?

Let's assume you bought 100 shares of a stock at $30 per share, and it has dropped in price to $20. There are those who recommend that you buy another 100 shares at $20. This would give you an average cost per share of $25 on the 200 shares.

I feel you can average yourself right into the basement of the poor house. I never mind paying a higher price than my original purchase price if there are earnings justification. It just means the market has confirmed my own good judgment.

They Don't Ring a Bell • Are you bearish or bullish for the next 2 months? How about the next 8 months? What about the next 18 months? (That's long term for the dynamic market we have. As a matter of fact, I find that most people consider six months and one day long term.)

Are you bearish for the short term and bullish for the long term? If so, you probably have lots of company. The only problem is that they don't ring a bell at the bottom (or the top) of the market, and those who wait often continue to wait until the market has climbed to new highs. They then panic on the upside and say, "What a fool I was not to have bought back when the market was low. I've already waited too long, but there must be plently of good buys left." And they hop in with both feet.

With the continuously growing appetite and importance of the institutional investor, it is well to consider if the individual investor can successfully compete.

• THE INSTITUTIONAL INVESTOR

The institutional investor is one who usually buys in large blocks at advantageously lower negotiated commissions. He is the large life insurance company, the large bank, the large pension fund manager, the large college endowment fund manager, the large mutual fund.

There is considerable evidence that their demand for stock will be a strong force in the market place. Projections show that in the 1980s nonprofit institutions will have in their portfolios $4 billion worth of stocks, life insurance companies $5.5 billion, private pension funds $13.3 billion, open-end investment trust $90 billion, and state and local government retirement plans $1.5 billion (even under our new pension laws).

There are just not this many new quality issues coming into the market to fill the demand. As we learned in basic economics, if demand is greater than supply, the price will rise.

Logic would seem to indicate that with this much money in the hands of trained, informed, unemotional money managers, this would lend a high degree of stability to the market. I'm sorry to say that I don't think this is what will be happening. Their equipment for becoming better informed has reached a high degree of electronic sophistication. Unfortunately, they all seem to be availing themselves of the same tools. They are all reading the same computer printouts from their very advanced monitoring equipment. This shows all of them the same buy and sell signals at the same time, causing simultaneous buying and selling that results in sudden and often precipitous price changes.

An example might be found in the stock of Wrigley. Their commercials may have been a bit staid—"Double your pleasure, double your fun"—but you always knew Wrigley was there. Then suddenly at 1 p.m. on that fateful day in October, trading was halted by the New York Stock Exchange. When it reopened around 2:30, there was no pleasure and no fun. Wrigley was off 27 points, almost a 20 percent drop. Just like that. By year's end it had shed another 15 points.

Had the bottom suddenly fallen out of the chewing gum market? No, as a matter of fact, third-quarter earnings were well above the previous year's earnings, but they were not what Wall Street expected. Wall Street becomes nervous when its expectations are not met, and 20,000 shares were dumped. That is what is called "bombing" a stock.

• YOU CAN COMPETE

Can you as an individual investor compete with so many institutional buyers in the market?

Yes, if you will conscientiously do your homework and keep reasonably calm. One of your greatest assets is flexibility. There will be times when you will be skittish about the economy and believe it wise to convert some positions to cash reserves.

It may be more difficult for the professional money manager to unload a block of 200,000 shares of the kinds of stocks institutions hold without depressing the market in that stock.

For example, suppose you decide IBM's multiple (the stock's price relative to its earnings per share) is too high, and you'd like to sell your 50 shares. Fine. No problem. But could Morgan Guaranty, which may hold over $2 billion in IBM stock, do the same? They are locked in, unless they want to see their last shares sold at prices much lower than their first.

Very often, the way to make big money in the market is to find small, well-managed, rapidly growing companies. Most institutions are too big to be able to take advantage of that strategy. You can buy meaningful positions in smaller companies that the "big boys" cannot touch. (An investment company trust cannot by regulation own more than 10 percent of the shares outstanding of any one company.) You would hope, however, that as the company grew, the institutions would be able to move in, which in turn should help move up the price of the stock you "discovered."

• KEEP YOUR PERSPECTIVE

When news seems at its worst, remember good news has always followed bad news. Things do move in cycles and waves. (I know you feel some of them may engulf you.) Interest rates do adjust downward. The crisis shortages are solved. A nation that can go to the moon can also produce energy, good food, and unpolluted air and water. Inflation is something you should learn to live with. It may slow slightly, but you should accept it as a continuing fact of life.

It's important to be in the stock market for it offers you opportunities for gains, favorable tax treatment on these gains, and liquidity. Yes, there are risks. But all of life is a risk. Investing will always be a delicate balance between risk and reward.

• WHICH STOCKS FOR THE DECADE AHEAD?

Don't I wish I knew. And don't you wish I knew and would pass on the secret to you?

From all indications, it can be a very good one, but emphasis will be in different areas than before. It will probably be an economy of shortages of natural resources with higher capital investment requirements than in the 1970s. While the 1970s were consumer oriented, the 1980s will probably be investment oriented. We will have greater emphasis on how to manufacture products more cheaply and to conserve our natural resources such as oil and gas, lumber, iron ore, and copper. Greater emphasis will be on technology—of building smaller cars that consume less fuel; homes that are smaller and better insulated and probably located nearer to places of employment; heating and air conditioning units that are designed to consume less electricity. "Recycling," "recovery," and "reuse" will be words we'll use often in our day-to-day conversations.

In the 1980s we should move away from planned obsolescence and build things to last. Eating habits may change. As the prices of animal feeds increase, we may see more meat substitutes. There will be a raft of changes. But is this bad?

The decade ahead will offer you a dynamic challenge—a challenge you cannot afford to turn down. It is a challenge you must accept. Do so with intelligence, knowledge, vigor, and enthusiasm! You may find that the "world is your oyster" (from pollution-free oceans).

Application

A good way to become knowledgeable about growth industries is to be alert to current trends. In which areas should you be attuned as you read the daily newspaper? How will you become informed about the management of the corporations in the industries that you feel offer the most growth potential? How do you determine the right time to invest? How will you time your sales?

{ 7 }

The
Stock Market
Is
Like a
Yo-Yo

- ## IGNORANCE AND FEAR,
  ## DETERRENTS TO INVESTING

If stocks over the long term have been a good investment, why do so many of our citizens miss the opportunity to own their share of American industry and the growth of income and capital that has occurred through their ownership?

Ignorance and fear!

As I mentioned earlier, our school system seems to have allowed an educational void in this particular field. Millions of dollars are spent yearly to teach our youth how to equip themselves for a vocation so they can earn the money necessary to provide a living. Yet, they are not taught what to do with this money once it is earned.

Every day I'm appalled at the basic ignorance of money management that exists. Yet, I'm exposed to only a small portion of the total. Most of those with whom I counsel have at least recognized that they have a problem and have attended a financial planning seminar to try to correct it. Recognition that you have a problem is a giant step toward its solution.

The vast majority of people are ignorant of what money must do to accomplish their financial objective. Even if they have calculated the rate of return their money must accomplish, they are ignorant as to how to accomplish that rate. This kind of ignorance yields two unfavorable results:

1 · A lack of financial independence at 65 and, therefore, dependence on friends, relatives and charity.

2 · A lack of interest in preserving the free enterprise system since they do not participate in its ownership.

I find that those who become owners of individual stocks or mutual funds look at American industry in a different way. They are more interested in their productivity and the productivity of their fellow workers for they feel they have a stake in the results. They feel they are robbing themselves if they goof off on the jobs for which they are being paid. One of the major cures for inflation is worker productivity.

A second major reason our citizens do not own shares of the very same companies they literally "vote for" every time they go to the grocery store is fear—fear that if they invest, they will not be returned the same number of dollars they put into the stocks.

• INTRINSIC VALUE

People fear anything they do not understand. What they do not understand is that the market is made up of two basic ingredients. The first, and only ingredient of long-term importance, is intrinsic value. Intrinsic value is the true worth of a company's stock. This is dependent upon the company's assets, its ability to produce a product or service that is wanted or needed by a sufficient number of people, and its ability to market that product or service at a profit. One of the best measuring sticks of our country's total overall productivity is the gross national product. The gross national product is the total value of the goods and services produced in our nation within a year. It also comprises the total expenditures by consumers and government, plus gross private investment. In other words, it is everything we as a country produce in a one-year period. It is all that you produce, your neighbors produce, your co-workers produce. Also included are the government's production and expenditures. If you hire a maid and pay her a salary, this salary is included in the gross national product. If you do your own housework, this productivity is not included.

Let's go back to the depths of the depression—1933. At that black period in the nation's history, economic conditions were so depressed that we have a tendency to believe that nothing was being produced. However, this country produced $56 billion in GNP in 1933. This amount has steadily increased until, in 1971, the GNP of the United States crossed the $1 trillion mark (1.055), and 1972 ended with $1.155 trillion, and 1973 with $1.289 trillion.

It took our nation 195 years to reach the first trillion. Do you know when economists predict we will reach the second trillion? In 1980!

Can you visualize the magnitude of just $1 trillion? If you ever get discouraged about the U.S. economy, get out a sheet of paper and pencil and start writing. First you write "1"; then start adding zeros. When you write the twelfth zero, you've reached a trillion. By then, perhaps you, too, will have become optimistic about our economy.

Our increase in GNP in 1971 was greater than the total GNP of Canada. In 1972, our GNP increased $99.7 billion, and their total GNP was $102.9 billion.

A simple illustration would look something like this:

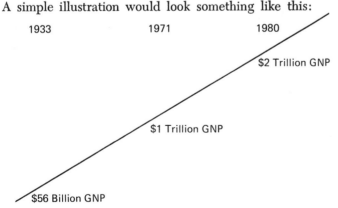

Here are the actual GNP figures for 1933 through 1973. Start reading GNP figures in your daily newspaper. They are truly exciting if you'll take the time to relate to just what this productivity means.

In the chart below, I've added two other factors to help you identify with the events around the figures!

Year	Events since 1933	Cost of living 1933 = 100	Gross national product in billions
1933	Depression, bank holiday, FDR begins first term, NIRA	100.0	$ 56.0
1934	Millions on relief, dollar revaluated, Hitler becomes Fuehrer	103.4	65.0
1935	Italy attacks Ethiopia, P.W.A., Public Utility Holding Co. Act	106.1	72.5
1936	Civil War in Spain, Germany reoccupies Rhineland	107.2	82.7
1937	Business "recession," stock market break	111.0	90.8
1938	Munich, Austria invaded, Czechoslovakia partitioned	109.0	85.2
1939	War begins, U.S. neutral, $552 million for defense	107.4	91.1
1940	Nazi "blitzkrieg," France falls, U.S. Selective Serv. Act	108.3	100.6
1941	Atlantic Charter, Pearl Harbor, U.S. enters war	113.7	125.8
1942	African campaign, Guadalcanal, stock market reaches low	126.0	159.1
1943	Casablanca, Quebec, U.S. advance in Pacific, withholding tax	133.8	192.5
1944	D-Day in Europe, Guam recaptured, Philippines invaded	136.0	211.4
1945	Yalta, Potsdam, FDR dies, atom bomb, war ends, U.N.	139.1	213.6
1946	Nationwide strikes, inflation, market decline	150.8	210.7
1947	Marshall Plan, Taft-Hartley Act	172.7	234.3
1948	Israel formed, Berlin blockade, Truman elected	185.9	259.4
1949	NATO, Red China formed, Russia explodes atom bomb	184.1	258.1
1950	India independent, war in Korea	185.9	284.6
1951	Excess profits tax, wage–price freeze, transcontinental TV	200.7	329.0

Year	Events since 1933	Cost of living 1933 = 100	Gross national product in billions
1952	Living cost at new high, U.S. H-bomb, Eisenhower elected	205.2	347.0
1953	Korean armistice, U.S.S.R. hydrogen bomb, mild recession	206.9	365.4
1954	First atom submarine, taxes reduced	207.6	363.1
1955	Israeli–Egyptian clashes, Eisenhower's heart attack	207.1	397.5
1956	Nasser seizes Suez Canal, Eisenhower re-elected	210.1	419.2
1957	Sputnik, business declines, European Common Market formed	217.4	442.8
1958	Middle East troubles, business recovery, first U.S. satellite	223.3	444.5
1959	Castro wins, Russian moon shots, longest steel strike	225.3	482.7
1960	African turmoil, Polaris launched underwater, JFK elected	228.8	503.8
1961	Berlin and Congo crises, business activity at new peaks	231.1	520.1
1962	Manned space orbits, stock market break, Cuba quarantined	233.7	560.3
1963	Stock market and earnings up, Kennedy assassinated	236.6	590.5
1964	Business expansion continues, tax cut, LBJ elected	239.7	634.4
1965	Vietnam crisis, Gemini 6 and 7	243.7	684.9
1966	Stock market break, Vietnam War	250.8	749.9
1967	Israeli–Arab war, devaluation of British pound	257.9	793.9
1968	Apollo crew circles moon, Nixon elected	268.7	865.0
1969	Moon explorations, stock market break	283.1	931.4
1970	De-escalation of Vietnam, stock market dips lower and starts recovery	299.8	974.1
1971	Wage–price freeze, stock market recovery continues	312.4	1055.5
1972	Election year, inflation rampant	315.8	1155.2
1973	Watergate, energy crisis	347.0	1289.1
1974	Recession		

As you will note, in only 3 of the 40 years did the GNP fail to increase over the previous year. These years were 1946, 1949, and 1954. In 37 of those 40 years it increased. (It's also shattering to see that the cost of living went up in 38 of the 40 years.)

• HUMAN EMOTION

If we can agree that our GNP is an indication of the true long-term intrinsic value of stocks, and this figure has increased almost each year, then why does the stock market fluctuate? Because the market includes another ingredient—human emotion. We become overly optimistic and overly depressed. Our confidence factor reflects this picture and goes back and forth across the intrinsic value line. This can be illustrated in this way:

Intrinsic
Value
GNP

Human Emotion

The market to date has been like a man with a yo-yo walking up the stairs. If you could get your eyes off the yo-yo, you had the opportunity to climb a high flight of stairs. If you could not, you may have condemned yourself to staying in the financial basement. The market is very much like the human body—it runs and rests, runs and rests.

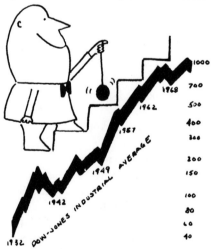

• OPPORTUNITY
OR DISASTER

When the market dips, do you say, "Oh, what a disaster!"? Or do you say, "Oh, what an opportunity!"? Your response to this question may very well determine where you will be financially 10 years from now. If you say, "What a disaster!", the basement may be yours. If you say, "What an opportunity!", you may have the opportunity to climb the financial stairs.

What difference does it really make in accomplishing your long-term financial objective if the market fluctuates? For example, if you have 10 years before you plan to retire, and your funds are invested in a well-managed mutual fund or you continuously select and manage a diversified portfolio of quality stocks yourself, the fact that their market value fluctuated during the period shouldn't bother you. Your concern should be "What will the market value of my securities be at the end of the 10-year period?"

Let's take a look at the record of the particular middle-of-the-road mutual fund that we have named the Seminar Fund. (Remember, this is what has happened in the past, with no future guarantees! But what is?)

Figure 5 is a bar chart covering the Seminar Fund over its life. It covers years when the market went up and years when it went down. The general trend, as you can see, has been upward. You must decide for yourself what you feel will be the trend in the future.

Take time, right now, to really study this chart. If you are a speed reader, don't zap past this. It deserves your conscientious study.

• THE YO-YO
AND THE STAIRS

Now that you've studied the chart, what are your reactions? Remember, it covers a long period of time. As a matter of fact, it covers a 40-year period from 1934 through 1973. Do you agree that this is a fairly graphic picture of a man with a yo-yo going up the stairs? What difference did it make to him how many times the yo-yo yo-yoed during the life of the fund? The stairs he climbed reached quite a height. If you had invested $10,000 on January 1, 1934, reinvested all your capital gains distribution (classified as a part of capital by regulation), and on December 31, 1973, decided to cash in your shares at that lower spot in the market, you would have received $269,739 net to you after all costs had been taken out, with the exception of your federal and state income tax responsibility. In addition, during that period you would have received cash dividends of

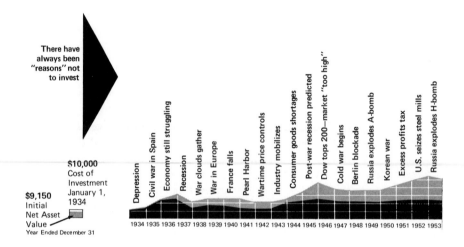

FIGURE 5.   Bar Chart

$123,471. If you had reinvested both the capital gains and dividends, your $10,000 would have grown to $955,780. (Just think how many life insurance policies, by contrast, have been sold to a man age 27 with the idea that the $10,000 placed in the cash value would be growing for his retirement income.)

We, of course, do not know what the next 40 years will bring, but if our economy is no better or no worse than the past 40 years, surely this performance can be one of the possibilities you could consider.

Now, if you just can't get your eyes off that yo-yo and absolutely must have your dollars "guaranteed," take out your pencil and draw a straight line from left to right on the preceding illustration of the Seminar

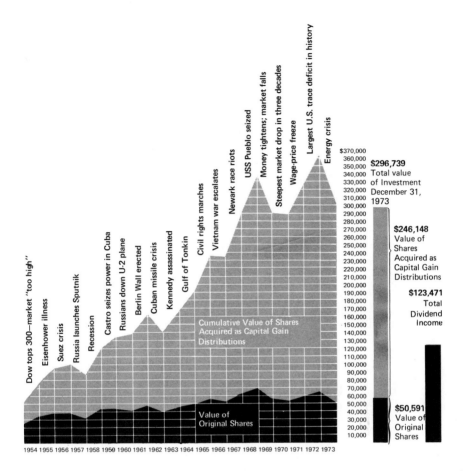

Fund and connect the $10,000 marks on each side. This is your basement position from which you can look up the flight of stairs (remember, in this example, we are spending the income from either source). This means that in the savings institution, you were guaranteed that you could always go back and get your $10,000. It also means that that is all you could get, regardless of what inflation had done to the purchasing power of your money, and regardless of how much the savings institution had made investing your money for themselves. You can't be critical of them, however, because you, of your own free will, loaned them your money. In return, they "guaranteed" the return of the same number of dollars plus a fixed rate of return.

• DIRECT OR INDIRECT INVESTING?

All money is invested in American industry either directly or indirectly. The direct method can be accomplished by putting your money to work in an investment similar to the Seminar Fund. An indirect method would be to lend your funds to a savings institution and let them invest in American industry. When you choose the latter, you in effect place a filter along that $10,000 line in our example. The screen in that filter has in the past been equipped with a very fine mesh, and very little has filtered through to you.

Remember, to become financially independent you must save and let your money grow. (Many of our citizens save and let financial institutions grow. They are building some magnificent structures of marble, glass, and steel that add beauty to our downtown business areas and to our suburban shopping centers.)

To participate in the profits of American industry, you must get your eyes off the yo-yo and on the stairs.

• ALL ASSETS FLUCTUATE IN VALUE

Why should you let daily fluctuations bother you? Everything you own fluctuates in value. The market value of any asset you own is only what someone is willing to pay you for it.

Your home fluctuates in value every day, but the newspaper doesn't carry a market page quoting its value. What if it did? You come home on Monday, pick up the newspaper, and find that the market value of your house is quoted at $25,000. On Thursday evening you come home, pick up the paper, and find it is quoted at $22,000. Would you panic and begin crying? Would you be alarmed and begin to weep over your $3,000 loss? The loss is just as real if you need to sell. Fortunately for your peace of mind, the values of your home and other assets are not published every day; therefore, you are unaware of their fluctuation in value, saving you the agony of existing in a state of panic as some do when they own securities.

Don't succumb to the yo-yo panic! If you do, you may find it very costly.

• THE EMOTION
CURVE

The emotions prevent many a person from being a good investor. The reason he has not invested is fear of loss, which is a much stronger motivator than desire for gain. So he stays out of the stock market because of fear and ignorance. You never really trust or are "for" anything you do not know.

However, as time goes on, he hears bits of scuttlebut and glorious claims made by others on the cocktail circuit about big gains in the market. At that point interest begins to become more intense, and hope begins to replace fear. As the headlines get bigger and the TV commentator nightly reports, "The market soared again today," greed begins to rear its head. That's when he'll jump in with a mighty splash and shout, "Buy!" Then when there occurs a correction in the market, hope begins to wane. But surely his stocks will recover shortly. He just could not have made a mistake. As the market continues its decline, then fear seizes him and he cries, "Sell!"

These stages on the emotion curve can be illustrated in this way:

If you follow his example, you have assured yourself of the most infallible way I know to lose money in the market—buy high, sell low!

• HOW NOW,
MR. DOW?

When clients call to ask "How's the market?", what they are really asking is the level of the Dow Jones Industrial Average (DJIA). To answer the question, I punch the appropriate symbol, IDJN, on my Bunker-Ramo and give them the plus or minus at the moment. Actually, the level of the Dow probably makes no difference if they are invested in individual stocks. What does make a difference is how their particular stocks are doing.

The Dow Jones Average is not the best indicator, but we've used it for so long that it will probably be with us for a long time.

There are really four Dow Jones Averages—the Industrial, the Composite, the Utility, and the Rails. However, the best known is the Industrial Average, which has 29 industrials and 1 utility—American Telephone and Telegraph.

Charles S. Dow published his first Dow Jones Average on July 3, 1884. It first appeared in his financial news bulletin called the *Customer's Afternoon Letter* (a forerunner of *The Wall Street Journal.*) It was distributed to brokers and bankers from an office behind a soda fountain in the basement of 15 Wall Street. In 1896, *The Wall Street Journal* began publication of the first Industrial Stock Average of 12 stocks. It has had a long climb. It took 60 years to reach the first 500 points, 16 more to go to 1,000 and retreat. The table below shows some Dow Jones milestones and how it has climbed over the years:

	First close over	
100	Jan. 12, 1906	100.25
200	Dec. 19, 1927	200.93
300	Dec. 31, 1928	300.00
400	Dec. 29, 1954	401.97
500	Mar. 12, 1956	500.24
600	Feb. 20, 1959	602.21
700	May 17, 1961	705.52
800	Feb. 28, 1964	800.14
900	Jan. 28, 1965	900.25
1000	Nov. 14, 1972	1003.16

The Dow Jones Industrial Average is not an average anymore. When it first began, the average was computed by adding the price of the stocks in the Average and dividing by the number of issues. The divisor has been changed over the years to adjust whenever a component stock was split or declared a stock dividend. Also, 18 stocks have been added.

The Stocks in the Dow • Here are the 30 stocks in our present Dow Jones Industrial Average. They are:

Allied Chemical
Aluminum Co. of America
American Brands

American Can
American Telephone and Telegraph
Anaconda

Bethlehem Steel
Chrysler
du Pont
Eastman Kodak
Exxon
General Electric
General Foods
General Motors
Goodyear Tire and Rubber
International Harvester
International Nickel
International Paper

Johns-Manville
Owens-Illinois
Procter and Gamble
Sears, Roebuck
Standard Oil of California
Esmark (Swift and Co.)
Texaco
Union Carbide
United Aircraft
United States Steel
Westinghouse Electric
Woolworth (F.W.)

" That value controls the Dow Jones Average "

The size of the company has no bearing on its weight in the Dow Average. AT&T, with $60,625,045,000 in assets, has the same weight as Esmark, Inc. (Swift & Co.) with slightly less than $500 million in assets.

Only two stocks remain that were in the original average. They are American Tobacco, now American Brands, and General Electric. IBM was once in the average, but "Who is interested in office equipment?" our forefathers reasoned, so it was dropped. Just think where the Dow would be now if IBM had been left in!

Seventy Years with Mr. Dow • Figure 6 illustrates the Dow Jones Average in graph form showing both highs and lows.

THE STOCK MARKET IS LIKE A YO-YO

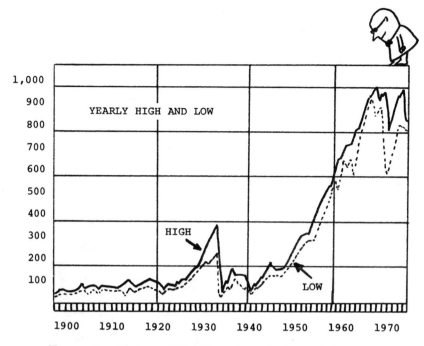

FIGURE 6.   History of the Dow Jones Industrial Average

Where Will the Dow Be by 1980? • I do not know! But, let's see if we can make a sensible estimate. If you have an opinion about the future course of the American economy, it's also a stock market prediction.

Before deciding where we're going, let's consider where we've been. From 1959 to 1969, the gross national product rose from $484 billion to $932 billion—a 6.6 percent compound annual growth rate. A shade over one-third of this gain represented price increases, but two-thirds was real growth. Thus, price inflation averaged 2.3 percent per year, and real growth was 4.3 percent per year.

Several government agencies and outside forecasters are predicting greater real growth for the future.

But you be the predictor. Do you think we will have a lower rate of growth, the same, or higher? If you feel a lower rate, choose "A" below; if the same, choose "B"; or if higher, choose "C."

A • Lower rate (5.5 percent a year).
B • Same rate (6.6 percent a year).
C • Higher rate (7.5 percent a year).

Based on the growth rate you selected, you can now calculate your estimate of the 1980 GNP.

A · 5.5 percent compound annual growth rate will produce $1.678 trillion.

B · 6.6 percent compound annual growth rate will produce $1.883 trillion.

C · 7.5 percent compound annual growth rate will produce $2.069 trillion.

In the past, our experience has been that the DJIA earnings averaged about 6¢ per billion of GNP. Assuming this ratio continues, our forecast then would be:

Forecast	1980 GNP will be	DJIA earnings
A	$1.678 trillion	$100.70
B	$1.883 trillion	$113.00
C	$2.069 trillion	$124.15

During the postwar period the DJIA has sold at an average of around 15 times earnings. It has ranged from a low of under 6 times to a high of just over 20 times. Based on your estimate of the price–earnings ratio, the 1980 DJIA becomes:

		Price–Earnings ratio		
Earnings estimate	10×	15×	17×	20×
A $100.70	1007.00	1510.00	1711.00	2014.00
B $113.00	1130.00	1695.00	1921.00	2260.00
C $124.15	1241.00	1862.00	2110.00	2482.00

Assuming you chose the middle course, your estimate of the DJIA is 1695. The future Dow price–earning ratios may go higher or lower than any of these. The relationship between GNP and the Dow earnings may be subjected to wide fluctuations. Inflation may be more or less than estimated.

Your earnings predictions may differ from any of the ones we have used. You may feel that the P/E ratios will be higher or lower than they have been in the past. Table 13 will help you pick the combination you believe the future may hold.

Despite the many areas of possible fluctuation, this exercise in forecasting vividly demonstrates that it is difficult to be pessimistic about long-term stock prices if you are at all optimistic about the economy!

Table 13. Relationship of Price to Earnings

Possibilities for the Dow-Jones Industrial Average in 1980

Dow-Jones Earnings per Share	9	10	11	12	13	14	15	16	17	18	19	20	21	22	23	24	25
$130	1170	1300	1430	1560	1690	1820	1950	2080	2210	2340	2470	2600	2730	2860	2990	3120	3250
125	1125	1250	1375	1500	1625	1750	1875	2000	2125	2250	2375	2500	2625	2750	2875	3000	3125
120	1080	1200	1320	1440	1560	1680	1800	1920	2040	2160	2280	2400	2520	2640	2760	2880	3000
115	1035	1150	1265	1380	1495	1610	1725	1840	1955	2070	2185	2300	2415	2530	2645	2760	2875
110	990	1100	1210	1320	1430	1540	1650	1760	1870	1980	2090	2200	2310	2420	2530	2640	2750
105	945	1050	1155	1260	1365	1470	1575	1680	1785	1890	1995	2100	2205	2310	2415	2520	2625
100	900	1000	1100	1200	1300	1400	1500	1600	1700	1800	1900	2000	2100	2200	2300	2400	2500
95	855	950	1045	1140	1235	1330	1425	1520	1615	1710	1805	1900	1995	2090	2185	2280	2375
90	810	900	990	1080	1170	1260	1350	1440	1530	1620	1710	1800	1890	1980	2070	2160	2250
85	765	850	935	1020	1105	1190	1275	1360	1445	1530	1615	1700	1785	1870	1955	2040	2125
80	720	800	880	960	1040	1120	1200	1280	1360	1440	1520	1600	1680	1760	1840	1920	2000
75	675	750	825	900	975	1050	1125	1200	1275	1350	1425	1500	1575	1650	1725	1800	1875
Price Earnings Ratio	9	10	11	12	13	14	15	16	17	18	19	20	21	22	23	24	25

Weighing possible risks and rewards, the future of common stock investing appears bright to me—provided the investor holds a diversified list of selected common stocks, either directly or through a professionally managed common stock mutual fund.

Application

Be constantly alert to the increase or decrease in the Gross National Product. What do you predict will be the GNP in 10 years? At what price earnings do you predict the stocks in the Dow will be selling? What do you think will be the future correlation between the GNP and the Dow Jones Industrial Average? What action should you take to apply your opinions to your own financial future?

{ 8 }

Mutual
Funds:
Pro and
Con

By now you've taken a good hard look at some of the requirements necessary to become a successful investor in individual stocks. But you may be protesting that you do not have that kind of time and expertise. You are a topnotch professional in your chosen vocation, and the reason you are is that you devote almost every waking hour at being good at it, which doesn't leave time for studying the market. Yet, you realize that you must have your money working for you so your children can go to college, and so that you can some day retire in financial dignity. What should you do? If you do not have what I call the 3 "T"s and an "M," I recommend that you put professional money managers to work for you.

• TIME

The first "T" is for Time. Do you have the time to truly study the market trends. I don't mean, do you have a moment before you settle down to the next murder mystery or hospital drama on TV to take a quick glance at the evening newspaper to learn whether your stocks went up or down during the day?

Do you really have the time to spend studying balance sheets, profit and loss statements, market trends, economic indicators, changes in monetary policies, increases in government expenditures, decreases in other areas of government expenditures, shortages, surpluses, consumer buying trends, international competition due to lower labor costs, access to raw materials, and so forth?

If you can answer that you do have this time and feel that it would be more rewarding financially and emotionally to spend this time being a professional in the market, then you have the first "T."

• TRAINING

The second "T" is for Training. What is your educational background—accounting, statistical analysis, money and banking, marketing, economics, finance, human psychology? If you are thoroughly schooled in these areas and have developed some reasonable expertise in them, you qualify for the second "T."

• TEMPERAMENT

The third "T" is for Temperament. Are you temperamentally suited for successful investing in the stock market? Did you work very hard for your money? Were you a child of the Depression? Does your memory of hard times make you squeeze every nickel until it screams loudly?

I was raised in the hard times of the dust bowl of Oklahoma. That trying experience made an indelible impression on me. In my counseling I have observed many others from a similar background. In most of them I have found that it has caused their emotional decisions about money to be more black and white than they should be. Money decisions must often be based on various shades of gray. I find that if a person has experienced bad times, he either clutches a dollar very tightly to his bosom for fear of losing it, or determines that once he gets a dollar, he is going to put it to work aggressively to see if he can turn that dollar into an additional dollar. My reaction to my dust bowl experience was and still is the latter. It's not that I enjoy hoarding money or even spending it. My challenge has been to take one dollar and make two, and then take the two and make four, and so on.

Analyze your own personality. This is not an easy thing to do. Some basic books on psychology may be of help to you. One I have enjoyed is Dr. Muriel James' book on transactional analysis entitled *Born to Win.* The whole field of psychology can be fascinating, and through it you may discover why you and others react to certain stimuli and conditions the way you do. In the world of finance this knowledge can pay handsome dividends.

Can you act when you have reasonable facts before you? You'll never know all the facts. If you wait until you are 100 percent sure, your decision will invariably be too late. I find most investment decisions are made far too late rather than too soon. Don't ever deceive yourself into thinking that if you don't make a decision, you haven't made a decision. You have. You have decided that where your money is right now is the best place for it to be.

I've found the difference between mediocre and superb performance in the market is the ability to evaluate and then take the appropriate action.

I observe many who plant good fruit trees in the form of good stocks, and refuse to harvest the fruit, letting it rot on the trees.

Don't become enamored with a stock because it has made you an unrealized capital gain (meaning it went up). Don't be afraid of taking a profit if it appears that the stock has topped out and will probably be flat for six months to a year. Don't back off from taking a profit just because you'll have a capital gains tax to pay.

There is a time to buy and a time to sell—regardless of which stock you own. Can you move when it's time to do so? If so, you have the third "T," Temperament.

• MONEY

You have analyzed your three "T"s. Now let's look at how you fit the "M." "M" represents Money. Do you have enough money to diversify your holdings? Diversification is one of the first rules of successful investing. Do you have sufficient funds to enable you not to put all your eggs in one basket, but to have at least 10 baskets—one basket for office equipment, another for natural resources, still another for beverages, another for retail stores?

You may feel the need to subscribe to an advisory service. You should calculate this cost in money and in the time needed to digest the contents.

If you have the 3 "T"s and an "M," you will find being your own pro fun and rewarding. Therefore, you should plan to devote considerable time and energy to this important facet of your financial future. If not, let the pros do it for you.

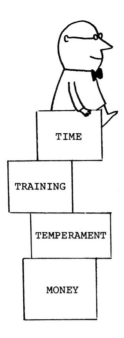

• LETTING THE PROS DO IT

You may find letting the professionals do your investing for you very hard to do. It is especially hard for some professionals. You would think it would be otherwise since they are so aware of how much time, training, and experience it took to bring them to their present level of proficiency. The admission that someone can do something better than they can do it often is just too hard an admission for some persons to make. The same doctor who would be aghast if I should suggest removing my own appendix will hop into the stock market arena without any more preparation.

Even when the professional becomes a pro in the market, I usually find that the good full-time pros outperform the part-time pros.

Let's assume you are willing to let the professionals help you. What choices are available to you?

Private Professional Management • There are two ways to obtain professional management. If you have a large amount of funds to invest, you may qualify for private professional management through an investment advisory service. There are some that will accept as small an account as $50,000 for a fee of 1 percent of the net assets per annum.

Most of your top services will not accept an account of less than $300,000. The team that manages the Seminar Fund will not accept a private account of less than $20 million. On this size account one-half of 1 percent of the net asset value is the usual management charge.

Let's assume you have sufficient funds to qualify for private professional management. What should you do?

First, do an in-depth study of the professional teams available. Become acquainted with their personnel, and take a good hard look at their past performance. After all, you are buying brains. You might as well get the best "brains" you can for the money you are paying.

Second, you will sign an agreement giving the management service discretionary power to buy and sell for your account. This can be canceled or amended at your discretion. In the agreement you will designate the stockbroker of your choice.

Third, you will need to transfer the agreed amount of money or stocks to the bank or broker that is to act as the custodian of the assets in the account. They will then make the proper delivery of stocks and money at the directions of the advisors.

After these necessary steps have been taken, you will begin to receive confirmations from your broker on each buy and sell. Your service will also make a monthly or quarterly report to you, giving you a résumé of all transactions, a report on gains and losses, and often a comparison of your portfolio's performance against that of the popular averages.

You may withdraw the account at any time.

Public Professional Management • If the amount you have for investment is less than $100,000, you should consider using public professional management, through the investment medium of the investment company trusts, commonly called mutual funds.

I would prefer calling them by another name. Not that the term "mutual fund" does not give an indication of their nature, but I find that so many confuse them with mutual savings and loan or mutual insurance companies, and worry that they can be assessed, which of course is not true.

The Feeling Is Mutual • "Mutual" means you may mutually benefit from pooling your resources with others. For example, let's say you have $1,000. Alone you could not obtain diversification or professional management. But let's assume there are 999 others who each have $1,000 and have the same financial objective that you do. If all of you pooled your funds, you would have a million dollars. With a million dollars you would have sufficient money to spread your risk among a number of different industries. You would also have enough money to hire some top professional money managers to select and constantly supervise your holdings. A mutual fund then should do for you what you would do for yourself if you had sufficient Time, the proper Training, the right Temperament, and sufficient Money to diversify. It offers the same advantages to the small investor that the wealthy have always had. The wealthy have enough money to diversify and enough money to hire the pros.

In a previous chapter we concluded that there were three basic requirements for successful investing: diversification, proper selection, and constant supervision. Let's examine these three to see if a quality mutual fund with excellent management will fulfill these requirements. (There is a wide range of expertise in managements. Spend considerable time and study choosing the one or ones you will use.)

Diversification · You have explored the desirability of not putting all your eggs in one basket—but spreading your risk with the hopes of reducing your possibilities of loss and increasing your potential for gain. Do some mutual funds offer these characteristics? Yes, I believe they do.

The Investment Company Act of 1940 provides that a mutual fund may not have more than 5 percent of its assets in any one company, nor own more than 10 percent of the outstanding shares of any one company. By this regulation you know that you should always have at least 20 stocks in your mutual fund portfolio, and also that any one of the 20 will not represent more than 10 percent of the outstanding shares of that company. This in itself insures a fair degree of diversification.

You will find as you explore the large number of funds available that most of them have from 100 to 150 different stocks in their portfolio, and will cover a wide spectrum of industry groups.

As I've mentioned before, I use the Seminar Fund as an example of how a fund works, not as a recommendation. I use this fund because it does have a reasonably good performance record, but by no means is it tops. I avoid showing a top performing fund. I find that most of those in attendance have been receiving only a very meager return on their money, so if I show them something that seems too good, they may develop a credibility gap. When you have those who have been reasonably happy with 5 percent and you start talking of an average of 12 percent, they have trouble believing that the investment could be sound. I make a point of never using a fund as an example that does better than 12 percent for this very reason.

Incidentally, I remember using this fund one night at a seminar

when a lady, whom I had evidently impressed with the possibilities the
fund could offer, came up to me and blurted out, "Whatever will the
savings and loans do?" When I asked her what she meant, she said
she feared everyone would now take all their money out of them, and
they would not have money to lend for home mortgages. I calmed her
fears by assuring her that much of the money would remain there and
she need not be so concerned. Since that time they have suffered, not
through competition from the stock market but from the government
itself when it offered investors 9 percent on Treasury bills while pro-
hibiting the savings institution from competing.

I always use a fund that has averaged 12 percent in the long term,
for I'm convinced that that's the minimum long-term performance you
should accept on your money. With our present rate of inflation and
progressive tax bite, you have to have that much to make any reasonable
progress.

Back to diversification. Here is the way $10,000 might be spread
in a portfolio. (If you only have $1,000, just drop the last digit.)

Alco Standard	$ 23	Crown Zellerbach	$ 75
Aluminum Company of		Delta Airlines	61
America	132	DeSoto	10
American Cyanamid	38	duPont (E.I.) de Nemours	96
American Telephone and		Exxon	338
Telegraph	193	Fairchild Camera and	
American Metal Climax	82	Instrument	86
Amfac	40	Federal National Mortgage	
Arizona Public Service	40	Association	271
Atlantic Richfiield	411	First Charter Financial	10
Bethlehem Steel	90	First Chicago	138
Braniff International	46	First National City	61
Burlington Industries	127	Florida Power	76
Burlington Northern	30	Ford Motor	123
Capital Cities Comm.	60	General Electric	5
Carter-Wallace	13	General Motors	16
Chrysler	35	General Telephone &	
Colt Industries	37	Electronics	30
Columbia Broadcasting		Getty Oil	18
System	39	Great Northern Nekoosa	81
Communications Satellite	52	Great Western Financial	58
Connecticut General Insur-		Hart Schaffner & Marx	22
ance	307	Heinz (H.J.)	102
Consolidated Foods	40	Host International	11
Continental Telephone	26	Houdaille Industries	18
Control Data	142	Howmet	2

I-T-E Imperial	$ 16	Philip Morris	167
Ideal Basic Industries	39	Phillips' Incandescent	
Imperial Corporation of		Lamps	$ 58
America	26	Pittston	20
Imperial Oil	40	Public Service Co. of	
Interco	57	Colorado	58
Interlake	5	Pullman	67
International Business		RCA	258
Machines	61	Revlon	33
International Paper	33	Reynolds (R.J.) Industries	16
International Telephone		Rohm & Haas	58
and Telegraph	86	Safeway Stores	54
Jonathan Logan	30	Scott Paper	126
Kaiser Aluminum & Chemical	81	Singer	92
Kaiser Cement & Gypsum	15	Southern Railway	59
Leaseway Transportation	43	Sperry Rand	490
MCA	61	Standard Oil of California	233
Manufacturers Hanover	69	Stevens (J.P.)	30
Marathon Oil	19	TRW	19
Marcor	2	Tenneco	36
Masco	98	Texaco	204
Matsushita Electric		Tidewater Marine Service	39
Industrial	95	Time	62
Middle South Utilities	16	Unilever N.V.	36
Miles Laboratories	20	Union Pacific	129
Mississippi River	70	United States Freight	21
Mohasco Industries	24	Upjohn	76
Monroe Auto Equipment	24	Victor Comptometer	13
Monsanto	41	Wells Fargo	15
National Gypsum	7	Western Union	10
National Steel	27	Westinghouse Electric	12
Norfolk & Western Railway	118	Whirlpool	9
Northwest Airlines	30	Zenith Radio	64
Northwestern National Life		Other Stocks	105
Insurance	19	Total Stocks	$ 7,827
Ohio Edison	5	Corporate Bonds	13
Olin	2	Net Cash and	
Outboard Marine	18	Equivalent	2,160
Overnite Transportation	15	Total	$10,000
Pacific Gas & Electric	113		
Panhandle Eastern Pipe			
Line	22		

This array of stocks should fulfill the first requirement for successful investing—diversification.

Proper Selection and Constant Supervision   ·   The Seminar Fund has a picture in its guidebook of some very learned looking men and women sitting around a large conference table with research reports in front of them. They are having one of their daily conferences to determine which stocks to add and which to take out of the portfolio, or to just be as certain as they can that the stocks they presently hold fulfill the requirements that the shareholders designated when they chose this particular fund.

A staff of analysts, each a specialist in his own field, constantly reports to the investment committee. There will be specialists in the oils, the chemicals, the automotives, and so forth. Not only do they read, analyze, and project figures on each company in their industry specialty, but they also make on-the-spot studies and conduct fact-finding interviews with the top officers of these companies.

I remember an officer of an oil company calling me to invest in a particular fund after one of the fund's analysts had called on him. He was very impressed with the analyst's thorough knowledge of the oil industry and especially of his company.

The thoroughness and training of these specialists fulfill the two other requirements of successful investing—proper selection and constant supervision.

In addition to these three requirements of successful investing, the properly selected mutual fund can provide 10 other valuable characteristics.

Convenience, an Essential Ingredient   ·   The first is convenience. We all do what is convenient for us. Mutual funds can offer this convenience with a plan that will fit almost any pocketbook. You may start an investment program in a mutual fund with a relatively small amount of money; in fact, some funds have no minimum initial investment. Others will accept as small an amount as $100. You may then add in many funds any amount or as small an amount as $25. In addition, you have the privilege of automatically reinvesting both your dividends and your capital gains, usually without commission. Some funds charge to reinvest dividends. None charges to reinvest capital gains. If you were to receive these same dividends from individual stocks in your private portfolio and you realized capital gains from stock buys and sells and wanted to reinvest, you would be charged a commission. With a mutual fund you can have immediate reinvestment of small or large amounts of money, giving you an opportunity to speed up your compounding potential.

Dollar-Cost-Averaging as You Earn   ·   The second item in the list of 10 additional advantages that a mutual fund may offer is that you can truly dollar-cost average. This means putting the same amount of money into the same security at the same interval. One certainty of the stock market is that it will fluctuate. So put this characteristic to work for you instead of worrying so much about it. Choose an amount you can comfortably invest each month (not too comfortably or you may not save anything) and invest that amount on the same day each month.

Many funds provide a bank draft authorization so that the bank can automatically draft your account each month. I find this to be an extremely satisfactory arrangement for my clients. Banks never forget! I find my clients often do.

The mutual fund will carry your share purchase out to the third decimal point, which allows you to truly dollar-cost-average. This makes this investment medium a good one to use for this purpose.

The chapter entitled, "Is There an Infallible Way to Invest?" covers this in more detail.

Where Do You Fit on the Triangle? · Do you remember our triangle of finance that we used when we were discussing individual stocks? It is applicable here, too. A fund must state in its prospectus its financial objective. This objective cannot be changed without the consent of the shareholders. The fund rarely changes its objective. If it is presently an income fund and management also desires to manage a growth fund, they will establish a new fund and add it to their family of funds. They may also add a middle-of-the-road fund, a corporate bond fund, or a convertible bond fund. The financial triangle would look something like this:

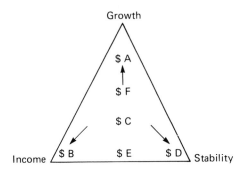

As you can see, you can't be a Paul Revere who hops on his horse and rides off in all directions. You must decide which direction you want to go. When you maximize "Income," you move farther from "Growth." The same is true if you select "Stability" as your primary concern.

A fund management group may have a family of funds, attempting to provide a fund for each place on the triangle, or it may have only one or two.

There are approximately seven kinds of mutual funds: growth (aggressive and moderate), income, balanced, bond, convertible bond, specialty funds, and reserve funds.

Growth Funds · The growth fund would place your dollar nearer to the top of the triangle at (A) because its objective is long term growth. Intermittent volatility should not be of great concern. You should not be interested in dividends when you invest in a growth fund. As a matter of fact, if it were possible for the fund managers to select stocks that paid no dividends and just grew in value, with no need to buy and sell and realize capital gains, this would be ideal for you. What you really want is for $1 to grow to $3 at least in 10 years. You would prefer not having any tax liability in the meantime if such were possible.

When I've asked a prospective client his financial objective and he has answered that it is growth, I may recommend a particular quality growth fund to him. When he asks me, "How much does it pay?," meaning what the dividend is, I know I have not communicated properly what a growth fund is designed to do.

Income Funds · There is a good selection of quality income funds. Their portfolio managers choose stocks that have paid good dividends in the past, have a record of increasing dividends, and have a reasonable expectation of continuing good dividends and market stability of their shares. If your need is for income now rather than later, this is the type of fund you should consider. Your location on the triangle would be (B).

Balanced Funds · In position (C) on the triangle you will find balanced funds. These are funds that invest approximately 60 percent of their funds in high-quality bonds and the remainder in high-quality, income-producing "blue chip" stocks. In periods of market decline they offer a safer haven than the growth funds. Conversely, in a rising market they usually lag behind.

Bond Funds · When you invest in a bond fund, you are placing your dollar in the lower right-hand side of the triangle (D). Bond funds have been around for many years; however, in the growth craze of the 1960s they attracted very little attention. With the agonizing reappraisals of the early 1970s they became increasingly popular. The magic word was no longer "growth," but "income."

Bond funds invest most of their funds in debt-type securities. These are corporate bonds and debentures, perhaps a few convertible bonds, treasuries, commercial paper, etc. Instead of taking an equity position in the market, you become a lender of money.

When you invest in a bond fund, do not think that the price of the shares will remain fixed. It will not. It does have some fluctuation, though usually not as great as in other security investments.

If your fund is composed of bonds with an average yield of 8 percent and the going interest rate is 9 percent, then the fund will not be able to sell the bond at par; therefore, the price of your shares could decline. On the other hand, if the going rate drops to 7 percent, they probably can sell the bonds at a premium (above par) and the price of your shares would increase. If they purchased a bond at par (usually $1,000) that carries a rate of 8 percent, which matures January 1, 2000, this does not mean they must hold the bond until the year 2000 to turn it into cash. It means on January 1, 2000, the person holding the bond is guaranteed $1,000. Between now and that date, the value will usually fluctuate with the country's going interest rate.

Convertible Bond Funds · In an effort to obtain the best of two worlds, some management groups have established convertible bond funds. These funds were designed to have a relatively good yield—around 5 to 6 percent —and have the potential of growth. They listed the characteristics of their fund by showing the advantages and disadvantages of bonds and stocks, and proposed that they would combine the best from both. Your dollar with them would be placed around (E) on the triangle.

As discussed earlier, its characteristics are supposed to be the best of two worlds: the guarantee of principal and rate of return of a bond, and the potential for growth of common stock.

The theory runs that even though you may be placing a bit of a damper on maximum growth potential, there is down-side protection for the convertible bond should only drop in price to a level where it will take on the characteristics of a bond yielding the current interest level.

The theory sounds good, but its performance has not been outstanding. The number of quality convertible bonds available in the market place has been limited. This tends to make a thin market (not enough traders to make it competitive). Also, many of the firms offering convertible bonds are not the blue chip companies. They had to offer convertibles to "sweeten the kitty" to sell their bonds to the investing public. So the convertible bonds were tied to less stable securities causing more volatility than the shareholder who invested in the convertible bond fund was willing to accept.

Specialty Funds · Personally, I would rarely, if ever, select a specialty fund. In my opinion, they destroy one of the main reasons you would

choose to invest in investment company shares, and that reason is diversification. I have not placed it on the triangle for it has maverick characteristics. I would place it, according to risk, at the top of the triangle along
with "go-go funds." I believe the investment community is better off
without either of them. Specialty funds have specialized mostly in either
insurance stocks or bank stocks. They have for that reason been rather
cyclical in their performance.

One exception has been a particular fund with 85 percent of its
assets in gold stocks. During the "gold rush" of 1973, it grew in value
100.4 percent and has continued to give an excellent performance.

Reserve Funds · During the extremely high interest rates of the mid-
1970s a new kind of fund appeared. Its purpose was to offer its investors
a haven for their money until the storms of the stock market subsided.
They placed funds in relatively risk-free, fixed-income instruments such as
bank commercial paper, certificates of deposits, Treasury bills, and federal
agency paper. Many of these had no sales charge and a relatively low
management fee.

Common Stock Funds · The middle of the road fund that seeks a balance among income, growth, and stability is the stronghold of the mutual
fund industry. It would fit in the middle of your triangle and is the place
most investors feel the greatest amount of comfort.

When deciding where you should be on the triangle, you should remember that your temperament is important in your investment program.
I find in my counseling that once I have sufficient information about a
client's time schedule, assets, and tax bracket, it is not difficult to choose
the investment I feel would fulfill his needs financially, but it may not fit
his temperament. Regardless of how much I think he should invest for
maximum growth, if I detect that volatility would disturb his peace of
mind, then the best investment for him will probably be in the middle.
Peace of mind is a good investment, too.

Our Seminar Fund fits in the middle, and it is letter (F) on the
triangle. Let's say that (F) stands for "just fine" for most investors. Trying
to make it too fast is what causes most failures. Remember, those who
make it to their goal of financial independence have usually done it
slowly. If you select your fund well from this category, you should obtain
your 12 percent compounded over a 20-year period. The Seminar Fund
has in the past averaged 12 percent or better in fifteen of the nineteen
20-year periods.

When Your Financial Objective Changes · Another characteristic of
most mutual funds is that they have an exchange privilege. If you select

a fund that is a member of a family of funds, you have the privilege of exchanging that fund for another of their funds for only a $5 exchange fee that goes to the custodian bank to compensate them for setting up a new account and canceling your old certificates and issuing you new ones.

You may consider doing this if your financial objective has changed. For instance, if you have been interested in growth but are now retiring, you may now be more interested in income. You have the privilege of changing from one fund to the other without a sales charge. You should be aware, however, that if you realize a gain on your shares, the IRS considers this a sale, and you'll have to pay a capital gains tax on your profit. A better way may be to just begin your check-a-month from your growth fund, hoping appreciation will replace the value of the shares redeemed.

You may also establish a loss for tax purposes using the exchange privilege. Let's assume the market has dropped below your cost. You are still confident of the investment ability of the management team and believe that temporary market conditions have adversely affected antici-pated performance. You are nearing the end of the year and have some capital gains already established for the year. You may want to exchange the fund you own for one of their other funds, thereby establishing a loss for your tax purposes. You would need to wait at last 31 days before moving back to your original fund, or the IRS would disallow the charge off as a "wash sale." Again, there is no commission, just a $5 fee to the custodian bank to exchange it back to your original position.

There is a mutual fund to fit most financial objectives. Study their management carefully before making your selection. Then sit back for a bit of time and "leave the driving to us," as the bus company ad says, and see how the pros do for you. Managements can change, so don't just throw your fund shares in your safety deposit box and forget about them. Do not try to second guess or panic on a day-to-day basis either. Be aware of any changes in management and systematically, at least once a year, take an inventory of their performance.

In our next chapter, we'll look at some other characteristics of mutual funds that should help you in your financial planning.

Application

Analyze yourself unemotionally. Do you have the Time, the Training, the essential kind of Temperament, and sufficient Money to diversify? Does your ego require that you "do it yourself"? (There is nothing wrong with ego, if it's recognized and you make your investment decisions accord-ingly.) Where do you fit on the financial triangle now? When should you change your position? How can this best be accomplished?

{ 9 }

How
the Professionals
Invest

• "WILL SOME
BRAINS"

I have a client who has been an excellent stock trader for years. We've made very good profits together. He has thoroughly enjoyed the challenge of predicting trends before they happened, buying the leading stocks in those industries, moving out of them before the trend ran out, and moving into the next trend ahead of the other traders. A few years ago he said that he wanted to invest in a particular mutual fund. Since he had never shown any interest in mutual funds over the years he had been my client, and since he obviously was very good at selecting his own portfolio, I asked him why he had now decided to avail himself of outside professional management.

He described to me his wife and daughter. He obviously loved them

118

very much and was proud of their accomplishments. Then he added, "They know nothing about money management. It's probably my own fault. Stock analysis and projections have been my avocation for many years, but I've never attempted to share this information with them. On the other hand, I don't really think it's their cup of tea. They are both creative, artistic, very social people who have taken delight in the luxuries my talent has provided for them, but I don't think they have ever given much thought to the source of the funds that provides these luxuries. I'm getting up in years now and want to will some brains to my wife and daughter so that they may continue to have professional management of their money in the event I'm not here to provide it for them."

The selection he made was good, and his reasoning was sound. He selected a management team with a 40-year record of consistent, prudent, and good performance.

• EASE OF ESTATE SETTLEMENT

Another reason that even the most talented trader may want to consider a mutual fund for a portion of his investment when he moves toward retirement years is that the older we become, the more likelihood there is of death. That's what a mortality table is all about. That's why life insurance costs you more each year that you live because you're that much more apt to die.

When death of a stockholder occurs, the assets represented by a portfolio of individual stocks are frozen awaiting probate and can only be changed with the court's permission. For example, let's say shares of U.S. Steel were in the portfolio of the deceased at the time of Steel's confrontation with the Kennedy administration, when for all practical purposes they were told they would not be allowed to make a profit. There had been earlier storm warnings on the horizon. Quick action to sell looked prudent. But the estate had not been probated and therefore was in limbo. Action could not be taken quickly enough to protect the estate.

Now let's assume U.S. Steel had been in the portfolio of a fund. The fund's portfolio managers were free to sell U.S. Steel from the fund and replace it with another stock The shares of the fund were frozen in the estate, but not the securities that made up the portfolio of the fund. Therefore, a mutual fund can provide professional management of the assets of the deceased while awaiting probate.

• DIVERSIFICATION MAINTAINED
AFTER PROBATE

Another characteristic of a fund that may be valuable at this time is the ease with which an estate can be divided. Also, there need be no disruption of diversification. Let's assume there are four heirs who are to share alike. The securities in the estate are in the form of 4,000 shares of the Seminar Fund. Each heir would receive 1,000 shares. There would be no disruption of diversification in each of the four portfolios. Each would still own probably 100 different stocks, all professionally selected and managed as if they belonged to one billionaire.

• BUYING BRAINS
AT A DISCOUNT

Earlier I said that mutual funds enabled the smaller investor to obtain the same advantages as the wealthier investor. The wealthier still have one advantage because they can buy at a discount. When they make larger purchases, whether in the form of a lump sum purchase at one time or over a 13-month period under a letter of intent, they are entitled to progressive discounts as they cross discount amounts. Most funds have discounts at $10,000, $25,000, $50,000, $100,000, $250,000, and $1,000,000.

The letter of intent allows the investor a 13-month period of time to cross one of the sales charge discount points. The letter of intent is not a commitment to buy but a privilege to buy at a discount during the 13-month period. For example let's assume you have $10,000 to invest today, but anticipate having an additional $15,000 to invest during the coming 13 months. You would then invest under a $25,000 letter of intent. When you do that, you receive the same discount on your $10,000 purchase as if you had invested $25,000. The custodian bank then escrows some of your shares. When the additional $15,000 is added, they release your shares. If you decide you do not want to add the remaining $15,000, that is your privilege. If the 13 months pass and you have not completed your letter, you have two choices: Return the discount which you would not have received anyway without the letter, or the custodian bank will sell enough of your escrowed shares to return to the fund the second discount you received and will send you the remaining shares. Your discount would be adjusted back to the $10,000 level. Therefore, it never cost you more and can save you money. You are not required to return the dividends and · capital gains on the extra shares you received during the period they were in escrow.

Typical "opportunity fees," called sales charges, are as follows:

Amount of purchase	Sales charge as percentage of the offering price
Less than $10,000	8.5%
$10,000 but less than $25,000	7.5
$25,000 but less than $50,000	6.0
$50,000 but less than $100,000	4.5
$100,000 but less than $250,000	3.0
$250,000 but less than $500,000	2.0
$500,000 or more	1.0

As you reached $500,000 above, you may have said, "Big deal. Who has that kind of money?" Contrary to what many people think, many large investors buy mutual funds. The average mutual fund purchase is over $27,000. If you are investing $100,000, your sales charge going in would be 3 percent, and there would be no charge to sell, regardless of the growth of your shares. Your dividends and capital gains would also be reinvested, if you chose, without charge.

Under what is called "rights of accumulation," you may also qualify for additional discounts. Let's assume you own shares that have a value of $20,000 and that you have $5,000 you would like to add to your account. You may do so under the "rights of accumulation" at the $25,000 discount level.

Let's assume the fund in which you have invested $100,000 has 100 stocks in its portfolio. Have you calculated your commission, in and out, if you were obtaining this same diversification through a portfolio of individually selected stocks? You may say that you have only $10,000, so the opportunity fee would be 7½ percent. Try getting comparable diversification with $10,000 in and out—or just going in, with the present minimum sales charge per ticket and the odd-lot differential when you are trading odd lots.

A study conducted by the National Association of Security Dealers indicated that an investment of $5,000 in 16 individual issues, which is what they deem is necessary for adequate diversification, would cost 7 percent in commissions, assuming an "in and out" transaction in listed securities. If you conclude that dividend reinvestment at asset value is worth 1 percent to the average investor, and that rights of accumulation are worth 0.5 percent, and that the exchange privilege is worth 0.4 percent, the total opportunity cost of the mutual fund investment would be 8.9 percent. They also found that the average sales charge on fund sales is 4.4 percent. This average is much lower than the 8½ percent that is generally mentioned.

I find many investors do not know about reduced sales charges on larger purchases and are amazed to find how low they are, having been led to believe that all carried an 8½ percent commission.

• WHAT DOES
IT PAY?

I find that a lot of people get hung up on what something costs them. I never worry about what something "costs" me, but I am vitally concerned about what it "pays" me. It makes no difference what it "costs."

Let's assume you turn over $1 to me to manage for you. I charge you no sales charge to do this. I will charge you, however, one-half of 1 percent yearly management fee. At the end of 10 years I return to you $2 net after all costs are taken out.

Now let's assume you turn over $1 to me, and I charge you 8½ pennies to put this dollar under my management, and again I assess you one-half of 1 percent yearly management fee. At the end of 10 years I return to you $3. Which was the best investment for you? Which really cost you the most? Did your efforts to save 8½ pennies "cost" you $1?

• DISTILLING THE
WISDOM OF THE AGES

If I were to distill all the wisdom of all the ages that I have acquired reading and observing, I could put it all in just nine words: "There is no such thing as a free lunch."

A savings institution would not have charged you to open a savings account for $10,000 10 years ago. As a matter of fact, they may have given you a handy Teflon skillet or a fuzzy wuzzy blanket for doing so. But how much did it cost ? If you had averaged 5 percent, which you could not have done at most savings institutions, your $10,000 would have grown to $16,436.

Had you taken the same $10,000 and placed it in our Seminar Fund during an average 10-year period, it would have grown to $31,403. Even in their worst period (1937–1946) this mutual fund still outperformed what you could have obtained in a *guaranteed* position.

• "OPPORTUNITY
FEE"

I call a sales charge an Opportunity Fee. Here is my reason for doing so.

Let's assume you want to travel from Houston to Dallas. We find the only way to get there is by bus. We go to the bus station; the clerk writes out your ticket and says, "That will be $13, please." You answer, "I'm just not going to pay that." If you don't, you're just not going to Dallas.

It's not what something costs you, but what it pays you that should be your chief concern.

There are, however, a few well-managed funds that do not make a sales charge. Carefully examine their performance, too.

• HOW TO RECEIVE
A CHECK A MONTH

You've been working for your money, saving a portion, and putting it to work. Now it's retirement time. Time for you to change places with your money and let your money work for you.

A plan that I have found that works very well for my clients when they reach retirement age is to use a mutual fund withdrawal plan called a Check-A-Month.

This plan makes it possible for them to begin supplementing their income by drawing regularly upon their capital. In most cases they accumulated the capital for this very purpose. A systematic withdrawal plan enables them to use up a portion of their investment in an orderly fashion while keeping the remainder at work for them in a diversified, continuously managed portfolio of common stocks.

As hard as it may be for you to believe, it was not until the mid-1960s that mutual funds were allowed to show a check-a-month withdrawal record.

They can now be shown in the manner listed in Tables 14 and 15. Here is the record of the Seminar Fund. These tables cover the period from January 1, 1963, to December 31, 1972. I chose this period because it appears to have been an average period as far as performance is concerned. Fourteen 10-year periods outperformed this period, and six have not done as well.

First, let's look at $10,000 and then at $100,000 (our minimum goal for you).

The figures in these illustrations are based on the assumption that withdrawals were made first from income for the year, as measured by the investment income dividends reinvested that year, and then from principal, as represented by the original shares acquired.

Common stock prices fluctuated during this 10-year span, but they were generally higher at the end of the period than at the beginning. It is assumed that shares were purchased at the beginning of the period at the costs shown in each table and that the amounts indicated were

Table 14. If You Had Invested $10,000 (Initial Net Asset Value: $9,150) and Taken Monthly Withdrawal of $50 . . .

Year ended Dec. 31	Amounts withdrawn		Totals		Value of remaining shares			
	From income dividends	From principal	Annually	Cumulative	Remaining original shares	+ Acquired through cap. gain distributions	=	Total value
1963	$ 237	$ 363	$ 600	$ 600	$10,134	$ 457 *		$10,591
1964	250	350	600	1,200	10,515	1,173		11,688
1965	269	331	600	1,800	11,905	2,257		14,162
1966	329	271	600	2,400	10,625	3,069		13,694
1967	374	226	600	3,000	12,491	4,514		17,005
1968	445	155	600	3,600	13,432	5,793		19,225
1969	481	119	600	4,200	10,843	5,755		16,598
1970	501	99	600	4,800	10,171	6,191		16,362
1971	505	95	600	5,400	11,255	7,254		18,509
1972	513	87	600	6,000	12,231	8,566		20,797
	$3,904	$2,096	$6,000					

Results if plan had commenced January 1, 1972:

1972	$ 249	$ 351	$ 600	$ 600	$ 9,653	$ 301		$ 9,954

* Amounts of capital gain distributions taken in shares for the years 1963–1972 were $443, $678, $862, $1,066, $1,155, $724, $336, and $616. *Total:* $7,407. For the one-year period 1972: $296.

Table 15. If You Had Invested $100,000 (Initial Net Asset Value: $96,500), and Taken Monthly Withdrawals of $500 . . .

| Year ended Dec. 31 | Amounts withdrawn | | Totals | | Value of remaining shares | | |
	From income dividends	From principal	Annually	Cumulative	Remaining original shares	+ Acquired through cap. gain distributions	= Total value
1963	$ 2,506	$ 3,494	$ 6,000	$ 6,000	$107,248	$ 4,837 *	$112,085
1964	2,646	3,354	6,000	12,000	111,638	12,424	124,062
1965	2,856	3,144	6,000	18,000	126,788	23,946	150,734
1966	3,512	2,488	6,000	24,000	113,539	32,608	146,147
1967	4,002	1,998	6,000	30,000	133,906	48,011	181,917
1968	4,765	1,235	6,000	36,000	144,458	61,678	206,136
1969	5,169	831	6,000	42,000	117,025	61,353	178,378
1970	5,395	605	6,000	48,000	110,279	66,069	176,348
1971	5,455	545	6,000	54,000	122,524	77,456	199,980
1972	5,545	455	6,000	60,000	133,651	91,565	225,216
	$41,851	$18,149	$60,000		$102,126		

Results if plan had commenced January 1, 1972:

Year	From income dividends	From principal	Annually	Cumulative	Remaining original shares	Acquired cap. gain	Total value
1972	$ 2,631	$ 3,369	$ 6,000	$ 6,000	$102,126	$ 3,188	$105,143

* Amounts of capital gain distributions taken in shares for the years 1963–1972 were $4,684, $7,189, $9,167, $11,358, $8,684, $7,647, $12,385, $7,786, $3,628, and $6,672. Total: $79,200. For the one-year period 1972: $3,128.

withdrawn each month. The results reflect the operation of a withdrawal plan under which all income dividends and capital gain distributions are reinvested in additional shares at net asset value, and sufficient shares are sold from the shareholder's account to provide for each withdrawal payment. Continued withdrawals in excess of current income will eventually exhaust principal, particularly in a period of declining market prices.

The results shown should not be considered as a representation of the dividend income, the capital gain or loss, or the amount available for withdrawal from an investment made in the fund today. Only that portion of the total amount withdrawn designated "From Income Dividends" should be regarded as income; the remainder represents a withdrawal of principal.

The Kettle of Nutritious Broth • You might picture this as a kettle filled with nutritious broth. This broth represents housing, clothing, food, etc., for your retirement years.

Let's assume you've paid yourself first for the past 20 years and that you now have $100,000 at retirement. Let's further assume that you begin a 6 percent withdrawal plan. We would place the $100,000 in the kettle, and then we would put a faucet or gauge at the bottom of the kettle and set it at 6 percent per annum on a monthly basis, based on the value of the shares at the time the withdrawal plan was started. Actually, the beginning net asset value used here is $96,500, for it has been adjusted for the commission. If you have been accumulating shares over the 20-year period and if you have $100,000 in share value, there would be no reduction at the beginning.

Your kettle would look like this:

$100,000

6% Spigot
$500 Per Month
$6,000 Per Year

You begin a 6 percent withdrawal based on a beginning value of $100,000. That would amount to $500 per month. (A convenient way to determine what 6 percent would be is to know that 6 percent is $5 per month on each $1,000.) This example shows you beginning your $500 check the very first month. (I usually recommend waiting for a few months with the hopes that the fund will increase in value before beginning the withdrawal.) Every time you receive your check, it is accompanied by a confirmation that shows the history of the account for the current year.

As the fund needs funds to send you your check each month, they will redeem shares. When the fund distributes dividends or capital gains, these are reinvested in additional shares. Therefore, the number of shares you own will change with any activity in your account. This is the reason you deposit your shares with the custodian bank when you begin your withdrawal program.

Your concern should not be with the number of total shares in your account but with the net asset value of the shares in the account.

In the above you will note that by the end of 1963, your share value was $122,085. The value was greater at the end of both 1964 and 1965. In 1966, it shows a decline in value. Now, this should not cause you undue alarm. Remember, we have learned the market has always fluctuated. By 1967, it had more than recouped the loss of 1966, and 1968 showed another gain. Then came 1969 and 1970. Both showed declines. Then came 1971 with a gain and 1972 with a gain.

Now let's take a look at your 10-year record. You started with $100,000. You withdrew a total of $60,000. Your remaining shares would have been worth $225,216 on December 31, 1972. (Remember this is the past. Remember all the hedge clauses throughout this book.)

Instead of using up your broth, the amount has increased. While you were taking out at the bottom, American industry was ladling the broth in at the top. It's often not necessary to fight the battle alone if you will let American free enterprise help you.

How Long Will Capital Last? • Let's assume that instead of the level of the kettle increasing, it decreased. There is nothing sacred about principal. There is nothing that says you are obligated to leave an estate to your heirs. The "sacred" thing is to make you and it come out together.

If you used capital at 7 percent while it was only earning 6 percent, do you know how long your capital would last? Thirty-three years! If you begin your withdrawal at 65, in 33 years you'll be 98 years of age!

Here's a handy chart to use in programming how long capital will last:

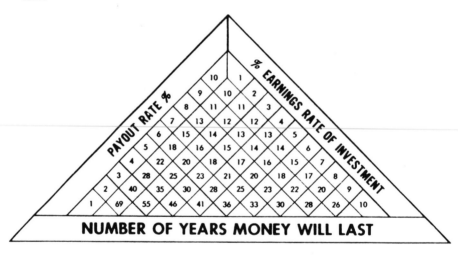

NUMBER OF YEARS MONEY WILL LAST

Another way to visualize how long capital will last is to use this table.

Suppose you have $100,000 that is growing at the rate of 7 percent a year, and you withdraw at an annual rate of 8 percent—$8,000 a year or $666.67 per month. Look at the box where these two percentage figures intersect, and you will see that principal will last 30 years.

• **YOU'RE NOT SPENDING
BUT REPOSITIONING**

I find that often a prospective client feels he is spending his money when he makes an investment.

How Long Will Your Money Last?

Total return per annum on balance of principal

Percentage of original principal withdrawn per annum	3%	4%	5%	6%	7%	8%	9%
			Principal will last . . .				
4%	46 yrs.						
5	30	41 yrs.					
6	23	28	36 yrs.				
7	18	21	25	33 yrs.			
8	15	17	20	23	30 yrs.		
9	13	14	16	18	22	28 yrs.	
10	12	13	14	15	17	20	26 yrs.

If you make an investment by withdrawing funds from a savings account, you are not spending your money but repositioning it, hopefully so it will work for you rather than for the savings institution.

If you should desire to redeem your shares you may do so on any business day. You may cash in all or part of your shares. When you sell your shares back to the fund, you will receive an amount representing your share of the value of all the securities and other assets of the fund at the time. It could be more or less than your cost. The amount you receive will depend on the investment performance of the fund.

If your need for money is temporary or if it is not a favorable time in the market, you may want to consider using your shares as collateral at the bank. You can usually rent time in this way with the hope that the value will increase at a later date.

Even if the market is progressing nicely, you may decide to borrow against the value of the stocks instead of disturbing the goose that you feel is producing satisfactory eggs.

The rent (interest) is deductible on your federal income tax return.

• WHO INVESTS IN MUTUAL FUNDS?

A recent New York Stock Exchange study compared 22 million investors who owned only common stocks with 9 million investors who owned mutual funds. (Five million owned both mutual funds and common stocks; four million owned funds only.) It contrasted the "stock only" investors with the fund investors and found:

1 · Fund investors are the better-educated clients; 65 percent are college graduates vs. 50 percent of the "stock only" clients.

2 · Fund investors are the wealthiest clients, with the largest assets; 23 percent have portfolios of more than $25,000 vs. 15 percent of the other clients.

3 · Fund investors are the highest income clients. Nearly one-half have incomes of $15,000 vs. only one-third of the other clients.

4 · And finally, to put away the idea that mutual fund investors lock up their money forever, fund investors are the most active clients, with one-fourth making more than six transactions per year vs. only one-tenth of other clients.

We are indebted to *Wiesenberger Financial Services Marketer* (an excellent publication) for this breakdown on mutual fund clients.

• IF IT'S A "BETTER MOUSETRAP"

If quality mutual funds have performed in the way I've enumerated in my examples, why haven't investors embraced them with great enthusiasm and in massive numbers?

The chief reason is that state securities boards, the Securities and Exchange Commission, and the National Association of Securities Dealers have prohibited them from telling their story. About all they have allowed those recommending mutual funds as a valid way to invest to do legally is to warn you that you might lose your money. That's not the best way to spread the good word, I'm sure you will agree.

A mutual fund prospectus giving full disclosure of all pertinent facts was rejected by one of the states because it showed a loaf of bread in color. Even though it had in bold print on the front of the prospectus these words:

THESE SECURITIES HAVE NOT BEEN APPROVED OR DISAPPROVED BY THE SECURITIES AND EXCHANGE COMMISSION, NOR HAS THE COMMISSION PASSED UPON THE ACCURACY OR ADEQUACY OF THIS PROSPECTUS. ANY REPRESENTATION TO THE CONTRARY IS A CRIMINAL OFFENSE.

I've had many clients call panic-stricken when they reread the above in the packet of materials after they have made an investment. Sometimes you are tempted to just throw in the sponge. Yet, you know they need to be informed so you spend hours explaining just what this warning means.

Also, there are other "delightfully" scary paragraphs. I pride myself on having informed investors, but many a prospectus is a detriment to intelligent investing.

The regulatory agencies also have not allowed sales literature that pictures people who showed any signs of reasonable solvency. I remember one brochure that was rejected because the man had cuff links in the cuffs of his shirt. They were not diamond studded but looked more like the dime store variety.

In 1971, for the first time in history, the Investment Company Institute was allowed, under very specific "don't rules," to publish the mutual fund performance record.

• THE RECORD

"The Record" was published first in 1971, and then an updated record was published for 1972. Below is "The Record" printed in its entirety as it appeared in our national magazines. (Permission to print their Record for later years has now been withdrawn—hence the use of the 1972 Record.)

What "The Record" Reveals • First of all, during the 22-year period, 1950 to 1972, you could not have averaged 5 percent on your "guaranteed" savings account. An earlier chapter shows the percentage you would have actually received with various savings institutions.

Now let me be sure to point out that if you had experienced this exact performance of "The Record" shown above, you would have had a "loss" in 1953, 1957, 1962, 1966, 1969, and 1970, a total of six years. The fear of loss I find to be a much stronger motivator than the hope for gain. Many will stop looking at "The Record" right after this discovery and fail to notice that there were gains in 16 of the 22 years.

Remember our example of the yo-yo and the stairs. If you can't get your eyes off the yo-yo and on the stairs, you may be condemned to stay in the savings institutions basement, where your $10,000 over a 22-year period, before income taxes (remember this yield was interest and fully taxable), only grew to $30,719, or a gain of $20,719.

If you had done no better than the average above (if you didn't, were you really working at it?), your $10,000 grew to $103,898, or a gain of $93,848—a difference of over 4.6 to 1.

Perspective on Performance • With respect to performance, I find it difficult to see how the mutual fund industry's long-term record could

The mutual fund record.
What other investment program
do you know that can match it?

Year	Initial Investment* $10,000	% Change	Gain	Loss	Compared with 5% interest compounded annually $10,000
1950	$11,089	+10.89	$1,089		$10,500
1951	12,734	+14.84	1,645		11,025
1952	14,166	+11.24	1,432		11,576
1953	14,150	− .11		$16	12,155
1954	20,233	+42.99	6,083		12,763
1955	23,805	+17.65	3,572		13,401
1956	25,604	+ 7.56	1,799		14,071
1957	23,023	−10.08		2,581	14,775
1958	32,088	+39.37	9,065		15,514
1959	36,198	+12.81	4,110		16,290
1960	37,403	+ 3.33	1,205		17,105
1961	46,911	+25.42	9,508		17,960
1962	41,484	−11.57		5,427	18,858
1963	48,519	+16.96	7,035		19,801
1964	54,866	+13.08	6,347		20,791
1965	66,256	+20.76	11,390		21,831
1966	62,785	− 5.24		3,471	22,923
1967	84,294	+34.26	21,509		24,069
1968	99,138	+17.61	14,844		25,272
1969	85,100	−14.16		14,038	26,536
1970	78,616	− 7.62		6,484	27,863
1971	94,008	+19.58	15,392		29,256
1972	103,898	+10.52	9,890		30,719

*Figures in this table are based on annual performance averages of funds listed in the Management Results section of Wiesenberger's *Investment Companies*, except for the categories of bond and preferred stock funds, tax-free exchange funds and international funds. Annual average performance was derived by adding each fund's performance and dividing by the number of funds. New funds were added as they appeared in the Wiesenberger volumes which were used. In 1950, 1961 and 1970, for example, the number of funds was 40, 145 and 307, respectively. Investment results assume initial investment of $9,150 following deduction of sales charge of 8½ percent and subsequent reinvestment of dividends and capital gains. 1972 numbers are preliminary.

be very much better, even when we add into the industry total the dismal record of the go-go funds, which I will discuss later.

The I.C.I. advertisement shows that $10,000 invested in the average mutual fund 23 years ago, with income compounded, would

As the table on the opposite page demonstrates, mutual funds, on the average, have piled up a pretty impressive record over the years.

$10,000 to $103,898

It shows how an investment of $10,000 in 1950, measured by the average performance of mutual funds, would have grown to $103,898 by the beginning of 1973.

That's a net gain of $93,898—after paying management fees and any sales charges.

In contrast, $10,000 at 5% interest compounded annually would have produced a guaranteed net gain of $20,719 over the same period.

(Note: Naturally, you don't have to invest $10,000. You can buy mutual fund shares with virtually any amount from $100 up. Or as little as $25 a month after a modest initial payment.)

Past performance, of course, is no guarantee of the future, and the record of any individual fund varies with its investment objectives.

Giving your dollars a chance to multiply

For people with long-range financial goals, such as retirement or a child's education, mutual funds can be particularly suitable.

Perhaps their greatest attraction is that, unlike savings accounts and other fixed-return investments, mutual funds are designed to grow with the economy.

The investment performance of mutual funds generally reflects long-term stock market trends as well as the overall conditions of the economy. However, mutual funds are based solidly on the premise that over the long haul, the U.S. economy will continue to expand and flourish. As it has, by and large, ever since 1776.

So they give your dollars a chance to multiply.

A chance to stay ahead of inflation.

What is a mutual fund?

Basically, it's a group of people with the same financial goals who invest their money together under the direction of professional money managers.

When you buy shares in a mutual fund, your money is combined with that of the other investors in a diversified group of securities, usually stocks. The securities are selected, and constantly reviewed, by the fund's managers on the basis of the fund's stated objectives.

There are several kinds of funds. One kind may specialize in securities the managers believe will increase in value (growth funds). Another may look for those with good income as well as prospects for growth (income plus growth funds).

Although there's some degree of risk in any investment, full-time professional management, plus diversification helps reduce the risks for mutual fund shareholders.

have grown to about $104,000 at the end of 1972. It may surprise you to learn that the performance figures are in fact unfairly negative, for the industry's average was heavily weighted by conservative funds in the early years, when it paid handsomely to speculate, and by aggressive funds in 1969–1970, when it paid to be conservative. Despite its statistical limitations, the advertisement understates the industry's record. If the table had been limited to equity funds in business throughout the entire period, the final value would have been approximately $120,000. The overall annual return of 10.7 percent reflected in the advertisement is not only wholly creditable but also wholly credible.

• COMPARED
TO WHAT?

Beginning in 1971, it became fashionable among financial writers to give a sharp jab to the stomach of the mutual fund industry. There are at least two reasons for this: First, I think the writers just got tired of reporting the same old news each day, which in substance said the market went down again. Second, the mutual fund industry had been a knight in shining armor. When spots of tarnish began to show, it was much more fun to kick the knight than to polish away the tarnish to let the shining metal beneath show through.

The incongruous part of this development was that these same financial writers were the ones who had placed the crown of victory on the heads of some of the "go-go" fund managers with such headlines as "_____ Fund up 113 percent for the Year!" (Regulations require that I omit the name of the fund.)

Headlines such as these and interviews quoting the "bright" young men who were managing a very small number of "hot" funds brought on a performance race like we've never seen before and hopefully will never see again. The older, well-managed funds, with seasoned money managers at the helm and with true dedication to sound investment principles, did not engage in these wild excesses as did the few gunslingers who had their field day in the speculative heat of 1967.

I'm convinced, as I've mentioned, that many of the agonizing reappraisals we have had in the stock market (that's stockbroker jargon for saying that the market went to pot) are in direct proportion to the amount of junk peddled by stockbrokers during speculative periods.

As a financial planner dedicated to faithfully helping my clients accomplish their long-range plans, I have had one whale of a time trying to justify why I recommended a fund that only increased 39 percent in 1967, after they have read a headline that year stating "_____ Fund Up 113 Percent." My warning about "letter stock" (stock that could not be sold until a certain time had elapsed) fell on deaf ears. I had to either sell the fund to the client or know he would buy it from some other broker. With us, we could at least warn him when we saw the storm warnings.

Please don't think I'm inferring that we never make mistakes. We do. I've had management teams change on me during this performance craze. The fund would be sold to another management group whose performance did not begin to measure up to that of the previous managers.

A large number of funds was sold to life insurance companies during this period. The more sophisticated investors were beginning to see the error of placing their savings in cash surrender value of life insurance policies. This caused the insurance companies that had built their vast empires on high cost, low protection, cash surrender value policies to become extremely nervous. They were beginning to lose the "savings" dollar. They began to look for equity products, with possible hedges against inflation, that their agents could sell. They hoped to keep their agents and to train them to add this new product to their line of wares. They found, however, that it was very hard to undo all the indoctrination they had subjected their agents to when they had taught them to sell "guarantees."

• THE GUNSLINGERS
OF THE GO-GO ERA

There were excesses in 1967. The young gunslingers who were the "portfolio managers" of a minority of "go-go" funds, as these performance-crazed funds were called, were too young to remember a severe market decline. They thought the only direction the market could go was up.

Even the more temperate managers were tempted to chase rainbows. Fortunately, the majority did not succumb to the temptation. When the plug was pulled in 1969–1970, the go-go era went down the drain. Along with it went its idols and much of the capital of those who idolized them. While only a small percentage of industry assets was engulfed in the go-go era, regrettably this portion was very visible. The press had a field day.

Don't be too sure you would have avoided these excesses if you had been in the thick of the 1967 frenzy.

When I have someone say to me, "Mutual funds are not doing so well," again, I ask, "Compared to what?" Compared to what the average speculator did on his own—even as badly as these few funds did—they still fared better than he did, due mostly to the funds' diversification. So again I ask, "Compared to what?" Compared to the man who bought Ling-Tempco-Vought (LTV Corp.) at 169½ and later sold for 8¾.

We'll skip such "delicacies" as Four Seasons Nursing Home and National Student Marketing and look at some others:

Stock	Highs	Later lows
Wyly Corporation (formerly University Computer)	$187	$1¾
Kalvar Corp.	176½	2¾
Penn Central	86½	1¼
Tex-Sym (formerly Westec)	67⅛	⅜
Levitz Furniture	60½	1¾
Winnebago Industries	48¼	2⅜

• DID YOU KNOW THE DOW JONES AVERAGE IS NOT FOR SALE?

In some financial publications, I find mutual fund performances lumped together and actually compared to the Standard and Poor's 500 Stock Index, as if the Index were for sale. It's not for sale. Neither is the Dow Jones Average.

Your problem may be not what the Dow has done performance-wise, but how can you intelligently put to work $10,000.

The most common comparison I've seen in the press matches Standard and Poor's 500 Stock Index and the Lipper Average of 530 mutual funds. All the comparisons I've seen wholly ignore the critical fact that the market index is weighted by the value of each company's common stock and that the Lipper Fund Average is not. Twenty-five giant "blue chips" account for about one-half of the weight of the Index, with the 475 remaining securities accounting for the other half.

• COMPARING INDEX APPLES AND LIPPER ORANGES

In the fund figures, the situation is reversed. While 52 percent of industry assets are represented by the 25 largest funds, they have a weighting of only 2 percent in the Lipper Average. Contrarily, 209 small growth funds, generally highly volatile, account for 40 percent of the weight of the average, but only 2½ percent of industry assets.

Does it matter? Of course it does. For while it purports to compare "the market" with "the fund industry," it is really, to use a trite phrase, comparing "apples and oranges." Thus, in a year such as 1972, when large companies are the best market performers and small funds are the worst industry performers, we had a comparison showing a 15½ percent gain for "the market" (the Standard and Poor's 500) and only

9½ percent for "the industry" (the Lipper 530). And on the basis of that comparison, despite its obvious unfairness, a theory gained credence in the press that might be described as the "idiot theory of performance" —if fund managers fall that far short of the market, they must be idiots.

But if market "apples" can be compared with fund "oranges," so can market "oranges" be compared with fund "apples." This would then give the "genius theory of performance." Using 1972 as a criterion, the fund managers could claim brilliance. In 1972 the average stock on the New York Stock Exchange (unweighted by inflation) rose by just one-half of 1 percent. The fund industry, taking into account all its assets and weighting each fund's performance by its assets, rose by 13 percent —a gain 26 times larger than the New York Stock Exchange Index. If we were so foolish as to rely on this comparison, the fund managers could be acclaimed as genius. This comparison never made any head-lines.

Obviously the fund managers are not geniuses, nor are they idiots. However, most of them did outperform what the average person did on his own in the same period.

• HOW DID THE SEMINAR FUND MEASURE UP?

How did the Seminar Fund do in comparison to the average? (Remember that the averages are not for sale and that the comparison below is past history.)

	To December 31, 1973				
	Latest 10 yrs	*Latest 15 yrs*	*Latest 20 yrs*	*Latest 30 yrs*	*Latest 40 yrs*
Seminar Fund	+78.8%	+148.3%	+495.3%	+1079.7%	+3143.0%
Standard and Poor's 500 Stock Index	+30.0%	+ 76.7%	+293.2%	+ 735.9%	+ 865.8%
Dow Jones Average of 30 Industrial Stocks	+11.5%	+ 45.8%	+202.9%	+ 526.1%	+ 751.7%
New York Stock Exchange Composite Index	+29.8%	+75.4%	+281.0%	+ 625.8%	NA

• HOW DID YOUR STOCKS MEASURE UP?

Why don't you make a tally and see how your stock selection compares? If you've outperformed the Seminar Fund, you'll be very pleased with yourself. If you have not, perhaps you should employ professionals to manage a portion of your funds.

Application

Are you more concerned about what something pays or what it costs? What program will you start today to attempt to provide at least a minimum $100,000 investment for your check-a-month at retirement? What is your life expectancy based on your family's record? Will your present life-style tend to increase or decrease your life expectancy in comparison with your family's history? How does your record of performance compare with "The Record" of the average of the mutual funds? How does your record compare with the Seminar Fund? Should you do your own investing, or turn it over to professionals? If the latter, should you turn all or a portion over to them?

{ 10 }

Is There
an Infallible Way
To Invest?

- ## DOLLAR-COST-
  ## AVERAGING

Is there an infallible way to invest in the stock market? Perhaps not. But then what in life is infallible?

However, there is one way of investing I've found that comes closer than any other. It's called dollar-cost-averaging. This concept has been widely practiced by astute investors for years. Instead of trying to time the "highs" and "lows" for their purchases (which as we've learned already is a lot easier said than done, since you never seem to know what the low is until it's too late to do anything about it), they have learned the value of investing a fixed amount of money on a regular schedule and letting the principle of dollar-cost-averaging work for them.

This plan does not require brilliance or luck, but the discipline to save and invest over a long period of time. How dull—no brilliance or luck, just discipline. That doesn't make your adrenal gland surge, make bells ring in your cerebrum or bring a sparkle to your eyes. Nor will it lend itself to sharing enticing tidbits at the "happy hour" about your marvelous astuteness in the market.

But let's assume you are going to get your kicks in other ways and that you feel becoming financially independent does have some compensating features. Just what is dollar-cost-averaging, and why should you consider it as one method for attempting to build your estate?

When you dollar-cost-average, as you will remember, you invest the same amount of money in the same security at the same interval over a long period of time, with the assumption that the stock market will fluctuate and eventually go up. (These two things have always happened in the past.)

Let's assume you can discipline yourself to save $100 a month, a quarter, any regular interval, and that you have the earning capacity and the discipline to do this for a long period of time. Then get started immediately because it makes little or no difference in your end results whether the market is going up, down, or sideways when you start.

If you are paralyzed into a state of inertia as to when to buy, what to buy, and when to sell, which has caused you to be in the delay–linger–wait syndrome, skip buying a particular stock and choose a mutual fund that has an excellent reputation for good management and a commendable record of past performance. A fund is especially adaptable to dollar-cost-averaging because under an accumulation plan you can buy fractional shares carried out to the third decimal point. You may also invest monthly in a Monthly Investment Program (MIP) Plan in a stock listed on the New York Stock Exchange. However, you may find the MIP Plan in the end more costly and without sufficient diversification.

Let's assume you have $100 per quarter to invest. For the sake of simplicity, we will assume the investment company trust you have chosen is selling at $10 per share. You invest $100 and receive 10 shares. Then a correction occurs in the market and the fund you are investing in goes down to $5 per share. You still plop in your $100 for the quarter. (You're not masterminding this program, once you've made your decision regarding the investment to be used, but you are investing each quarter, regardless of what the market is doing.) At $5 per share you would receive 20 shares for your $100. Let's assume by the next quarter the market has returned to where it was when you started and is now selling at $10 per share. You will now receive 10 shares for your $100.

An overly simplified illustration would look something like this:

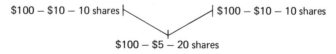

$100 – $10 – 10 shares $100 – $10 – 10 shares

$100 – $5 – 20 shares

Let's take an inventory:

Regular investment	Share price	Shares acquired
$100	$10	10
100	5	20
100	10	10
TOTALS $300	$25	40

Results: Total invested $300. Total shares owned 40.

Ending market price per share $10: 40 × $10 = $400.

You have made a $100 gain with the market dropping 50 percent and only returning to where it started. Average price per share ($25/3) = $8.33. Average cost per share ($300/40) = $7.50. You bought more shares (20) at a low cost ($5) than at a high cost ($10) and received an average cost for your securities. In the past, when I have followed this program, I've always made money.

If you are investing in a mutual fund, it should have a tendency to fluctuate with the market because of its wide diversification, and if our long-term upward trend continues, you should benefit from this fluctuation.

If you are one of those who enjoys playing with numbers, here are three hypothetical examples started at different points in varying business cycles. I've simplified and somewhat exaggerated the examples to more clearly demonstrate the principles of dollar-cost-averaging. In actual application you should take into consideration the period of your overall program.

In a declining market

Regular investment	Share price	Shares acquired
$ 300	$25	12
300	15	20
300	20	15
300	10	30
300	5	60
TOTALS $1,500	$75	137

Average price per share ($75/5) = $15.00

Dollar-cost-average per share ($1,500/137) = $10.95

This example shows the importance of continuing your investment program throughout a declining market. When the share value dropped from $25 to $5, the greatest number of shares was acquired. So any recovery above the dollar-cost-average of $10.95 would establish a profit.

In a steady market

Regular investment	Share price	Shares acquired
$ 300	$12	25
300	15	20
300	12	25
300	15	20
300	12	25
TOTALS $1,500	$66	115

Average price per share ($66/5) = $13.20

Dollar-cost-average per share ($1,500/115) = $13.04

Even in a relatively steady market, dollar-cost-averaging can work to your advantage. As the above example shows, the actual per share cost is 16¢ less than the average price of $13.20 per share.

In a rising market

Regular investment	Share price	Shares acquired
$ 300	$ 5	60
300	15	20
300	10	30
300	15	20
300	25	12
TOTALS $1,500	$70	142

Average price per share ($70/5) = $14.00

Dollar-cost-average per share ($1,500/142) = $10.57

As the above example shows, the dollar-cost-average per share of the five regular investments is $10.57. When compared with the current $25 per share value, it does demonstrate the importance of fluctuations in prices to the success of dollar-cost-averaging.

The practice of dollar-cost-averaging does not remove the possibility of loss when the market is below the average cost, but it clearly demonstrates that the successful pursuit of the system will lessen the amount of loss in a declining market and increase the opportunity of greater profit in a rising market.

So you see, dollar-cost-averaging doesn't give you the fun of sharing your brilliance at the coffee klatch; but if it helps you to increase your assets, it could make it possible for you to enjoy a fattening, gooey Danish pastry later.

If your real reason for investing is to make money, dollar-cost-averaging is the most infallible way that I have found to approach the market.

• INVESTING
FOR GAIN?

You would be surprised how many people are in the market not to make money but for the thrill it offers!

One afternoon a dentist and his wife came to my office to open a brokerage account. They said they did not expect or want my advice. All they would require of me were good executions. They explained that his profession kept him extremely busy with little time off and "playing the market" would be their diversion. Their chief goal was not to make money but to use their brokerage account as a mini-Las Vegas.

This case history reminds me of another. One of my young CPA clients stopped me on the street one day to tell me he would be calling me in about a month to make an investment of some funds he would be receiving. A month passed—then two months passed. One afternoon our paths crossed again, and I asked, "Tommy, have you received your money yet?" A sheepish grin appeared on his face. He said, "Yes, but tax time was so busy, we just couldn't get away for our planned trip to Las Vegas, so I put the money in the commodity market and lost it."

I'm going to assume you are reading this book because you want to become financially independent and not for the kicks gambling may give you.

• EGO,
THE DETERRENT

Let me again remind you that one of the greatest deterrents to successful investing is the three-letter word, EGO. Dollar-cost-averaging will not do a thing to bolster your ego. Ego causes investors to hold a stock long after it has gone sour because their ego will not let them admit that they could make a mistake. They harbor the hope that by some miracle it will return to what they paid for it; then, they tell me, "I'll sell." Don't say to me, "I've never had a loss," and expect me to be impressed. It means to me that you've probably never been in there trying or that your ego made you hold long past the time when you should have let go.

One of the major reasons many refuse to use professional management is that it's an admission that someone can do something better than they can do it. Again, EGO. . . .

• TEN YEARS BEFORE
THE GOLDEN YEARS

Let's assume your masculine or feminine prowess is not threatened by the admission that someone can do something better than you, and you've decided to let the professionals managing the Seminar Fund do your investing for you. You are age 55 and plan to retire in 10 years. You begin your investment program with $250 and faithfully add $100 a month, rain or shine, market going up, market going down, Elliot Janeway's predictions of bust or Kiplinger's *Changing Times* headline of "Boom Ahead!" For 119 additional months, you faithfully send in your money to the custodian bank or service corporation. How will you come out? I don't know. I can show you (Table 16) how you would have done during thirty 10-year periods between 1934 and 1973 using the Seminar Fund. The last column on the right shows the results.

• DOES LIFE
BEGIN AT FORTY?

Perhaps you are only a tender 40. Does "life begin at 40"? I don't know that it does, but I do know that if you come to me at that age, I have 25 years to be of help to you.

In 40 years there are sixteen 25-year periods, and Table 17 shows what happened during those years. Again, the right-hand column tells the results.

• ARE YOU
A TENDER 25?

Let's assume you are a mere 25 years of age. Table 18 is the total record that was attained by dollar-cost-averaging over a 40-year period. The total results from January 1, 1934, to December 31, 1972, were $978,843, and to December 31, 1973, after a severe market decline, $815,271 after all costs were taken out, with the exception of federal income taxes.

Again the now-familiar disclaimer: This table covers the period from

Table 16.   Performance of the "Seminar Fund"

Jan. 1– Dec. 31	Income dividends reinvested	Total cost (including dividends reinvested)	Capital gain distributions taken in shares	Ending value of shares
1934–43	$2,827	$14,977	$2,079	$19,502
1935–44	2,726	14,876	2,059	20,800
1936–45	2,511	14,661	2,995	24,615
1937–46	2,766	14,916	3,897	22,443
1938–47	3,325	15,475	4,491	21,827
1939–48	3,556	15,706	4,286	19,757
1940–49	3,658	15,808	4,222	19,705
1941–50	3,746	15,896	4,049	21,250
1942–51	3,719	15,869	4,129	22,125
1943–52	3,438	15,588	3,946	21,055
1944–53	3,340	15,490	3,485	18,676
1945–54	3,238	15,388	3,795	25,845
1946–55	3,307	15,457	4,959	29,026
1947–56	3,453	15,603	6,245	29,338
1948–57	3,451	15,601	6,502	22,961
1949–58	3,368	15,518	6,261	29,346
1950–59	3,127	15,277	6,670	28,469
1951–60	2,928	15,078	6,452	25,351
1952–61	2,754	14,904	6,363	26,868
1953–62	2,560	14,710	5,720	20,118
1954–63	2,298	14,448	5,029	20,990
1955–64	2,073	14,223	4,761	20,743
1956–65	2,020	14,170	5,042	23,424
1957–66	2,078	14,288	5,553	21,287
1958–67	2,137	14,287	5,528	24,406
1959–68	2,167	14,317	5,051	24,716
1960–69	2,278	14,428	5,277	19,828
1961–70	2,332	14,482	4,896	18,380
1962–71	2,377	14,527	4,222	19,527
1963–72	2,319	14,469	3,793	20,098
1964–73	2,229	14,379	3,148	14,845

January 1, 1934, through December 31, 1973. While this period, on the whole, was one of generally rising common stock prices, it also included some interim periods of substantial market decline. Results shown should not be considered as a representation of the dividend income or capital gain loss that may be realized from an investment made in the Fund today. A program of the type illustrated does not ensure or protect against depreciation in declining markets.

Table 17.   Performance of "Seminar Fund" in 25-Year Periods

Jan. 1– Dec. 31	Income dividends reinvested	Total cost (including dividends reinvested)	Capital gain distributions taken in shares	Ending value of shares
1934–58	$41,486	$71,636	$66,061	$215,616
1935–59	39,852	70,002	70,191	213,955
1936–60	38,687	68,837	70,543	195,526
1937–61	39,727	69,877	75,928	222,902
1938–62	41,551	71,701	78,992	182,441
1939–63	40,791	70,941	77,887	200,715
1940–64	40,220	70,370	80,885	209,495
1941–65	39,388	69,538	85,067	236,579
1942–66	38,769	68,919	89,499	210,085
1943–67	37,145	67,295	85,757	230,930
1944–68	37,073	67,223	82,127	236,150
1945–69	37,155	67,305	83,389	185,608
1946–70	37,647	67,797	80,537	170,624
1947–71	38,471	68,621	73,377	181,774
1948–72	37,979	68,129	71,209	187,210
1949–73	37,216	67,366	65,124	137,581

• LUMP SUM INVESTING

You can also use dollar-cost-averaging for larger lump sum investments. For example, you have $25,000 for investment, but you are uncertain as to whether this is the right time to commit so large a portion of your assets to the market.

You may select the fund or list of stocks that fits your financial objective. If you are using a fund, you may file a letter of intent with the fund as discussed in the chapter on mutual funds. This gives you the privilege of investing at two discounts over the full offering price. There is usually a discount at $10,000 and a second one at $25,000. You have 13 months to cross one of these discounts.

The lump sum method is also helpful when you do not have the $25,000 now but will have it within the 13-month period. You may be selling some of your assets at a capital gains or cashing in some government bonds with a large amount of accrued interest. If you space their disposition over two tax years you may be able to save some tax dollars.

Realize that dollar-cost-averaging takes time because it means placing your investment dollars in your chosen securities month after month, year after year, sweating out recessions, confidence crises, and so forth. Compared to the horse races or a turn at the crap table, it's disgustingly dull. If the thought of retiring in financial dignity and enjoying the Golden Years brings you joy, perhaps dollar-cost-averaging is for you. Our formula still remains:

Time + Money + American Free Enterprise =
Opportunity To Retire in Financial Dignity

• JOHN WORKED FOR THE TELEPHONE CO.

I've been using a lot of impersonal figures. Many minds clap shut when a row of figures or a chart rears its ugly head. I hope you are still with me.

To help you relate to the figures in Table 19 below, let me give them the identities of John, Martha, and Julia.

John reached the historic day when he became 50. His wife, Martha, gave a big birthday party for him, and loads of friends came to help him celebrate. They had a great time that evening.

However, the next day, John began to have some somber thoughts. "I'm 50. I'll retire from the telephone company in 15 years. We haven't saved much toward retirement. I wonder what my pension will be?" John went to the personnel office to inquire about his pension and found it would be only $200 per month.

That night, as they sat at the kitchen table, John told Martha of his unhappy findings and said, "Martha, that will not be enough to allow us to retire in dignity."

The kids were all out on their own by then, and, after scrutinizing their budget, they decided they could save $100 a month. So each month after that John wrote a $100 check to the bank and requested that they invest it for him in shares of the Seminar Fund.

Table 18.   Performance of "Seminar Fund," 1934 to 1973

COST OF SHARES

Year Ended Dec. 31	Total Periodic Investments (cumulative)	Income Dividends Reinvested Annually	Income Dividends Reinvested Cumulative	Total Cost (including dividends reinvested)
1934	$1,350	—	—	$1,350
1935	2,550	—	—	2,550
1936	3,750	$102	$102	3,852
1937	4,950	272	374	5,324
1938	6,150	52	426	6,576
1939	7,350	207	633	7,983
1940	8,550	373	1,006	9,556
1941	9,750	586	1,592	11,342
1942	10,950	617	2,209	13,159
1943	12,150	618	2,827	14,977
1944	13,350	726	3,553	16,903
1945	14,550	705	4,258	18,808
1946	15,750	1,092	5,350	21,100
1947	16,950	1,569	6,919	23,869
1948	18,150	1,771	8,690	26,840
1949	19,350	1,806	10,496	29,846
1950	20,550	2,193	12,689	33,239
1951	21,750	2,407	15,096	36,846
1952	22,950	2,549	17,645	40,595
1953	24,150	2,935	20,580	44,730
1954	25,350	3,109	23,689	49,039
1955	26,550	3,837	27,526	54,076
1956	27,750	4,230	31,756	59,506
1957	28,950	4,728	36,484	65,434
1958	30,150	5,002	41,486	71,636
1959	31,350	5,388	46,874	78,224
1960	32,550	6,281	53,155	85,705
1961	33,750	6,496	59,651	93,401
1962	34,950	7,097	66,748	101,698
1963	36,150	7,514	74,262	110,412
1964	37,350	8,389	82,651	120,001
1965	38,550	9,515	92,166	130,716
1966	39,750	12,214	104,380	144,130
1967	40,950	14,481	118,861	159,811
1968	42,150	17,879	136,740	178,890
1969	43,350	20,034	156,774	200,124
1970	44,550	21,639	178,413	222,963
1971	45,750	22,672	201,085	246,835
1972	46,950	23,776	224,861	271,811
1973	48,150	26,541	251,402	299,552

John did this for 15 years. Then came John's retirement day. He then wrote a letter to the same bank. His letter said, "I'm retiring now and won't be able to send any more money. Would you be so kind as to send me my dividends quarterly as they are declared and my capital gains each year that you have any to distribute."

VALUE OF SHARES

Acquired through Periodic Investments	Acquired as Capital Gain Distributions (cumulative)	Sub-Total	Acquired through Reinvestment of Income Dividends (cumulative)	Total Value	Capital Gain Distributions Taken in Shares*
$1,416	—	$1,416	—	$1,416	—
4,443	—	4,443	—	4,443	—
6,565	$986	7,551	$102	7,653	$976
4,532	617	5,149	271	5,420	67
6,760	1,119	7,879	392	8,271	321
7,640	1,341	8,981	581	9,562	231
8,168	1,391	9,559	922	10,481	149
8,141	1,242	9,383	1,356	10,739	29
10,155	1,482	11,637	2,161	13,798	104
14,054	2,086	16,140	3,362	19,502	202
17,387	3,293	20,680	4,617	25,297	877
22,834	6,589	29,423	6,503	35,926	2,469
21,185	8,169	29,354	6,790	36,144	2,379
20,565	9,234	29,799	7,796	37,595	1,732
20,155	9,790	29,945	8,941	38,886	1,202
21,467	11,386	32,853	10,893	43,746	1,508
25,021	14,250	39,271	14,396	53,667	1,576
28,216	18,229	46,445	18,031	64,476	2,754
30,237	21,972	52,209	21,169	73,378	3,214
29,458	22,586	52,044	22,806	74,850	1,990
43,784	38,093	81,877	36,406	118,283	5,439
50,666	53,787	104,453	45,118	149,571	10,321
51,782	65,736	117,518	49,298	166,816	11,965
42,551	61,583	104,134	43,852	147,986	9,119
58,972	91,508	150,480	65,136	215,616	7,437
62,486	111,684	174,170	73,215	247,385	16,223
61,163	121,831	182,994	76,790	259,784	13,955
70,881	155,819	226,700	94,248	320,948	16,616
58,508	137,440	195,948	83,610	279,558	12,507
68,360	172,505	240,865	103,881	344,746	14,195
74,338	208,030	282,368	119,593	401,961	23,011
87,801	274,134	361,935	149,579	511,514	30,737
81,305	287,654	368,959	148,699	517,658	39,270
98,529	377,055	475,584	192,846	668,430	31,547
108,521	445,398	553,919	229,167	783,086	28,275
89,333	405,114	494,447	206,034	700,481	47,301
85,927	415,376	501,303	218,770	720,073	30,768
97,083	479,304	576,387	267,499	843,886	15,273
107,386	554,018	661,404	317,439	978,843	28,932
85,081	456,205	541,286	273,985	815,271	21,582

John lived for 20 more years, and when he was 85 he went home to be with his maker.

A few weeks later a friend of Martha's, whose name was Julia, also lost her husband. She came to Martha saying, "I've received these life insurance proceeds, and I have such a strong sense of stewardship about

Table 19. John and Martha's Investment and Use

15-Year Share Accumulation Illustrations
Total Investments: $18,150

Jan. 1–Dec. 31	Income Dividends Reinvested	Total Cost (including dividends reinvested)	Capital Gain Distributions Taken in Shares†	Ending Value of Shares
1934 - 48	$8,690	$26,840	$10,738	$38,886
1935 - 49	8,552	26,702	9,831	37,087
1936 - 50	8,510	26,660	8,949	38,995
1937 - 51	9,107	27,257	9,627	43,026
1938 - 52	9,870	28,020	10,797	45,963
1939 - 53	9,968	28,118	10,270	41,613
1940 - 54	9,980	28,130	11,467	58,635
1941 - 55	10,020	28,170	14,202	65,397
1942 - 56	9,858	28,008	16,425	63,534
1943 - 57	9,277	27,427	16,104	47,549
1944 - 58	8,954	27,104	15,383	60,213
1945 - 59	8,664	26,814	16,702	60,357
1946 - 60	8,645	26,795	17,204	56,473
1947 - 61	8,726	26,876	18,277	63,277
1948 - 62	8,506	26,656	17,650	48,841
1949 - 63	8,166	26,316	16,963	52,979
1950 - 64	7,593	25,743	16,705	52,836
1951 - 65	7,090	25,240	16,887	57,514
1952 - 66	6,892	25,042	17,548	50,395
1953 - 67	6,720	24,870	16,837	56,025
1954 - 68	6,528	24,678	15,287	55,640
1955 - 69	6,336	25,486	14,829	42,418
1956 - 70	6,410	24,560	13,903	38,945
1957 - 71	6,489	24,639	12,394	41,138
1958 - 72	6,445	24,595	11,523	42,695
1959 - 73	6,239	24,389	10,043	31,312

† The value of the shares acquired with these capital gain distributions is reflected in "Ending Value of Shares."

20-Year Use of Investment
$41,613—Net asset value of shares accumulated as of December 31, 1953*

Year Ended Dec. 31	Cash from Income Dividends	Cash from Capital Gain Distributions	Ending Value of Shares
1954	$1,692	$ 2,916	$59,971
1955	1,872	5,040	67,818
1956	1,872	5,256	67,890
1957	1,872	3,600	54,572
1958	1,800	2,664	73,938
1959	1,800	5,400	76,962
1960	1,872	4,248	73,938
1961	1,800	4,608	84,305
1962	1,800	3,240	68,322
1963	1,800	3,384	78,474
1964	1,872	5,112	84,089
1965	1,944	6,263	97,984
1966	2,232	7,343	89,561
1967	2,448	5,328	107,271
1968	2,736	4,536	116,846
1969	2,808	7,055	95,104
1970	2,808	4,176	90,209
1971	2,808	1,872	100,720
1972	2,808	3,384	110,223
1973	2,952	2,376	86,321
Totals:	$43,596	$87,801	

*If all the shares had been purchased at offering price (which includes the sales charge as described in the prospectus) on December 31, 1953, instead of accumulated in the shareholder account, the cost would have been $44,276.

them that I'm endeavoring to invest these funds prudently. I've been considering a particular mutual fund and remembered that you and John owned it. Were you happy with it?" Martha said, "Oh yes, and I still have it." Julia replied, "I know it's a personal matter, but how well have you done?"

Martha began walking toward a drawer in the kitchen saying, "I don't mind sharing this information with you at all. John kept excellent records, so let's take a look."

When they looked at John's records, this is what they found. They had received $43,596 in dividends and $87,801 in capital gains distribution during the 20 years of John's retirement. Martha said, "I especially remember these capital gains distributions because John liked them the best. He kept reminding me that they were "half tax-free." Then she added, "Would you believe I still have all the shares we had at the time John retired? We often looked up their net asset value in the paper together, so I know how to calculate their value."

When Martha and Julia multiplied the number of shares times the net asset value per share they found they had a value of $86,321.

All John and Martha had ever done was save $100 a month from age 50 to 65!

• THE SECRET

Again let me repeat, the secret of financial independence is not brilliance or luck, but discipline!

Do you truly want to retire in financial dignity? Do you believe in the future of the American economy? If your answer is Yes, get busy dollar-cost-averaging!

Application

How many years do you have before retirement? How much can you save each month for this purpose? Which day of the month is most convenient for you to make your investment? If you decide to use mutual funds, which would be best for you? What other method have you found to attain financial independence that has a greater likelihood for success? What is the secret of financial independence?

$$\left\{ \begin{array}{c} 11 \end{array} \right\}$$

Investing
in
Real Estate

There are three major areas you should consider when determining how to best employ your investment dollars. These are, first, shares of American industry. You have just looked at the criteria you must learn and follow in accomplishing success in this area. The second major area is real estate, which we will examine in this chapter. The third is natural resources, with which you and I will become more familiar in a later chapter.

In times of uncertainties, such as occurred in the early 1970s, investors tend to "return to the earth." This exhibits itself in revived interest in investments closely allied with the land—either under, in, or attached to the land.

Let's first consider which, if any, of these areas offers a valid investment media for you.

• RAW LAND— THE GLAMOUR INVESTMENT

Often a young couple who has attended one of my seminars will come to my office for counseling, as each person who attends a seminar is entitled to do. They will be very starry eyed about their future and say, "We want to invest in land. They're not making any more of it, you know."

Yes, I know they're not making any more of it—with perhaps the exception of the Dutch reclamation from the sea. That does not mean, however, that land is a valid investment consideration for them. To begin with, young couples usually have no more than $5,000 in liquid assets, they frequently have two or more children, and they have a very small equity in their home. It will be very difficult for them to take a meaningful position in raw land. Larger tracts—which they do not have the resources to secure—offer the best profit potential. Taxes must be paid while they wait for the land to "mature"—meaning waiting for the ultimate commercial user. Also, if they borrow money to finance the purchase, interest payments must be paid. In their lower tax bracket Uncle Sam can not give them much help. They must also forgo liquidity while waiting. Investing in "land" becomes more of a wistful dream than a valid investment possibility for this couple.

Your financial situation may be quite different. You may possess liquid assets and have a high cash flow from other income sources to service the interest on the loan and to pay taxes while you wait. This makes raw land investing a valid possibility for you. Your next consideration should be whether to invest on an individual basis or to join others in a land syndication.

Historical Perspective • Although America has built most of her cities, building is still going on at a rapid pace. Far more vacant land remains available than you might think. Not counting reserves of government property or the Alaskan wilderness, there are over five acres of land per person in the United States. Much of this land is usable and accessible.

Our present land boom began after World War II and appears to have years to run. Most of the war babies who made such a demand on school facilities in the 1950s and the colleges in the 1960s are now having babies of their own and are entering the market for homes. This will cause a great demand for places to live and for the land upon which to build the places to live. It is estimated that the demand for housing will increase steadily in the next decade. Housing construction brings other real estate activities. Shopping centers, office buildings, and industry follow new centers of population into expanding suburbs.

There are many indications that land and its development holds greater profit potential than at any time since the building boom of the 1950s.

Land has always been the glamour growth stock of real estate. It comes unfettered with buildings to manage and tenants to satisfy. However, you must also realize that an investment in empty land is the most speculative kind of real estate venture.

Principles To Follow • If you decide that investing in raw land is for you, there are six basic principles you should remember. The first principle is: Don't follow the population. Get out in front of it. The second is to realize that timing of land purchases is all important. The third is to be prepared financially to service your holdings. The cost of property taxes, liability insurance, and interest on financing makes it necessary to have around a 10 percent a year increase in the price of the land just to cover expenses.

It is important that you fully comprehend the nature of the ultimate land use, which will determine what a developer can afford to pay for your property. It is also necessary for you to understand the timing of the return of your invested capital. For a property to double in value may seem to be good; however, if the property should take 20 years to double, it will not be quite so attractive. Successful real estate investment requires a forward-looking investigation and an understanding of the nature and character of the property being considered.

Fourth, keep your down payment low—paying down as little cash as possible. Sellers are often willing to accept 29 percent or less down and to finance the remainder to spread out tax payments on capital gains.

If you want to take the risk of maximum leverage, you should endeavor to negotiate the smallest down payment you can get—perhaps as low as 10 percent. If you take this course, you will need to obtain around a 20 percent annual appreciation. In other words, you would be counting on the price of the land doubling in a little over four years.

Fifth, be prepared to wait. The price of raw land seldom climbs steadily over a long period. Instead, values tend to remain fairly level for years.

When prices are rising, it may be easy to sell land, but if the price doesn't rise, money invested in land may be tied up for years while the expenses of ownership roll on. Even if a buyer can be found, financing may be difficult. Many banks will not carry mortgages on undeveloped land. You, the seller, may have to finance the buyer over a period of years. This may very well make land the least liquid of investments.

Some of the saddest plights I have seen have been widows who could not find a buyer for their raw land and had to sacrifice essentials to pay the taxes and interest payments on the land.

Sixth, if you make a land purchase and incur a large indebtedness, be sure to buy adequate term life insurance to cover the indebtedness to avoid a possible hardship on your heirs. Even if you own the land outright, without any indebtedness, land is not liquid. Insurance proceeds will allow your heirs to have enough ready cash to pay inheritance taxes and avoid a forced sale at the wrong time.

If you have already accumulated a substantial net worth with some liquidity, raw land may be a viable investment consideration for your investment dollars. If not, as glamorous as owning raw land may appear, you should probably pass up the temptation.

Raw Land Syndications • In recent years raw land syndications have enjoyed considerable popularity. Should you consider owning a small interest in a syndication? It all depends. Here are some criteria you should carefully examine:

1 • Who is the general partner or syndicator? What is his track record? Is it excellent or just fair? Syndications can be good or very poor depending on the know-how of the syndicator to buy right and to find a satisfactory buyer when it's time to sell.

2 ·   Ask yourself, "Is it a good investment?" If the answer is Yes, then look at the tax savings potential. Too many syndications are structured to save taxes and have slim chances of earning you a good return on your invested dollar.

3 ·   Examine what your after-tax cost will be on the investment, and then calculate what you feel your yearly return will be on your cost basis.

Recreational Lots   •   Should you buy recreational lots at the seashore, on the lakes, in the desert, in the mountains? Probably not. Some work out well, but the majority have been marked up so much before being offered to the investor that the opportunity to sell at a profit is minimal. Liquidity is a definite problem after all the lots have been sold and the aggressive sales force has moved on to other developments.

•   REAL ESTATE INVESTMENT TRUSTS

If you have a smaller amount of available capital to invest, need to spend your time staying or becoming more professional in your chosen vocation, and desire liquidity without some of the responsibilities of land ownership, an investment medium that may be ideal for you is the Real Estate Investment Trust (REIT).

In 1960, Congress altered the tax laws to encourage formation of the Real Estate Investment Trusts so that smaller investors could benefit from the potential profits and real estate tax benefits previously available only to large investors. REITs, as they are called in stockbroker jargon, make it possible for you to put some of your money into real estate without taking a speculator's high risk or being bothered with demands from your tenants. Share prices have been in the $10 to $20 range, and the average yield has been from 9 percent to 14 percent.

REITs are investment companies much like mutual funds. They specialize in mortgages, income-producing properties, or a combination of both. As closed-end companies, they issue a limited number of shares that are then traded in the market.

I do not recommend that you invest in the REITs that invest primarily in mortgages. Interest rate fluctuations can adversely affect their performance. Also, if a default occurs, they do not usually have the management know-how to manage the property profitably.

If you invest in REITs, don't place all your investment dollars into only one—spread your money among several.

A Particular REIT • Let's examine a particular trust that has done a satisfactory job for our clients in the past. It is managed by an extremely capable team of real estate specialists. Their investment policies, in the judgment of many who have made their fortunes investing in real estate, are extremely conservative, bordering on dull.

I first became aware of this trust during the stock boom of 1967. It had been established in 1963 and had an excellent performance record. Unfortunately, at that time in the market the words "income" and "conservative" were the kiss of death to an investment recommendation. "Growth" was the magic word. Promises of 20, 30, 40 percent gains per year were rampant in the stockbrokerage community. You were "Dullsville" when you mentioned reasonable income and reasonable growth.

There are times when any conscientious financial planner must resign himself to selling what clients demand. Not to follow this course means the planner's practice will not survive; and consequently he will not be around to help his clients "put the pieces back together" after their adventure. Therefore, I shelved the REIT that had appealed to me until a greater degree of sanity was restored to the market place.

Later as the market grew progressively worse I called the trust's management and said, "I think the world is now ready for you."

We held a seminar and presented the trust information together with the required prospectus that would have scared away the most avid gambler in Las Vegas! I presented this investment as one that appeared to me to offer a cash flow of around 8 percent, with some tax shelter and growth potential. The shares were $10 each, with a 100-share minimum original investment and the privilege of adding to it in smaller purchases, plus the privilege of reinvesting the quarterly distributions at no cost. With these minimum requiremnts the small investor could participate in prime income-producing real estate along with the larger investor.

How Has This REIT Performed? • If you had invested $10,000 in December 1971, your distributions for 1972 would have been 88¢ per share, or $880. This amounts to 8.8 percent, 73 percent of it nontaxable as a return of capital. (We'll explain how depreciation is passed on to the investor later.) Your annual dividend would have been increased with the 38th quarterly report to 96¢ (24¢ for the quarter) and to $1.20 annually (30¢ for the quarter) with the 39th quarterly report. This would give you a cash flow of $1,200 or 12 percent on your original investment of $10,000 at $10 per share.

In June 1973 a new underwriting was offered at $12.50 per share.

The $1.20 dividend at the new offering price represented a 9.6 percent cash flow, 76¢ of which was tax sheltered. The money crunch of 1974 had a devastating effect on mortgage REITs and the resultant publicity also lowered the market price of this REIT, as well as other equity REITs. Many investors cannot distinguish between the investment viability of the two.

The IDEAL Investment? • Although there is no such thing as an IDEAL investment, the real estate trust does have some ideal characteristics from an investor's standpoint!

I — Income with tax shelter
     Inflation hedge

D — Depreciation pass-through
     Direct investment
     Diversification—types and geographically

E — Equity built-up

A — Appreciation potential
     Accounting service provided

L — Leverage
     Liquidity

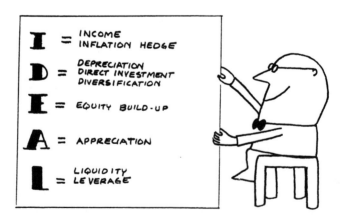

Income With Tax Shelter Through Depreciation Pass-Through • Two factors go into computing the usable income that you receive from investments—the amount that you receive and the amount that you are allowed to keep after taxes. Any improved property in a REIT portfolio may be depreciated over a number of years, and that depreciation credit is passed on to you. The rate at which properties are depreciated varies according to the nature of the property. The portfolio of properties may contain apartment complexes, shopping centers, office buildings, warehouses, restaurants, hotels and motels. The government allows the owners to depreciate furnishings such as drapes, carpets, and refrigerators over a 3-year basis (this is called component part depreciation), such items as swimming pools and paving over a 10-year basis, and buildings over a 20- to 30-year basis. This depreciation is an allowable expense for federal income tax purposes, but it does not have to be subtracted from distributable income; therefore, a large portion of it is often distributed to shareholders.

Historically, quality commercial real estate, kept in good repair, has maintained or increased in value. Hence, depreciation is not treated as a real expense to determine distributable income. It is, however, permitted as an income tax deduction, which serves to shelter a substantial portion of the trust's distributions.

In calculating the cost basis of your REITs this depreciation should be deducted as a return of capital and your cost basis reduced accordingly.

Here is a comparison between receiving your income from a "guaranteed" savings account and this particular REIT in 1972 (principal not guaranteed, of course).

On a $10,000 investment you would have purchased 1,000 shares at $10 per share. During 1972, 73 percent of the distributions per share were nontaxable as a return of capital (depreciation). If you were in a 30 percent tax bracket ($12,000 single, $20,000 joint) your net after tax return was as follows:

	REIT	@ 5%
Income	$ 880	$ 500
Loss to Taxes	−71	−150
Net Spendable	$ 809	$ 350

This amounts to 8.09 percent after-tax cash flow in a 30 percent tax bracket.

In 1973 the dividend was raised to $1.20 or $1,200. The tax shelter rose to 76¢ which would have made your net picture look like this:

	REIT	@ 5%
Income	$1,200	$ 500
Loss to Taxes	−86	−150
Net Spendable	$1,114	$ 350

This amounts to 11.14 percent cash after-tax cash flow.
The offering the latter part of 1973 was at $12.50 per share. $10,000
would purchase 960 shares at that price, and your net after-tax results
in the 30 percent bracket would be as follows:

	REIT	@ 5%
Income	$ 960	$ 500
Loss to Taxes	−69	−150
Net Spendable	$ 891	$ 350

If you are dependent on cash flow for your groceries and the cost
of food continues to rise, you'll have to either increase your income or
reduce your intake. (The dividends in this trust have increased 10
times in 10 years.) The tax shelter gives you more after-tax income,
which is the only kind of income you get to spend when you go to the
grocery store.

Direct or Indirect Investor · It has been an interesting psychological
study to me during counseling with prospective clients to find that many
who make deposits in savings and loan institutions feel that the officers
of those institutions are somehow standing with a loaded shotgun protecting their nest egg to guarantee its safety. It never seems to occur
to them that while they are depositing their hard-earned money at the
teller's window, the loan officer at a desk a few steps away is lending
out the same money to be invested directly into real estate.

If you are a depositor in a savings and loan association, you are
an *indirect* investor in real estate. You are "guaranteed" your sliver of
the interest the borrower pays plus your original deposit, and the institution is entitled to what very well may be the larger portion of the pie.

I feel that a trust gives you an opportunity to put a portion of
your money *directly* into real estate and gives you the potential of
receiving more of the full earning power of your money.

The restrictive money policies of the Federal Reserve Board during
1973 were extremely destructive to the market price of a large number
of stocks; however, these same policies often put some REITs in an
extremely attractive position.

Let's assume a developer has "bought" a piece of land for a shopping center. I say "bought"—what he usually has done is to make a
small down payment and persuaded the original landowner to carry the
papers. (Many developers seem short of ready cash.) He then has an
architect draw the plans for his shopping center. His next stop is at his
friendly banker for his interim financing. It will take from 18 months

to 2 years to build the center, and payrolls must be met and materials paid for in the meantime.

Because of the restrictive policies of the Federal Reserve Board during this period, the banker had to answer, "I'm sorry, we do not have any money to lend." At this point, what is the developer going to do? The interest he is paying on the land is "eating his lunch," and he has made a considerable investment in architectural drawings.

He then goes to a REIT trust for a loan. If you are a shareholder of the trust, the officers' first obligation is to you; so the trust officers, after careful study, may say, "Yes, we'll make you an interim financing loan. However, you must pay us the prime rate plus 4 percent. When the center is finished, you must return the interim loan, and give us half ownership of the center and 5½ percent of gross sales." The developer has one of two choices—lose the whole loaf of bread or end up with half a loaf. When faced with that alternative, he takes half a loaf, and you as a shareholder get your share of the other half.

Diversification · Diversification is an extremely important safety valve in any investment. A REIT offers two very important kinds of diversification: geographic and types of properties. For example, the particular trust I have used for several years has properties located in seven states and is permitted by its charter to go into the other 43. This adds a degree of safety since certain areas of the country can experience periods of temporary recession due to plant cutbacks, loss of aerospace contracts, and so forth. If property is spread over the faster growth areas of the United States, this helps give your investment some protection from these economic fluctuations.

The second kind of diversification is in types of properties. As already stated, the trust assets may be composed of investments in office buildings, medical buildings, apartment complexes, or hotels. Some of these types of properties may be overbuilt from time to time—but probably not all at one time. The diversification can give investors a cash flow to enable them to weather the economic cycles.

Equity Build-Up · You are probably familiar with equity build-up if you own your own home. Each month as you make your payment, you reduce your mortgage and increase your equity. At the beginning most of your payment will probably go for interest, but as you continue to make your payments over the years, less goes for interest and more to reduce principal, thereby increasing your equity.

The same is true when you are a shareholder of a trust. Equity is being built up as payments are made each month by the commercial users. This particular trust has several holdings on which they assumed existing mortgages. One piece of property has a 4 percent mortgage with only a few years left on the mortgage. Equity build-up on this property will be more rapid than property recently financed with the maximum loan.

Appreciation · Our study of inflation has made it evident that a steady and sizable appreciation is necessary to keep up with the shrinkage it causes. REITs are particularly attractive in this area because they can appreciate in a number of ways.

First, well-selected and -maintained property has had a tendency to increase in value as inflation increases its replacement cost. Studies show that commercial properties in growth areas of the United States have been appreciating in excess of 6 percent per year. Even if the amount of increase were less, this can yield an even greater gain in value than would first appear because appreciation occurs on the total value of the property, not just your equity in the property.

Second, many of the leases in the trust have escalation clauses—i.e., apartment and office building rents can be increased. In addition, the restaurant and hotel leases have base rents plus 5 percent to 5½ percent of the *gross* on foods and beverages, and 25 percent of gross room rentals, with perhaps a 50 percent ownership. This means that if prices soar, their income should increase, thereby increasing their cash flow.

One of the criteria for determining the market value of a piece of commercial income property is cash flow. For example, with an income of $100,000 a property may be valued at $1 million. With a cash flow of $150,000, its valuation may rise to $1,500,000.

Leverage · The amount of income that you receive from an investment and the amount it appreciates can both be increased by leverage. What do I mean by leverage? Leverage is technically the controlling of an investment with a sum of money smaller than its value—a complicated way to explain borrowed money. Let's use a simple example. You find a duplex and agree to pay $50,000 for it. With $10,000 to pay down, you find a mortgage company to lend you $40,000 on a long-term mortgage. This gives you a 4 to 1 leverage. Now let's assume your duplex appreciated 6 percent per year. The appreciation is not just on your $10,000 investment, but on the total $50,000. Therefore, the appreciation on your original $10,000 would be 6 percent × 4 or 24 percent.

This trust is conservative by most real estate standards and is only leveraged a little over 2 to 1. However, this still can provide you 6 percent × 2 or 12 percent appreciation on invested capital.

You should be aware, however, that leverage can work greatly to your disadvantage in less prosperous times. The more highly you are leveraged, the higher your monthly obligations for payment of principal and interest. In bad times, you may have to dip into your own funds to make the mortgage payments or lose the property. With the large holdings and diversification of an REIT, this likelihood is reduced but a negative cash flow possibility is certainly not eliminated.

Liquidity · Liquidity means that an asset can readily be turned into cash. The shares are marketable. During underwriting periods the distributors of the trust shares "support the market," standing ready to sell or redeem the shares at a particular price. During the 1973 underwriting period shares in our example sold at $12.50 and were guaranteed redeemable at $11.50. Between underwritings the shares are allowed to float free and are traded in the over-the-counter market. Many of the REITs, however, are listed on national exchanges, giving them a more active trading market.

In my opinion, REIT shares should be considered in the same long-term classification as any other real estate, not as a trading vehicle for quick capital gains. If the "liquidity" of REIT shares is needed, it is frequently better utilized as collateral for a bank loan.

Well-managed Real Estate Investment Trusts investing in commercial income properties can offer you a reasonable income and reasonable safety, with some tax shelter. If this fits your financial requirements, give some thought to investigating in a cross-section of the best managed ones.

• REAL ESTATE LIMITED PARTNERSHIPS

If you are in a higher tax bracket, you will want to consider investing in real estate through a limited partnership that is registered with the Securities and Exchange Commission.

There will usually be one General Partner who has the management expertise and assumes full liability. and a number of limited partners whose liability is limited to their investment.

The limited partnership approach to investing gives you more tax shelter going in and while you are in. However, you do give up liquidity. Although units can be transferred with the permission of the General Partner, you do not enjoy a ready public market for your ownership.

On the plus side you don't have to agonize about the market price each day because you won't know what it is. That can be a blessing, too.

Since you cannot quickly sell your shares, the bank probably will not accept them for collateral (though you can list them on your financial statement, which may influence the amount of credit your banker will extend to you).

You should be very selective in your choice of a limited partnership in which you invest. Management is the key to maximum success as it it in most investments. Select one that has an excellent past performance record and subordinates their profits to yours.

The types of properties may be similar to the trust, but you will not know which properties your funds will be invested in for these investments are usually not made until after the offering of partnership units is closed. This is called investing in a "blind pool."

Let's take as an example a particular management group. The units offered were $500 each. (In many states the minimum investment in a limited partnership is $5,000. If you live in one of these states, your minimum investment would have to be 10 units at $500 each.)

For example, let's assume you invested $10,000 (20 units) in one of the partnerships this management group has offered (they usually offer two a year).

What should you reasonably anticipate as your return?

Tax Write-Off • First, they structure the partnership to provide a 20 percent to 30 percent write-off in the year the investment is made. (The smallest write-off on these partnerships has been 20.5 percent and the largest 31 percent.) The limited partnership investor receives the benefits of these write-offs. The trust on the other hand is a corporation, and these benefits cannot be passed on in this manner.

Quarterly Distributions • Your second current benefit should be quarterly distributions, tax sheltered. This management subordinates the customary management fee charged for managing the properties until you have received 8 percent. This can provide incentive for good management and assures that they are not paid unless they manage the properties in such a way that the cash flow for you meets this minimum.

These two benefits would be your current ones, but they are not your main reasons for investing in the limited partnership. What you are attempting to do is to build up your assets tax sheltered until a later date when you will want to use them.

If the properties are sold at a profit, you should receive benefits from this equity build-up and capital appreciation.

Equity Build-Up • Let's look at equity build-up first, which I feel should be around 4 percent per year.

As the mortgage payments are made each month by the partnership from rent payments of tenants, your equity should be building up. The equity build-up, as we have just discussed, is less in the early part of the mortgage and more toward the end. You receive the benefits from this build-up upon the sale of the properties.

Capital Appreciation • Your fourth type of return is from appreciation. It also comes upon the sale of the properties.

You have already examined how leverage works in the section on real estate investment trust. It achieves like results here, though it has the potential of being greater because many limited partnerships have greater leverage. Let's assume that their well-maintained commercial income properties appreciate an average of 6 percent per year. What should you anticipate upon sale?

If your partnership is leveraged 3 to 1 and you have 6 percent appreciation (remember appreciation is on the total value of the properties, not just your down payment), then your appreciation would be 18 percent (6% × 3). Even if appreciation were only 1 percent, your results would still be 3 percent per year (1% × 3).

Upon sale of the properties this particular partnership subordinates their profits to yours. You must receive your original investment back and 12 percent annualized for each of the years you have held your investment before the General Partner is entitled to participate in the profits. When you have received this return, the General Partner then receives 5 percent of the net profits, and you as the limited partner receive your proportionate part of 95 percent of the profits.

For example, you invested $10,000. The properties were sold in six years. You must first receive $17,200. After that, the General Partner is entitled to 5 percent of the profits, and you are entitled to 95 percent.

This gives them a great incentive to keep the properties in good repair and to work diligently on improving cash flow, in that this is the best way to increase the selling price of a property, as you became aware when you were examining REITs.

When the sales are made, you will have a tax liability for the capital gains. This is determined by subtracting the original cost of the properties plus your tax-sheltered return from the sale price of the properties.

All of the properties will not be sold at the same time. Distribution will be made as the properties are sold. These proceeds are not reinvested as in the trust, but are paid out to you.

• SYNDICATIONS OF COMMERCIAL INCOME PROPERTIES

As I've mentioned, real estate limited partnerships are usually registered with the Securities and Exchange Commission. This does not mean that they are a safe investment or that they fit your needs. The registration statement should make all the facts available to you. Unfortunately, they are usually presented in such a way that if you are sophisticated enough to understand the prospectus, you probably are so advanced as to be eligible to consider syndications, if your contacts match your knowledge.

Syndications can be tailored to almost any real estate venture. However, most syndicates are formed for capital gains and tax advantages.

Small private syndications can be an excellent way to invest in local brick and mortar; on the other hand, they may be abused by promoters more easily than the larger registered limited partnerships can.

A private syndication with no more than 35 shareholders in many states does not have to be registered with the SEC. Registration is costly, but it can guard your investment against exploitation at the hands of those more interested in building their own fortunes than yours. Some sponsors even form syndications primarily to earn brokerage fees from the purchase and sale of property. They may also overprofit from front-end charges for setting up the syndication and from excessive management fees assessed against ventures that have never earned their investors any money.

Harder to find than an honest sponsor is a competent sponsor. It takes a great amount of expertise to manage apartment houses, office buildings, and shopping centers. Mismanagement can and has wrecked many syndicates.

You should approach syndicate offerings with extreme caution. The large national real estate firms can offer expert guidance and often a record of past successes; but private local ventures with friends and business associates may be the most comfortable for you and the easiest to check out.

• SUMMARY

If you have limited funds and desire to invest in real estate, you should probably choose either a registered Real Estate Investment Trust or a limited partnership. The first offers greater liquidity; the latter may offer more tax sheltered income and possibly more appreciation. If you have larger sums to invest, do not need liquidity, and have the staying power, time, and expertise to thoroughly investigate, you may find individual purchases or participation in unregistered limited partnerships or syndications more profitable to you.

Application

Do you have sufficient funds available to make raw land a viable investment for you? If so, what methods will you pursue to become knowledgeable about the best profit potentials? If the amount you have for real estate investment is smaller, is a real estate investment trust or a limited partnership a better solution for you? Do you need the liquidity and pledgeability of the trust? Can you take the longer term approach of the limited partnership? How do you correlate your tax bracket and your choice of investment?

12

The Roof
Over
Your Head

There is one kind of real estate about which you have no option—you must have a place to live during every period of your life. You do, however, have a number of choices about how you allocate your funds to meet this and other needs.

Food, clothing, shelter—the three essentials of life! That's what you learned in grade school, and as an adult you probably do not question these necessities. Since shelter is a necessity, but only one of your necessities, it behooves you to approach its provision as coolly and economically as possible for you will want to have funds left over for a few of the other goodies that put a bit of frosting on the cake of life.

There is much fuzzy thinking about how to best provide shelter. Many couples, particularly young ones, hate to rent even for a short period of time. They are convinced that rent receipts are pure waste, not realizing that rent money is no more wasted than the money spent for food or medicine. Many view house payments as almost pure "savings" and rent money in terms of a leaky faucet.

You may be one of those who are deliberately closing your mind to economic realities in order to own your own home.

• SINGLE-FAMILY DWELLING— HOBBY OR INVESTMENT?

To put this matter of renting vs. owning into proper perspective, let's look at the landlord–tenant relationship. A landlord renting a one-family dwelling would probably earn a net of 6 percent on his equity—the market value of the home less the mortgage. This could happen only if he kept the home rented most of the time and the renter paid the rent promptly. (He may, however, be enjoying some tax shelter by way of depreciation.)

If the landlord has a $5,000 equity in a $25,000 home, he might hope to earn about 6 percent net on his $5,000 each year or $300, or $25 per month. Or put in another way, if you had that much equity in your own $25,000 home, you'd be saving $25 per month by not renting the house from the landlord. However, you may not save that much because you can't claim as many deductions as the landlord.

Real estate ads often cite the fact that homeowners can deduct interest on their house loan and real estate taxes from their income taxes. The ads are true but do not give the whole story. The landlord also can deduct these items, plus many more that the IRS will not allow the home-owner to take. These cover insurance, repairs, painting, ligustrum bushes, depreciation, and so on (except to the extent that you use your home for business.)

Every house has a potential rental value—the sum that could be realized by renting to a tenant. As a rule of thumb, the rental value is about 10 percent per year of the market value. A $25,000 home then has an approximate annual rental value of $2,500, or a little over $200 per month. If you live in a $25,000 home, the real cost to you each year is about $2,500.

I have found that a single-family dwelling isn't much of an investment, in the real sense of the word, for either the landlords or the home-owners who are in the lower income tax brackets (with the exception of during the mid-1970s when high interest rates and high replacement costs greatly escalated home values.) Homes often are more of a hobby than an investment unless you have chosen a home in what later becomes a boom area where land values rapidly accelerated. This could then be an excellent investment. However, don't go overboard; inflation or a shift in location desirability may not bail you out of a costly real estate purchase. While you're waiting for the property to inflate in value, taxes and interest may put a very bad dent in your family budget.

• TAX
SAVINGS?

Lets go back to the fact that taxes and interest are deductible on your income tax. When you are considering buying a home, you may reason that Uncle Sam is helping you make the monthly payments, and you should not miss this help. This may well be true if you are in a high enough tax bracket. In the lower brackets the relief it brings may be only an illusion.

If your income is $10,000 per year, you may not get much of a tax break from the extra deductions. Even if you are in the middle income bracket, you will probably save no more than 15 percent of the net cost of your interest and property taxes by deducting them from gross income.

IRS allows each family a 15 percent flat deduction anyway (not to exceed $2,000), and unless you have enough deductions to itemize, including interest and property taxes, these last two costs become pure expenses.

You will need to have an income above $20,000 to approach any meaningful break on your tax return through home ownership.

There are many legitimate reasons for buying a home. You may feel it is a better place to raise your children. It may give you a sense of security, of belonging, or of status. A lovely home can be a true joy and a prestige symbol that adds to your self confidence.

However, don't plunge into home ownership only because others are doing it—a kind of follow-the-follower pattern of thinking—without truly weighing the pros and cons. Even though there are a number of valid reasons for home ownership, I find that most of them are sociologic and very few are based on genuine economic facts.

If you truly feel that owning your own home will bring you a greater enjoyment of life, will make you a more responsible citizen, and will offer you that additional privacy that may be important to you, then consider buying a home. But if your reasons are to boast about all the money you are saving, be careful not to boast to an economist.

• THE HYBRID
HOMEOWNER

If you want the advantages of owning your own home and the advantages of an apartment, perhaps you should consider owning your own apartment.

This can be done either in a co-operative apartment or townhouse, or a condominium. What's the difference?

In a co-op, you buy "shares" in the building and facilities, including recreational facilities. When shares are sold in co-ops, it must be by vote of the majority of the shareholders. You become both landlord and tenant, which means you take your share of both economic and managerial responsibilities.

Co-op ownership does give the tax advantages of home ownership together with recreational facilities and maintainance at a lower cost than an individual family dwelling.

In a condominium you own your own apartment and a pro rata share of the facilities rather than stock in the building. This means you have the same responsibility for common areas, but you may sell your apartment to whomever you wish. The tax and facilities cost advantages are identical to the co-op.

The methods of financing for both are similar to financing a one-family home.

What are some of the problems to these forms of home ownership? First, in co-op apartments, owners have occasionally had problems with the co-owners vetoing the sale of their shares which means, effectively, they could not sell their home. More important, poor maintainance of an apartment complex seriously lowers the value and saleability of your apartment so it is imperative to buy in a well-located, well-maintained building, just as you should buy a home in a well-located and well-maintained neighborhood.

• AVOID THE APPLES
AND ORANGES COMPARISON

The rather unemotional approach I've given home ownership should do one thing for you, and that is to make you aware that the monthly payments have little to do with the real cost of owning a home.

How do you go about comparing the cost of renting an apartment with the cost of buying a home? One way is to compare the annual rental for an apartment with 10 percent of the value of the home whose purchase you are considering. (If interest rates continue to soar, this should be adjusted to at least 12 percent and perhaps up to 15 percent.) If you foolishly compare the monthly payments on the house with the monthly payments on the apartment, you are, in effect, comparing apples and oranges. There is no comparative relationship. Mortgage payments have nothing to do with the cost of home ownership. Mortgage payments only relate to debt reduction.

The Real Cost • The real cost of home ownership includes upkeep and repair, fire and homeowner insurance, property taxes, equity investment, and depreciation (value loss). These expenses are just as real if you are a homeowner as if you are a landlord. The big difference often lies in the fact that a landlord recognizes them and includes them in the price he charges for the use of his property, whereas you may be tempted as a homeowner to pretend these expenses do not exist.

The landlord knows he must get at least 10 percent per year in rent on his property to cover his expenses and net him a profit. You, as a potential or present homeowner, would be wise to think as he does.

If you have been living in an apartment, feeling you just must buy your own home and save all that rent money, do slow down and take heart. The drain on your solvency may not be as bad as you have been thinking.

Mobility—The American Way • Another fact to recommend renting is that we are a very mobile society. Renting allows you to move more easily without the worry and delay of selling a home and the expense of sales commissions and horrendous closing costs.

At this point you may be thinking that if you owned a home, you would have built an equity in return for your payments as the years go by, whereas now you have nothing but rent receipts.

But, remember, I've been comparing the cost of renting with the cost of owning. You can save money and acquire net worth in other ways than by paying on a mortgage. You could open a savings account or start a monthly investment program with the difference.

The Case of Mrs. Bailey • An elderly widow client of mine lives in a house that is debt free and has a market value of $20,000. She asked if she should sell her house and rent an apartment. I told her that if she would bring me a list of her expenditures for the past year, I would be happy to advise her from a financial point of view. She gave me a list of her utilities, yard work expenses, house repairs, insurance, and taxes. I then added the 6 percent "guaranteed" return she could obtain on the $20,000 that would be available for investment after the sale of the house. When we added all of these together, we found that she could live in a $200 per month apartment more cheaply than she could live in her own home. In addition, she did not have to worry about watering her yard or possible vandalism during trips out of town.

I advised her, however, not to rush into selling her home. Answering a question on a financial basis is one thing; answering it on an emotional basis is quite another matter. Sometimes we need to consider that some expenditures are an investment in living.

• WHAT PRICE HOME CAN YOU AFFORD?

If you decide to purchase a home, it may be the largest single investment that you will make in your whole lifetime; therefore, invest carefully and within your budget.

There is no magic rule as to what percentage of your income should be spent for a roof over your head; however, I have found that usually this expenditure should not exceed 25 percent of your income. We've already concluded that there are other things in life as important as housing. You may desire good clothing, nutritional and tasty food, excellent medical care, a sporty or at least an adequate automobile, and an annual vacation. This makes it necessary to apportion your income.

To determine what price home you can afford, compute one-fourth of your annual income and multiply that figure by 10. Let's assume you earn $12,000 per year. One-fourth of $12,000 is $3,000, which, multiplied by 10, comes to $30,000. That figure is probably what you can afford to pay for your home.

There is nothing sacred about the 25 percent rule. Home financing agencies will approach your housing percentage figures a little differently, though the figures will probably come out in the same general category. Most of them will use as their general rule 2½ times your annual salary. In my opinion, you may want to be a little more conservative and use only 2 times annual salary in your calculations so that you will have funds for other household expenses. Property taxes are going up yearly; interest costs have increased greatly; you probably now view a built-in dishwasher, disposal, oven, and stove, and perhaps even a trash masher, as essentials, to say nothing of central heating and air conditioning. These conveniences will often cause you to have high maintenance bills. Also, the taxes, insurance, and interest are usually in proportion to the cost of the home.

Toward the end of 1974, lending agencies began using the guideline that one week's income must equal the monthly house payment on the mortgage for an applicant to qualify for a loan. Prior to the new 1974 housing law, lending institutions excluded the salary of the wife during child-bearing years. Now they must include all of the wife's paycheck when they calculate how much a working couple can borrow to finance a home.

Monthly Payments • You may be asking, "Don't the monthly payments really determine how much home I can buy?" Yes, they do determine how much you can buy, but they don't measure your ability to keep the house insured, heated and cooled, and in good repair, and the taxes paid.

In the higher income ranges other factors should be considered. You may not need, or want, to spend the full 25 percent of your income for housing; 20 percent may be sufficient. On the other hand, you may have a large number of children. If so, you may need to buy a less expensive house with more bedrooms. If you are childless, you may want to buy a one- or two-bedroom elegant home and stretch your budget beyond the 25 percent.

Location • I once interviewed the head of the real estate department for Prudential Life Insurance Company. When I asked him what the most important considerations in choosing real estate were, he drew himself up to his quite considerable height and said that there are three requirements you must never forget. They are "Location, location, location!"

The same is true in selecting your home. The three requirements you should never forget are neighborhood, neighborhood, neighborhood! The homes and people around you not only affect the resale value of your home but also your enjoyment of it.

The Least Expensive in the Neighborhood • Resist the temptation to buy the most expensive home in the neighborhood. It is much wiser to own a modest home in an expensive neighborhood. Your modest home may gain in value by being surrounded by more expensive homes, but an expensive home in a less expensive neighborhood will probably suffer.

Distance from Work · Distance from work should also be seriously considered. Before you yield to the temptation to move far out from town to escape high land and tax costs, consider the cost of driving long distances to work. This cost can easily wipe out any savings.

Saving $4,500 in the price of a home 30 miles from work could be used up in 2½ years or less if it were necessary to drive an extra 1,500 miles a year. With fuels in short supply, this cost could easily be increased or necessitate a change in home or job.

The time required to drive the extra distance should also be of prime consideration. Time is money. Extra time spent in driving may subtract from your earning power and sap your energy.

If you find, after considering all of these factors, that you still want to live farther out, may I suggest you utilize your commuting time by installing a tape cassette in your automobile. There are excellent tapes available on a wide variety of educational and professional subjects. I never get into my automobile without turning on my cassette player. I especially enjoy the Earl Nightingale series. His voice is motivating, and his ideas, if applied daily, can revolutionize your thinking and attitude. I have found his advice "You become what you think about" very true.

• SHOP FOR TERMS

Money is a commodity. It is a commodity like peanuts, warehouses, and even houses. Never be emotional about money. If you do, you won't make rational decisions about it. Put it in its proper commodity status. Therefore, go in a businesslike manner to secure your mortgage.

If you have a contact at a lending institution, be sure to avail yourself of any help this person can give you; it does make a difference whom you know. Do not accept the first loan offered to you. Shop for rates and terms. Each institution's circumstances vary from time to time, so their lending conditions and rates will vary accordingly.

Rates are important; but, as I will discuss later, the down payment and length of payment period far outweigh a slight differential in rates.

There was a time when the very word "mortgage" was tainted, and melodramas such as "Damsels in Distress" were presented from theater stages across the land portraying the villain as the man who held the mortgage. There is still a delightful rendition of this melodrama presented nightly on a riverboat moored on the banks of the Mississippi River in St. Louis. It's fun to hiss the villain and cheer the hero and heroine.

Today, instead of bringing visions of "The Perils of Pauline," mortgages are an acceptable and honorable way of American life; so go ahead and rent money, but do shop for the best terms available.

• TIMING
  YOUR PURCHASE

No doubt, some years are better than others for buying a home. If you buy your home when money is abundant, your interest costs will be lower, which will result in lower monthly payements for you. The quantity of money, which influences the cost, is regulated by action of the Federal Reserve Board, which in turn is based on consumer borrowing demands.

But what if you decide that you've reached that period in your family's life when you should buy a home, and it turns out that this is the time the Federal Reserve Board's money policies are restrictive and have driven money rates to a high level? Should you postpone your purchase?

The answer is probably No. Such Federal Reserve Board action is usually taken only to slow down inflation. This means you are looking for a house during a period of constantly rising building costs. During these times costs are probably rising faster than the carpenter can drive a ten-penny nail. If you wait until interest rates are lower, the price of the house will by then have inflated; and your monthly payments will be just as great or greater. Since the part that is interest is tax deductible and the part that is principal is not, you may be better off with the combination of lower price and slightly higher interest.

So if you feel you must buy a home, go ahead regardless of present interest rates.

• DOWN PAYMENT—
  LARGE OR SMALL?

If you have decided, after looking at all the facts, that a home of your own is best for you economically and/or emotionally, then you must decide on the amount of down payment you should make. To help you decide, let's look at two couples of similar circumstances. Study their attitudes and their realities, and determine which couple most closely fits your temperament.

Both couples have found a new home that fulfills their housing requirements. The cost of each home in $30,000. Each couple has $30,000 in savings in the bank, an income of $20,000 per year, and two healthy children of approximately the same ages.

The Allens • The Allens were reared by parents who programmed them with such admonitions as "Always pay cash," "Never owe money," "You might come upon hard times, so have your house paid for so you'll have a roof over your head."

When it was time to close on their home, the Allens felt the most prudent way was to pay cash, which they did. They then complimented themselves on saving "all that interest" and not having to make house payments each month.

The Bakers • The Bakers were reared by parents who were business oriented and held the earning power of a dollar in high respect. They had taught their children to use or rent each dollar they could and to put it to work at its maximum potential. So when it came time to close on their home, they felt that the prudent course for their family was to move in with the minimum down payment and to obtain the best mortgage available.

Then they began shopping terms and rates. First, they went to a life insurance company—choosing the kind that has enticed their policy-holders to do their "banking" with them in the form of cash surrender value. These companies, consequently, have large sums to lend at a much higher rate than the interest rate they are paying their policyholders. In fact, it is interesting to note that life insurance companies are the largest single underwriters of real estate mortgage money in America today.

The Bakers also shopped the savings and loan associations, which also have vast sums of lendable funds. These funds have been placed on deposit with them by those who wanted a "guarantee" of only a portion of the earning power of their money. These depositors were willing to settle for indirect investing in real estate by investing in the mortgage of the Bakers' home. The Bakers found the rates and terms varied from one savings association to the other, depending on the amount of lendable money each had at that particular time and the value judgment of each of their loan officers as to the Bakers' ability to pay.

They also shopped mortgage companies and found the rates varied by the same criteria as did those of the savings and loans.

The Bakers decided on a financing plan that would allow them to make a $5,000 down payment, with a $25,000 mortgage for 30 years at 8½ percent from a life insurance company, with monthly payments of $207.61, principal and interest. (Their taxes were estimated to be around $50 per month and the insurance around $20. This makes a total of $277.61 per month.)

Assuming a Mortgage • Since the homes were new, it was necessary for the Allens and Bakers to either buy with cash or obtain a new mortgage. Had the homes been "used," a third option might have been available and desirable. This is to "assume" a mortgage—that is, to take over responsibility for the mortgage the seller has on the house. Frequently an older mortgage has a lower interest rate than a new mortgage, and the closing costs are considerably less if the home is in a community in which banks charge "points" for a loan (a "point" is 1 percent of the amount of the loan). The purchaser pays the seller for his "equity" (the difference between the sale price and the mortgage) and then assumes the monthly payments. Ultimate legal responsibility for the mortgage, however, lies with the original buyer, so it is important for the seller to check the buyer carefully.

Which Couple Made the Right Decision? • Let's look at the Allens. They will not have a monthly house payment, and they will not have to pay interest on $25,000. They reasoned that over the 30-year period they will "save" $49,739 in interest on the $25,000 loan. They felt smugly proud of their decision.

The Bakers, on the other hand, felt they had made the right decision.

Which do you think made the right choice? Measure your value system against each of theirs and see where you feel you will be the most comfortable. This will help you to decide which course would be best for you.

Looking at the two cases from the point of view of a financial planner, I would choose the course taken by the Bakers for the following reasons.

Inflation rewards those who owe money, not those who pay cash. I realize this is a sad commentary on life, but it is a fact you must learn to accept.

If the government is successful in slowing the rate of inflation to 4 percent (and there is great doubt among most of our economists that this can be accomplished), you would be paying off your "loaned" dollars in 10 years with 60¢ dollars, in 15 years with 40¢ dollars, and in 20 years with 20¢ dollars.

Think how long your Dad had to work for a dollar 30 years ago, and then compare it with the minutes of work you'll have to do today. Any time you can postpone paying back a dollar that you have obtained on a long-term basis at a reasonable rate, always avail yourself of the opportunity. You must, of course, invest the money you have not paid down on the house in such a way as to earn more than the after-tax cost of renting it.

Making the House Payments • The Allens do not have to concern themselves with paying monthly house payments. The Bakers do. The

Bakers also have the responsibility of investing $25,000. How should the Bakers invest these funds to provide the extra amount of $200 needed monthly for house payments?

There are various investment possibilities they should consider. One that is worthy of close examination is an investment in a quality Real Estate Investment Trust such as the one we discussed previously. At $12.50 per share $25,000 would purchase 2,000 shares of the trust. With a current dividend of $1.20 this would amount to $200 per month, which they could use for their monthly payments. In the meantime their shares have an opportunity to grow, the income is mostly tax sheltered, and the interest they are paying on their $25,000 loan is tax deductible.

Another approach that our clients have used quite successfully has been to make a $25,000 investment in a middle-of-the-road quality mutual fund, similar to the Seminar Fund, and then take a check-a-month withdrawal. If $200 per month is withdrawn, that would be a 9.6 percent withdrawal. These withdrawals may come from four possible sources: (1) dividends, (2) realized capital gains, (3) unrealized capital gains, and, if these are insufficient, (4) the original investment. You cannot know what the future will bring. For example, if your fund grows at 12 percent and you take out 9.6 percent, or $200 per month, your original investment will grow. If it does not grow at 9.6 percent, you will use a portion of your original investment and, in time, perhaps all of it. If all of it is consumed, you obviously would have to look to other sources for your monthly house payment.

Had the Bakers placed their $25,000 in the Seminar Fund on December 31, 1944, it would have purchased 5,031 shares. Had the fund sent the mortgage company a check for $200 each month for the next 30 years, the fund would have paid the mortgage company $72,000, and there would have been 12,859 shares left in the account, which would have had a value of $154,180 on December 31, 1973 (even at that grim point in the market). Of course, if you were to follow the example of the Bakers, you may not do so well or you may do better.

Meeting an Emergency • The Allens paid cash for their home remembering their parents' warnings about possible hard times. However, if the Allens have an emergency, they will not be able to redeem a few square feet of their house. If they live in a state with a homestead law, they can't even pledge it as collateral for a loan. The loan-free home may have given them joy at the time of purchase, but if they should have a real emergency, they may find that their home is a dead asset that does not offer liquidity.

The Bakers, on the other hand, could redeem a few shares of their stock or take their shares to the bank and use them for collateral to borrow any needed funds.

• AVAILING YOURSELF OF
AN OPPORTUNITY

In money management, always put yourself in the driver's seat. Leave options open to yourself. Using your stock as collateral at the bank does not necessarily require an emergency. A good business opportunity may present itself. You'll have to pass it up if you don't have available funds. With collateral you can obtain these funds.

• INTEREST
IS DEDUCTIBLE

To give you an idea of how much of the Bakers' monthly payment is interest, which is deductible, the percentage schedule for the first five years of their loan was: 99.2%, 98.4%, 97.5%, 96.6%, and 95.5%. For the first year, 99.2% × $207 = $2,053 interest.

The IRS lets the Bakers deduct interest payments, so if they are in a 25 percent tax bracket, Uncle Sam bears 25 percent of their interest cost.

Of the 8½ percent interest they are paying, their net cost is only 6.38 percent (8.5 % × 25% = 2.125%; 8.5% − 2.12% = 6.38%).

• SALABILITY

We've mentioned earlier, as one of the reasons you should consider renting, the fact that Americans are a mobile lot. Recent studies show that the average family moves every seven years. The letters IBM, in our neighborhood, stand for "I've Been Moved." If moving is necessary, you may find it easier to find a buyer with $5,000 for a down payment rather than one with $30,000. A $5,000 equity is a salable equity whereas the $30,000 one is probably not. The Allens will have higher selling costs because seller's points on the new mortgage can amount to several hundred dollars.

There are reasons other than transfers for moving. The children may have become grown and left the nest, making a large home a burden rather than a necessity. The desirability of the neighborhood may have changed, or your company offices may have moved to another section of town. The reasons for moving can make a lengthy list.

• RATE OF GAIN ON INVESTED CAPITAL

It is estimated that homes have appreciated an average of 6 percent per year over the past 10 years.

The Allens have $30,000 invested in their home. Six percent appreciation would increase their net worth by $1,800 per year.

The Bakers' $30,000 home has also appreciated the same 6 percent or $1,800, but they have only $5,000 invested. An increase of $1,800 is 36 percent on their invested capital, as compared to the Allen's 6 percent. (The figure for the Bakers must be adjusted for their net after-tax interest expense.)

How much the Bakers' $25,000 will have grown over the 30 years we do not know, but to give a fair comparison of the Allens and Bakers, we must realize the Allens would have $200 a month to invest since they will not be paying this amount out each month for house payments.

If the Allens invest their $200 a month at 5 percent for 30 years, it should grow, exclusive of taxes, to $167,425. At approximately 3 percent after taxes this would amount to $117,606.

If the Bakers manage to obtain a 5 percent appreciation on their $25,000 investment, it would grow to $108,022; at a 6 percent appreciation it would grow to $143,587; and at a 10 percent appreciation it would grow to $143,587; and at a 10 percent appreciation it would grow to $436,235 (exclusive of taxes.)

• SUMMARY

1 · It may be less expensive to rent a multifamily dwelling than to own a single-family dwelling. Your costs are fixed, making budgeting more precise. Rental frees down payment money for other investments, and also allows you mobility to move to larger or smaller quarters or another location quickly and easily.

2 · Unemotionally calculate your true housing costs, remembering that the mortgage payment is only one of several major items in your housing costs.

3 · Monthly house payments should not exceed one week's earnings.

4 · If you anticipate moving, buy a home similar in style to that of your neighbors. This does not do much for your sense of creativity, but it may help you avoid taking a shellacking on resale. A good rule to remember when making an investment in any asset of considerable value is "Be a conformist." The more conventional you are, the better your chances are of increasing the value of your assets. Preserve some of your individuality, but don't go overboard. You may find it quite expensive if you do.

5 · Avoid paying too much for gimmicks. The builder may have spent an extra $1,000 on gadgets for flashy first-impression eye appeal and be able to sell you the house for an extra $3,000. As the years go by, you will want to build in your own charm, and the "gook" the builder originally added may turn out to be a hindrance rather than an enchantment.

6 · Avoid paying too much for a view. Surroundings are important, but after a year you'll probably take the view for granted and wish that this extra expenditure had been avoided.

7 · Keep your down payment as low as possible: Inflation lets you repay with cheaper dollars; resale should be easier; return on invested capital can be higher; and liquidity or pledgability can be available in times of emergency or investment opportunity.

Your home can be your castle or, under unfortunate circumstances, your prison, so use both your heart and your head in choosing how you'll provide that roof over your head.

Application

Unemotionally consider all the facts and then ask yourself: "Is it less expensive to rent or to own?" If you decide to own, should you buy a house or condominium? How much is available for a down payment? Do you more closely identify with the Allens or the Bakers in this chapter? What price home can you afford based on our formula?

What kind of neighborhood best fits your way of life? What housing is available in that neighborhood in your price range?

Whom do you know, or what contacts can you make, to obtain the most favorable financing?

Is the prime rate at this time dropping or climbing? If you choose to make a low down payment instead of a higher one, how will you employ the remaining funds? What items should you include in your housing checklists to make your home a joy instead of a burden?

13

Life Insurance— The Great National Consumer Fraud?

- ## THE GREAT MYSTERY

The great mystery of life is the length of it. You should have a plan with the hope you will live a normal lifetime. You should also have a plan in the event you should die prematurely. You do not know which will occur; therefore, you should prepare for either eventuality. It is not difficult to acquire financial independence if you apply your talents and if you have sufficient time.

How can you be sure you will have this time? You cannot. There is a way to "buy" time, however, and it is called "life insurance." This is the name given to it by life insurance companies who desire to sell it. A better term would be "protection for dependents." There is nothing that can insure your life.

• THE PURPOSE OF
LIFE INSURANCE

Life insurance is a wonderful thing. There is no substitute for it until a sufficiently large estate has been acquired to protect those dependent upon you. It provides a way that you can guarantee your dependents the financial means to continue living in the event you should die prematurely. It can be an economic extension of yourself. You should provide this protection for your dependents before you begin an investment program.

At the beginning of this book I stated there are five main reasons why most of our citizens reach 65 flat broke: (1) procrastination, (2) failure to establish a goal, (3) ignorance of what money must do to accomplish that goal, (4) failure to understand and apply our tax laws, and (5) they were sold the wrong kind of life insurance. I say "sold" because I believe that had they been told how to obtain protection properly, they would not have made such glaring errors.

So that you will not fall victim to being sold the wrong kind of life insurance, I hope to give you a clear understanding of how policies are constructed. This should enable you to properly buy the time you will need to acquire a living estate.

There is only one kind of life insurance, and that is pure protection based on a mortality table. All other kinds are pure protection plus banking. It is the banking portion that can be the culprit, so it is necessary for you to thoroughly understand this part of a vast number of policies that are presently in existence and are being sold today.

As a rule of thumb, you can avoid most of the errors in this area if you will refuse to bank with an insurance company under conditions you would not bank with your regular bank.

The purpose of insurance is to protect those dependent upon you in the event you should die before accumulating a living estate. After you have accumulated a living estate, your need to protect their livelihood has already been accomplished. You should plan to be self-insured by age 65. Life insurance is to protect your economic potential. You have either made it by 65, or you'll probably never make it.

• NAMES GIVEN TO
LIFE INSURANCE POLICIES

There are four major names given to life insurance policies sold in the United States today. They are ordinary or whole life; limited payment life; endowment; and term. Each can be participating and nonparticipating. In addition there are "special" policies that provide combinations of the above, usually at an additional premium. Let's take a look at each policy and the usual presentation given by those who want to sell the policies.

Ordinary or Whole Life • Whole life is the most commonly sold type of insurance in America today. The face amount of the policy remains constant as long as the premiums are paid, and the premiums remain identical during each year of the life of the policy. The term "whole life" means that you are to pay premiums for your whole life if you desire to keep the policy in force and that it will endow when you reach age 100.

This type of policy accumulates cash surrender value from a portion of the premiums paid. The cash surrender value can be obtained in two ways: by cashing in the policy and thereby losing the protection, or by paying 4½ percent to 6 percent to borrow the cash deposited in the account. If death occurs while the loan is outstanding, the amount of the loan is subtracted from the face amount of the policy. The cash value is not added to the face value of the policy upon payment of a death benefit.

Currently, the typical cost for a whole life insurance policy for a 35-year-old man is around $18 per thousand, or $1,810 per year for $100,000 of coverage. Contrary to popular opinion, rates vary widely from company to company.

Limited Payment Life • Another type of life insurance policy you may encounter is one on which you pay for a limited period of time. This type of coverage is called limited payment life. It provides lifetime coverage, with premiums payable for the specified period of time: 20 years, 30 years, and paid-up at age 65 (which would be a variable number of years depending on the age of the policyholder).

The premiums on this type of policy are naturally higher than those for a whole life policy. Typically, premiums for a man at age 35 are around $27 per thousand or $2,714 per year for $100,000, 20-pay.

A great disservice is done to a family when this type of policy is sold to them, especially when the father has several small children. This young family usually has only a limited number of dollars to spend for life insurance, and this type policy offers very limited coverage in the years when the family most needs protection so that they can pay little or no premiums when their need for coverage has lessened and their ability to pay has probably increased. In addition, with our pattern of inflation they have used "expensive" dollars while they are young so they can use less inexpensive ones later on.

Endowment • Endowment insurance is a combination of limited pay life insurance to be paid on death and an annuity that pays part of the premium monies back to the policyholder in a given period of time. Many are designed to endow at age 65, although I'm amazed at the number of policies I come across that endow at age 80. Yes, 80! The method of payout varies. It may be a lump sum or a set monthly payment for the period of the policyholder's life, in which case the benefit dies with him, or for a set number of years. In the latter case, the monthly payments will be less, but in the event of death payments will be made to a beneficiary for a certain number of months. The premiums on endowment policies are, as might be expected, very high, with a typical 20-year endowment policy costing a male at age 35 around $42 per thousand or $4,210 per year for $100,000. Since these premiums are paid with after-tax dollars and the cash surrender value often compounds at a very low rate, they can make an endowment policy an expensive way to invest for retirement. (Current interest rates are from 2½ percent to 4 percent.)

Pure or Term Insurance • There are four basic kinds of pure protection commonly called term. They are level term, annual renewable term, deposit term in combination with these two, and decreasing term covering various periods of time.

Level Term • Level term means that the face amount remains level for the term of time chosen. The most common periods are 5, 10, 15, 20, 25, and 30 years and level term to 65.

The rate for level term to 65 for a man at age 35 is around $10.74 per thousand, or $1,074 per year for $100,000 of protection. If coverage is needed after that age, there are conversion privileges, without evidence of insurability, for a longer period of time.

Deposit Level Term • There is another type of policy called deposit level term that merits your consideration. You make a deposit to assure the company you will keep the policy for a specified period of time. This type policy came into being because the lapse rate on conventional policies is quite high. Reportedly, of every three written, one is dropped or lapsed. This lapsed policy is expensive to the insurance company. They have paid a sales commission to the salesman, have gone to the expense of setting up the policy on the company's computer, and have done other expensive clerical work. If the policy is then dropped in the first few years of its life, it is an unattractive investment for the company. To protect themselves from this potential loss, they set the premium rates high enough that the two "good guys" who keep their policies pay for the "bad guy" who drops his.

If the insurance company could be sure that you would be a "good guy," they could afford to sell you your policy at a lower cost. How can they be sure you'll be a "good guy"? They have you make a one-time deposit, usually of $10 for every $1,000 of protection. At age 35, for a $100,000, 10-year-level-deposit term policy, you would make a deposit of $1,000, and your premium would be $4.37 per thousand, or $447. (There may also by a $10 policy fee per policy.) If death should occur, your beneficiary would receive $100,000 plus double the deposit, or $2,000. If you had taken out a 20-year-deposit term, your policy would have cost $7.23 per thousand for 20 years or $733 per year, and if death should occur, your beneficiary would be paid $100,000, plus five times the deposit, or $105,000. If you continue to live and keep your policy, you have obtained your insurance coverage at a considerable savings and doubled your deposit on a 10-year policy or the equivalent of 7.2 percent compounded and tax free. On the 20-year policy the original deposit is multiplied by 5. This is equivalent to 8.3 percent per annum compounded and also tax free.

Annual Renewable Term · In all policies the true cost of life insurance will be going up. Rates are based on likelihood of death, and each year you become older and this likelihood is increased.

In annual renewable term, the face amount of insurance remains the same and the rate increases. (The same is true in a cash value type of policy because the face amount remains the same, but the rate is increasing as you decrease the company's liability every time you increase your cash value.)

At age 35 your annual renewable term rate would be approximately $2.50 per thousand, or $260 per year for a $100,000 policy. This rate would increase each year.

Deposit Annual Renewable Term · Deposit annual renewable term is annual renewable term on which you have made a deposit for the same reasons it was made in deposit level term. Let's assume a 10-year-deposit annual renewable term best fits your family's needs and you are age 35. You would make a deposit of $4 per thousand, and your premium the first year would be $2.75 per thousand. The rate gradually increases each year. On a $100,000 policy you would be requested to make a deposit of $400 and your premium would be $285. If death occurs, the $100,000 is paid to your beneficiary, and the deposit is returned to them. At the end of 10 years your deposit is returned to you doubled ($800), and you can then choose from many options.

Let's assume you still need protection for your family. You can renew for another 10 years and can continue doing so until age 65. At that time there is again a wide variety of conversion privileges, all without evidence of insurability.

Before 65 one of the options available to you, if you so desire, is to convert to whole life, which would pay the beneficiary the face amount plus the cash value until you are age 65. After 65 only the face amount will be paid.

Other options that are available to you at the end of each 10-year period are convert to level term, convert to decreasing term to age 100, convert to decreasing term for 15-, 20-, 25- and 30-year periods, or decreasing term to age 65.

Decreasing Term · Another type of term insurance you may want to consider is decreasing term. It often fits the needs of a young family. When you are young and have a family dependent upon you, your need for life insurance will probably be at its maximum. As your family grows up and leaves home and your assets simultaneously increase, your need for "outside protection" will probably decrease. Decreasing term insurance can fit this picture very well.

A decreasing term to 65 policy for a man of age 35 is around $4.22 per thousand. The rate for this policy remains the same while the insurance coverage is decreasing. (The same occurs on cash surrender value policies.)

If you desire insurance for your life expectancy (at age 35 that is 72), your rate would be $6.18.

If you need to cover an indebtedness that is to be paid off over a certain period of time, say 10 years, you may want to consider a 10-year decreasing term for $2.92 per thousand.

Unfortunately, many agents present term insurance as "temporary" insurance and whole life as "permanent." A better explanation would be to reverse these descriptions.

With your decreasing term program, you should have an investment program to replace the protection that is diminishing. You are in effect substituting a living estate for a death estate, which is the direction you want to go, isn't it? You don't want a death estate, but until you have had time to accumulate a living one, it is often a necessity.

So that you can obtain a vivid mental picture of the basic types of policies, I have made a simple diagram of each and rounded off the premiums (Figure 7). Study these carefully, and then we'll look further at the purpose of life insurance.

(1) Level Term to 65

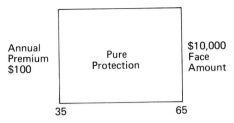

(2) Whole or Ordinary Life

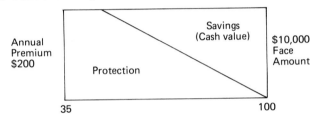

(3) 20-Pay Life

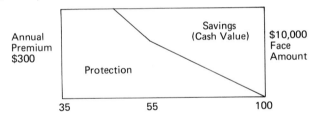

(4) 20-Year Endowment

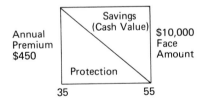

FIGURE 7. Four Basic Types of Level Coverage

Participating • A common variation in sales presentation and premium costing is participation. In policies with participation clauses, the policyholder receives a "dividend" annually from his premium. The premium dividend may be received in cash or, more frequently, left at interest with the insurance company or used to buy additional insurance coverage. (All types of life insurance, including term, can be set up to be participating.)

Participating policies have a nice ring to them, don't they? After all, aren't "dividends" desirable? What is a "dividend" from a company that sells participating policies?

A "dividend" is a return of an overcharge. I refer you to the United States Treasury Decision No. 1743. When the Tarill Bill of 1911 proposed an income tax on life insurance dividends, representatives of life insurance companies protested the tax. I quote from the decision arrived at after the protest:

> Reduced to final analysis the contention of the various companies are. . . .
> That dividends declared by participating companies are not dividends in a commercial sense of the word, but are simply refunds to the policyholder of a portion of the overcharge collected, which overcharge is merely held in trust by the company issuing the policy. Annually, or at stated periods, all, or a portion thereof, is returned to the person holding the policy. . . .
> It was vigorously contended by counsel representing certain of these companies that it was necessary in order to secure new business, to convince the prospective policyholder of the desirability of the same, and that this commercial necessity had resulted in the companies making misrepresentations of facts as to dividends to prospective purchasers of insurance, and that names and designations, having a single specific meaning in the commercial world and which were therefore attractive to prospective policyholders, had been adopted to represent transactions which they now hold are entirely different from that their name implies and represents, and from which the policy holder himself believed he was receiving and that business necessities had caused a continuance of these misnomers. *It was represented that, in fact, there were no dividends, but merely a refund of overcharges, which, for reasons above stated, were usually referred to as dividends.*

• BUYING INSURANCE

Let's assume an agent came to you intent on selling you the policy that would benefit *his* wife and children the most. His sales presentation might run like this: "At age 35 I can provide you with a $10,000 level term to 65 policy for $100 per year." You may feel the price fits your budget and begin to say, "Yes," but the agent interrupts and says: "But your protection runs out at age 65, and you don't want that to happen, do you?"

At this point you stammer, "Why, no, I wouldn't want to be without life insurance."

So the agent says, "Here is a policy for only $200 that never runs out; it's called whole life." (He doesn't add, "You pay premiums your whole life and it endows at age 100.")

Just as you are about to agree to this policy, he asks, "You don't want to pay premiums all your life, do you? Here is a policy for $300 that you can quit paying on in 20 years when it will be all paid up. Isn't that great?"

But just before you sign up, he says, "But let me tell you about another policy for $450 called 20-year endowment. In 20 years you've only put in $9,000; we will give you $10,000; you've had your insurance free for 20 years and made a $1,000 profit. Isn't that great?"

Now let's analyze the purpose of life insurance. It's purpose we have established is to protect those dependent upon you in the event you do not live long enough to accumulate a living estate.

Since your purpose for buying life insurance is in the event you die, let's assume your death occurred in 10 years. In the first policy you would have spent $1,000 and your beneficiaries would have received $10,000. In the second, $2,000 would have been spent and they received $10,000. In the third $3,000 with $10,000 of benefits. In the fourth you had a first class demise; $4,500 was spent and your beneficiaries received $10,000.

How Much Goes for Protection? • How much of each of your premiums above would have been used to provide protection, and how much was earmarked for the deposit into "your" savings account or policy reserve? In the diagrams above, the answer is only about $50 for the insurance protection. You were paying for two things: protection and banking. But, if you die, your beneficiary will only get one—not the face amount plus the savings account, even though you have paid for both.

What if the agent had told you that for $50 you could buy a $10,000, 20-year-decreasing term policy and that if you did nothing more than take the $400 savings in premiums each year to the bank, and your banker would only pay you 4 percent on your savings, in 20 years you would have $12,400 instead of just the $10,000 you would have received from the endowment policy. If you obtained 6 percent from your banker, your $400 savings per year would have grown to $15,596 instead of $10,000. Your "free insurance and $1,000 profit" were indeed expensive. (Tax-free municipal bonds currently pay over 7 percent so don't be seduced by an agent's compounding tax free pitch on your cash surrender value.)

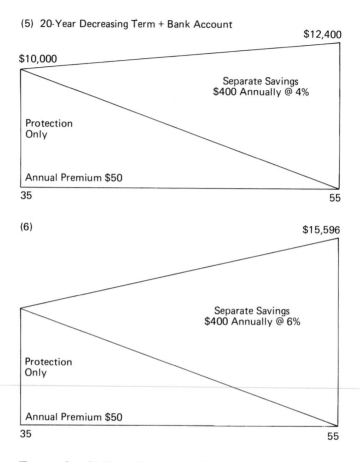

FIGURE 8.   20-Year Decreasing Term + Bank Account

Figure 8 diagrams this policy.

Banking with the insurance company, as you can see, can prove to be very costly.

Endowment vs. Decreasing Term • Figure 9 shows the difference between buying a $100,000 "endowment" at age 65 and buying "decreasing term to age 65" with premium savings invested separately at 3 percent, 4 percent, 5 percent, 6 percent and 8.5 percent. At only 8.5 percent (and I would not give you a very high score if that's all you averaged) you would have $305,662 in savings as compared to $100,000 in the endowment policy.

As you can readily see, it does make a difference where you bank!

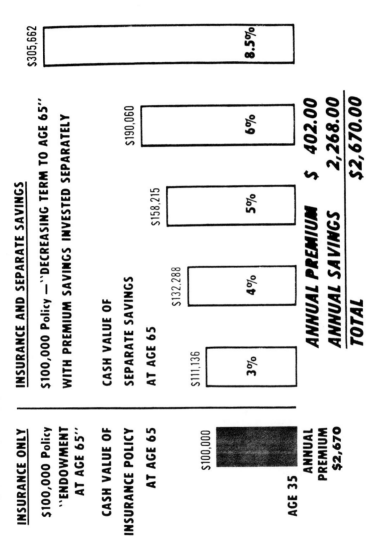

FIGURE 9. Investment Results

• LIFE INSURANCE AS AN "INVESTMENT"

Have you ever been told that life insurance is a good investment? Figure 10 shows the difference between placing $1,000 in annual insurance premiums toward an ordinary life policy as cash surrender value and investing that same $1,000 outside of the policies at various rates of return.

• WHY COST PER THOUSAND VARIES

Here is a chart (Figure 11) that may help you visualize why the cost per thousand varies from policy to policy.

As you can see, the chart illustrates a $100,000 policy at age 35. The first column shows that if you could get your coverage on the 1958 mortality table rate, you could obtain a $100,000 policy for $251 a year. But it's difficult to get a company to sell you insurance at the mortality rate. (Actually, they reinsure you today at only $1.47 per thousand or $147, and the reinsurance company still makes money.) You can, however, find a company that will sell it to you on a pure term basis. This would cost you $362 a year. Now if you want to have a "participating whole life policy" (and doesn't that sound great because you are supposed to be participating in the profits of the company), you can obtain an ordinary life policy for $2,185 per year. If you decide you do not want to "participate" in the "profits" of the company, they can sell it at a lower cost of $1,820.

Let's go on now to the 20 pay life in our illustration. Remember, that's the policy "you don't have to pay on all your life. It's paid up." Again if you want to participate in the profits, it will cost $3,316 per year, but if you're willing not to participate in the profits, you can buy it for $2,714. A participating endowment at age 65 is $3,076, and a nonparticipating is $2,670.

As you see, if you want to try to own a part of you know what, it could cost you $3,316 on a 20 pay life. Or you can buy pure protection for $362. In both policies the family receives $100,000. Why the difference in premiums? Let's examine our illustration: First of all, in the gray shaded area it says, "insurance, "insurance," "insurance" all the way across. The cost of insurance in each one of these policies is exactly the same. The other factors of savings and expense vary, so let's explore how rates are set.

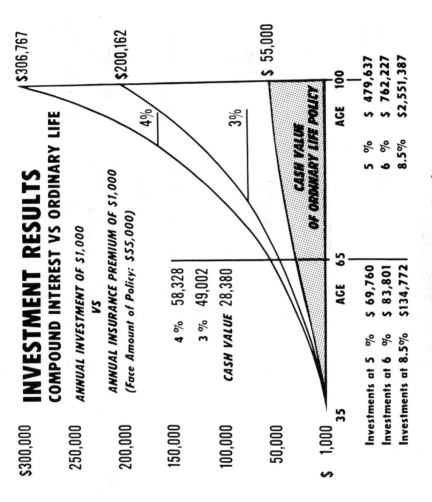

FIGURE 10.   Investment Results

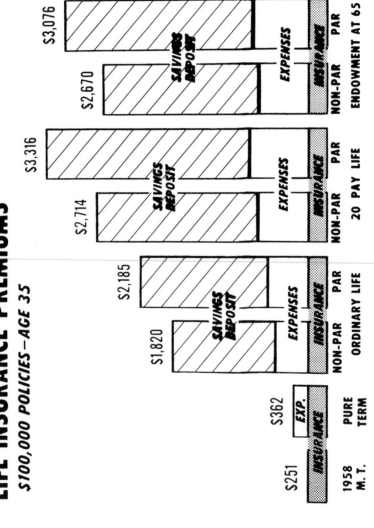

FIGURE 11. Life Insurance Premiums

• COST FACTORS
IN INSURANCE PREMIUMS

Three factors must be accounted for in setting the premium for your life insurance policy. The fourth factor, savings, is not found in all policies.

1 · *Mortality:* How much will the company have to pay out to its policyholder to provide the amount of death protection the policyholder wishes for the period of the policy?

2 · *Expenses:* How much does the company have to pay in sales expenses to acquire the business on its books, and administration expenses to carry the business thereafter?

3 · *Investment Income:* How much can the company earn from investing the policyholder's money during the period it has that money in its possession?

4 · *Savings Element:* How much does the policyholder want to invest in his policy's "reserve" to earn interest at a guaranteed rate of $2\frac{1}{2}$ percent to $3\frac{1}{2}$ percent?

The following simple arithmetic, therefore, is all that is required to determine a life insurance policy premium:

$$\text{Policy Premium} = \frac{\text{Mortality}}{\text{Costs}} + \frac{\text{Company}}{\text{Expenses}} - \frac{\text{Investment}}{\text{Income Earned}} + \frac{\text{Savings}}{\text{Element}}$$

Example:

a.	Mortality cost @ age 35	$2.51
b.	Less interest earnings	.06
c.	Net premium	2.45
d.	Plus company expense (assumed)	1.00
e.	Gross premium (selling price)	$3.45

From the above calculations, we have determined a natural premium, or the premium for a policy covering death only within a year. As this person gets older, the natural premium would increase each year.

The assumed interest is usually much lower than they will earn on the money. A very large mutual company has a booklet showing their rate of return. If you can obtain it, you will be very surprised at what a large rate of return they are obtaining. Also, the amount for expenses is often overstated.

Profits of an insurance company come from savings in mortality excess interest earnings, and reduction in expenses. As you will discover when you apply for a policy, the insurance company tries to eliminate those who are not a good risk, by carefully examining your state of health by requiring a physical and checking with any doctor you have seen over the past few years. They also conduct an "on the spot" inspection of where you live and may ask your neighbors about you to see if your life-style might contribute to earlier than anticipated death. They also check into your finances through the Retail Credit Bureau, hoping to eliminate those whose financial affairs might lead them to drastic behavior.

The Cost of Lapses • One other important factor figured into life insurance premiums is the cost of lapses. A life insurance company suffers a large loss if a policyholder keeps his policy for only a short time, and, for nonpayment of premiums, allows it to lapse.

1 • This loss results from the high costs incurred by a life insurance company in putting a new policy on its books: High, front-end commissions are paid to the agent; medical examination cost, the costs of credit checks, of entering a new policy on the books, etc., are also high.

2 • Unless the insured person pays premiums for a number of years, the company is unable to recover these initial costs. On average, a life insurance company recovers its first-year costs only after the policyholder has paid premiums for five to eight years.

3 • Into each premium, therefore, is added a cost attributable to the lapses a company expects to experience in the early years.

Mortality Tables • The "insurance" factor is the likelihood of death and is listed by age per thousand.

The first table used by insurance companies was the American Experience Table. It was based on statistics gathered between 1843 and 1858. During that time, of 1,000 men age 35, statistically 8.95 died. The second table the insurance companies were required to use was the Commissioners' 1941 Standard Ordinary Table based on death statistics between 1930 and 1940—before penicillin. During that period the death rate had dropped to 4.59 per thousand. Later, in 1966, the insurance companies were required to go on the Commissioners' 1958 Standard Ordinary Table based on death statistics between 1950 and 1954. Now woefully outdated, this is the last table regulatory agencies have required to be used. On this table, the death rate has dropped to 2.51 per thousand. It is my understanding that sufficient statistics have been gathered for a later mortality table, which should be in the neighborhood of 1.63 per thousand at age 35. So far, the life insurance companies have chosen not to use these later statistics.

If you are 35 years of age and have a policy on the American Experience Table, you are paying almost 400 percent more than you would need to on the 1958 CSO Table.

Insurance companies are not required to go back to old policyholders when a new mortality schedule is available. They continue to charge on the old. I find many policies in which the relatively young holder is still paying on Abraham Lincoln's mortality schedule.

The majority of the policies I see are on the 1941 table. As a matter of fact, lobbyists for a number of the large insurance companies have now gotten legislation passed in several states making it difficult for a financial planner to lower your insurance cost by providing you with a new policy on a current mortality table. This maneuver takes the form of complicated "comparison" replacement papers that frighten the prospective purchaser and discourage even the most conscientious agent.

Table 20 is a combination of all three mortality tables showing deaths per thousand at each age.

Expenses • Expenses on insurance policies fall into several classifications:

1 · Normal administrative costs that are the same regardless of the type of policy. These include such items as paying for your physical, office space, computer time, and salaries of employees.

2 · Variable costs include sales commissions, which are much higher on cash surrender value policies. Some large mutual companies pay a commission of 110 percent of the first year's premium paid over the first two years plus approximately 10 percent of the premium paid each year thereafter. These companies can usually afford to pay high commissions because this type policy can be extremely profitable to the company.

Table 20.   Deaths Per 1,000 in Three Mortality Tables

Age	American experience table	Commissioners' 1941 table	Commissioners' 1958 table
20	7.80	2.43	1.79
21	7.86	2.51	1.83
22	7.91	2.59	1.86
23	7.96	2.68	1.89
24	8.01	2.77	1.91
25	8.06	2.88	1.93
26	8.13	2.99	1.96
27	8.20	3.11	1.99
28	8.26	3.25	2.03
29	8.34	3.40	2.08
30	8.43	3.56	2.13
31	8.51	3.73	2.19
32	8.61	3.92	2.25
33	8.72	4.12	2.32
34	8.83	4.35	2.40
35	8.95	4.59	2.51
36	9.09	4.86	2.64
37	9.23	5.15	2.80
38	9.41	5.46	3.01
39	9.59	5.81	3.25
40	9.79	6.18	3.53
41	10.01	6.59	3.84
42	10.25	7.03	4.17
43	10.52	7.51	4.53
44	10.83	8.04	4.92
45	11.16	8.61	5.35
46	11.56	9.23	5.83
47	12.00	9.91	6.36
48	12.51	10.64	6.95
49	13.11	11.45	7.60
50	13.78	12.32	8.32
51	14.54	13.27	9.11
52	15.39	14.30	9.96
53	16.33	15.43	10.89
54	17.40	16.65	11.90
55	18.57	17.98	13.00
56	19.89	19.43	14.21
57	21.34	21.00	15.54
58	22.94	22.71	17.00
59	24.72	24.57	18.59
60	26.69	26.59	20.34

• THE MONEY MACHINES

Recent statistics for just one year showed that one well-known U.S. company had a net investment income of $1,332,086,856. (Yes, investment income! You see, their net policy reserves were $22 billion.) They received premium income of $3,694,135,298. Their claims for the year were $310 million. This would make a difference between receipts and claims of $4.716 billion for the year!

An excellent article on this subject appeared in the September 1, 1974, issue of *Forbes* entitled "Those Marvelous Money Machines!" and states:

> While other businesses produce products, the insurance industry produces money, capital. The industry is a wonderful money machine. At a time when presidents of successful companies spend their sleepless hours wondering where to get capital, insurance company bosses worry only about where to invest it. That's a high-class worry.
>
> The numbers are not easy to come by, but FORBES has made some sensible estimates. We figure the industry took in about $91 billion in premiums last year [1973] and earned about $22 billion from investments and other income. Against this it paid out maybe $79 billion in benefits, operating expenses and taxes. The remaining $34 billion or so was added to the industry's capital base—either as plowed-back profits or as additional reserves. By the year's end the industry boasted $336 billion in assets—against, for comparison, $26.3 billion for the whole U.S. steel industry.*

The life insurance business can be very profitable. You should ask, "For whom?"

Possible profits become very evident when you recognize that the insurance companies have sizable sums to invest, often at a rate of as high as 15 percent. In recent years they have also demanded and received as much as one-half interest in the real estate developments they finance. These funds are available because their policyholders have been enticed to "invest" through them.

Most policies show the company paying 2½ to 3½ percent on cash reserves. If you leave this cash value with them, I don't see that it makes

---

* Reprinted by permission of *Forbes Magazine* from the September 1, 1974 issue.

too much difference what percentage they pay, for your beneficiary receives only the face amount of the policy.

• WHOSE
CASH VALUE?

If you presently own a policy in which there is cash value, you may be under the impression that you are earning on "your" savings account. However, you do not receive any current economic benefit as the policy reserve in the hands of the insurance company earns interest. The policy provisions, if you'll take the time to study them, make this clear. There is no provision in the policy that says you own a part of the company reserves. The policy promises to pay benefits in certain events—usually upon death or upon living to a certain age or date. *Tax Facts*, published by the National Underwriters Co. states:

> The right to cash value upon surrender of the policy or the right to borrow against the cash value are, however, sometimes viewed as suggesting the ownership of a fund in the hands of the company upon which interest is being earned. Perhaps this misconception forms the basis of the conclusion that the policyholder is enjoying current interest income that should be taxed. It is true that in our sales talks and to some extent in our actuarial reasoning *we have attributed to the cash value of a life insurance policy some of the characteristics of a savings account. But this popular notion is without legal foundation.*

There is a good deal of confusion in the minds of insurance agents and the public as to the ownership of the cash values of insurance policies. This confusion has gone largely unchecked by any government agency such as the Securities and Exchange Commission, which regulates the securities industry, however, Senator Philip Hart has proposed a "truth-in-life-insurance" law.

In summary, it is a fact that the cash value in your insurance policy does not belong to you as you may have supposed. It does, in fact, belong to the insurance company issuing the policy. Consequently, any increase in the cash values of your policies, either by interest earned or by your deposits, serves only one purpose—that is the reduction of the insurance company's risk.

Cash Surrender Value Is at Jeopardy • I have a client who had a policy with a well-known company. His policy was an extremely expensive one and after he obtained the proper coverage much more cheaply, he wrote to them, enclosed his policy, and requested his cash value. They kept hedging and sending back letter after letter asking for further papers. Finally, he called them and demanded his cash surrender value. They assured him that his check was in the mail. When he received their letter, it stated they were sorry but they were insolvent and could not send him his cash surrender value. This man would have never banked with a bank that was not insured by the Federal Deposit Insurance Corporation; yet he was banking with an insurance company that was not protected at all. The death claim was never in jeopardy—only the banking element.

Did you also know that most companies have a provision in their policies allowing them the privilege of waiting six months to make a loan to you or to let you have your cash surrender value?

The Six-Month Wait • Did you ever wonder how the six-month waiting period happened to be a part of your policy if you have the cash surrender value variety? It has a very interesting history. During the Depression many people were cashing in their insurance policies, and many insurance companies were nearing bankruptcy. Around that time, President Franklin Roosevelt declared a bank holiday saying, in effect, "Sorry about that, but we can not return to you your bank checking and savings accounts." With this announcement, lights began flashing in the home offices of many insurance companies, and their executives said, "Oh, my goodness. Why didn't we think of that?" They got permission to suspend paying cash value, and ever since that date this six-month waiting period has been in most insurance policies. If you should ask an agent about this provision, the agent may assure you that his company would never make you wait. If he is so confident, why is the provision in the policy?

• NET COST

Now let's look at another term used so frequently and so inaccurately. It's called "net cost," a term to convince the unwary that life insurance is very inexpensive if bought the "permanent" way. The presentation will go something like this:

Total premiums paid ages 35–65	$6,000.00
Less Cash Value at age 65	5,000.00
Net Cost	$1,000.00
Average Cost Per Year	$ 33.33

Don't you believe it!

If death occured at 65, your net cost was the total of the premiums you've paid to date, $200 × 30 years or $6,000! Your beneficiaries did not receive the face amount plus your savings account. They received $10,000, not $15,000.

Let's go a step further, and see if the agent can prove there is a way that you can receive your insurance free and make a profit to boot. A minister who was also a part-time life insurance salesman gave me a similar pitch—unsolicited.

Net cost on a 20-year endowment policy:

Total premiums ages 35–55	$ 9,000
Maturity value at age 55	10,000
Net Profit	$ 1,000

As you can see, if they overcharge you enough, they can prove that not only have you had your insurance free, but that also you've made a profit.

What about the earning power of your money all those years? We have already learned that a dollar has fantastic earning potential and that it will work either for you or for the institution to whom you lend it.

• MY SEARCH
  FOR INFORMATION

Perhaps it would be well for me to share with you how I have developed such strong convictions about the insurance area of financial planning. Let me go back to the year 1958.

I began to have a gnawing feeling that there was something wrong with my family's life insurance program. (We had bought a policy from a friend some years before while we were still in college, struggling to earn enough money to finish and had asked him for a low-cost, high-protection policy.)

I began my search for information by first going to a college library and then to a large public library. To my surprise, information about life insurance was extremely scarce. This was puzzling. Millions of dollars were being spent annually on this commodity, but there was so little information available. I had heard of certain books about the subject, but they seemed to be "out of print." Laboriously, I began to piece together bits of information in an effort to solve this puzzle of how the various types of insurance policies differed and how they were put together.

Decreasing Term Plus Banking • During this searching period, I awoke early one morning, and like a bolt out of the blue I felt I had solved the insurance mystery. All the policies that were being so aggressively sold by the life insurance community were either pure protection alone or pure protection plus banking. Whole life, straight life, modified life, 20 pay life, 20-year endowment, executive life, and various other golden titles created by the marketing departments of the life insurance companies were actually decreasing term plus a savings account.

I now remembered that the word "term" had come up when we had asked the agent for a low-cost policy. He had recoiled in horror when we asked and said "term" is only "temporary" insurance, a poor substitute for "permanent" insurance. After all, you don't want to "rent" your insurance; you want to "own" it.

"Permanent" Insurance? • As I began to delve into how our policy was constructed, I began to question how "permanent" our "permanent insurance" really was. According to my understanding of the word "permanent," it is something that doesn't change; yet our insurance was decreasing each time we paid the premium and substituted some of our after-tax dollars for a portion of our insurance protection. The company's risk was decreasing as the burden was shifted to us through our increasing savings account.

"Our" Savings Account? • Was it really ours? If it were our savings account, what were its characteristics?

First of all, we found that we were using after-tax dollars and substituting them for insurance dollars we could buy for a few pennies. This did not seem to be brilliant economics. (And here I had a college degree in economics and finance!) Then we noticed from reading the cash surrender value table in the back of the policy that all of our savings the first few years had disappeared. (As I thought back over the explanation the agent had given us about the policy at the time of the sale, I couldn't remember his inserting the word "surrender" in his reference to the cash value. He referred to it as our "building up of cash for the future.")

We also discovered that as we continued to make deposits each year, we were being charged a commission to place money into our "savings account." Once the savings were deposited, we seemed to be losing all their earning power. I knew the agent said we were getting 3 percent on the cash reserve but as we examined the policy, it didn't seem too important what rate was being paid since, if death occurred, the insurance company planned to keep the savings and only pay the face amount of the policy.

We also found that if we wanted to borrow "our" savings, we would have to pay 5½ percent interest to borrow our own money. Really? Our own money? Again we asked, "Is it ours?"

We also found that if my spouse died with the savings there, the unilateral contract signed with the life insurance company specified that they got to keep "our" savings. The savings were part of the face amount, or death benefit, of the policy. Not an amount in addition to the face amount.

Funny Banking • It was then that we asked ourselves this: If we had gone to our banker and said to him, "We want to open a savings account at your bank." And he had said to us, "We're happy to have you open an account. However, we are required to tell you our rules. First of all, we will take all the deposits you make in your account the first year. After that, we will charge you to deposit money into your account. If you want to borrow from your savings, we will charge you 5½ percent interest to borrow your own money. If you refuse to pay us for the privilege of borrowing your own money, and withdraw your savings, you will have to give up your life insurance policy.

If our banker had said these words to us when we had inquired about opening a savings account, would we have opened the account? If we would not consider banking with our commercial bank under these conditions, why were we banking with a life insurance company?

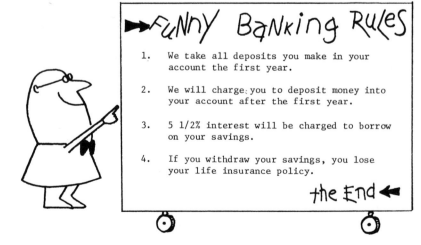

We then began to analyze our "banking." We examined four major areas: safety, yield, liquidity, and cost of doing business.

The first thing we examined, as you should, was safety. If your account isn't safe, none of the other characteristics are important. Once you've established that it's safe, you will then want to know what rate of return you are obtaining on your money because the rate of return is vitally important to any financial program. After that, you will want to know about liquidity—how readily accessible your funds are. Last, what is the cost of doing business?

Much to my surprise, here is how I tallied the two "banks" with regard to the savings portion of our policy:

	Savings with	
	Commercial national bank	Insurance company
Safety	Guaranteed by FDIC	Only as safe as the company
Yield	5–6%	2½%–3½% on cash reserve
Liquidity	On demand	Could wait six months and then pay only if they had the money
Cost of Doing Business:		
To Deposit	0	10–55%
To Withdraw	0	5–6%

What is your reaction to this comparison? With whom do you feel you should be banking? With the life insurance company? With the bank? We chose the bank.

We discovered that life insurance was for dying and investments were for living; and the combining of the two under one insurance policy only built bigger and better life insurance empires. And even though one insurance company is still allowed, in some states, to come into your living room via "living color" television and through national magazines to tell you that you, too, can own a part of a jagged, porous piece of real estate standing at the gateway of the blue Mediterranean, it is not literally true.

• BUY WHEN YOU ARE YOUNG

Have you heard, as we had, "Buy your insurance while you are young because it's cheaper?" We found that this is not true and that life insurance will cost more each year because it is based on a mortality table. We also found that the more recent the mortality table in use, the better the rates, because medical science is helping our population to live longer.

Did your agent tell you when he delivered your policy, encased in leather or plastic and embossed in gold, that your policy was sacred and should never ever be changed? Ours did. He said it would cost us dearly if we ever changed.

As I look back now, this is rather ridiculous. This would mean we had found the most knowledgeable agent who designed the best insurance package, that our needs would never change, and that no new mortality table would ever be in use.

When we analyzed our policies, we found that changing them was much to our advantage. We had a $25,000 policy for which we were paying $670.75 per year. It had $5,425 of cash surrender value; therefore, our net insurance was $19,675. What was our cost per thousand in this policy?

Face amount	$25,000.00
"Our" savings	5,425.00
Net insurance	$19,675.00
Premium	670.75
Lost earnings on $5,425 @5%	271.25
Total cost	$ 942.00

True cost per thousand: $942/19.7 thousand, or $47.82 per thousand

Our cost per thousand had increased from $26.83 per thousand, when we took out the policy, to $47.82.

I counted the loss of earning power on our savings because if the savings were in a bank at 5 percent (or in municipal bonds if we were concerned about taxes), the $5,425 would have earned us $271.25. We then made the startling discovery that $942.00 would purchase us $180,000 of annual renewable term life insurance.

During that year, if death had occurred, the beneficiaries would have received:

From the bank	$ 5,425
From the insurance co.	180,000
Total	$185,425

Our family's total (death and living) estate had been increased by $160,425 ($185,425 − $25,000) by just repositioning our assets.

How Did It Happen? • How did we ever happen to agree to this original policy? Would we have agreed to it if someone had told us about all the possible kinds of policies? Had we signed a contract without even reading it? We had asked the agent, who was a good friend of ours, for the lowest-cost policy with the maximum coverage. We later discovered he had not intentionally done us a disservice. He had sold us the kind of policy his company told him he should sell. (He was what is called a "captive salesman"—meaning he could only write insurance for the company he represented.) His general manager had also assured him this was the best policy for his client, for himself, and for the company. It was the best for him and for the company, but not for us.

It Made a Great Difference • In 1958, when we learned how life insurance policies were put together, we changed all our policies and were able to obtain a large amount of protection for the same premium and freed our cash value for investments.

On September 29, 1959, my husband was a passenger on the Braniff Electra that crashed near Buffalo, Texas, killing all aboard. My whole world crashed around me.

When everything was settled, I realized that my estate was much larger than it would have been if we had not made changes in our insurance program.

With intelligent investing of these proceeds since that time, I have moved along the road toward financial independence. I'm a financial planner today because I want to be, not out of an economic necessity.

• LIFE INSURANCE, A VERY PERSONAL MATTER

Your life insurance program should be designed to fit your needs at this particular time. Your needs will change from year to year, so your policies should be constantly reviewed. They are not sacred instruments.

Your need for protection may be less, the same, or more each year. Is there a new mortality table now available? If so, you will want to apply for a new policy at the lower rate. When you have the new policy safely secured (not before), then consider what should be done with your old policy. Policies can be changed, and riders can be dropped. Work with a creative financial planner to keep your insurance program finely turned to your changing needs. A good insurance program should not be expensive, if properly designed, and should be well within your family's budget.

- ## THE $100,000
  ## ESTATE

A minimum estate necessary to maintain a family today should be at least $100,000. At a 6 percent withdrawal, this is only $500 per month, which is not particularly generous, I'm sure you'll agree.

If you are a young family man, just beginning your journey down the road toward financial independence, your accumulated assets will probably be small. For example, let's assume you have accumulated $10,000. This is your "living estate"—meaning that no one has to die to make these funds available. If you need a $100,000 estate, you are $90,000 short. This will need to be provided by life insurance, which will be your "death estate" until you can substitute a "living estate" for it.

A diagram of your estate would look like this:

Death Estate	$90,000	**$100,000** **Desired** **Total Estate**
Living Estate	$10,000	

When your "living estate" has grown to $20,000, if your goal is still $100,000, you can reduce your "death estate" to $80,000. You keep substituting "living" for "death," "living" for "death," until you become self insured. This is your financial goal—not the acquisition of life insurance policies. Cash or its equivalent is far superior, I'm sure you'll agree.

All life insurance premiums are money down a rat hole unless you die. When you become self insured stop this waste.

- ## PROGRAMMING LIFE INSURANCE
  ## WITH INVESTMENTS

Let's assume you are a male, age 35, have saved $10,000, can budget $150 per month to cover your insurance program and your investment program, and desire to have a $100,000 estate.

If you place your investment dollars into a "guaranteed" position and obtain 5 percent, your programming would be as follows:

AGE	INSURANCE COVERAGE	$10,000	$117/Mo.	TOTAL ESTATE
35	$90,000	$10,000	$ 0	$100,000
45	70,740	16,289	18,547	105,576
55	42,480	26,533	48,747	117,760
65	0	43,219	97,943	141,162

If you find that you can invest at 10 percent:

AGE	INSURANCE COVERAGE	$10,000	$117/Mo.	TOTAL ESTATE
35	$90,000	$ 10,000	$ 0	$100,000
45	70,740	25,900	24,612	121,252
55	42,480	67,300	88,452	198,232
65	0	174,500	254,040	428,540

• WHICH LIFE INSURANCE COMPANY?

Does it make a difference from which legal reserve life insurance company you buy pure protection? No, it does not. Seek one that offers the best features at the best rates, designed to help you build a living estate. It should offer policies that are renewable and convertible, at your option, to any of their policies, without evidence of insurability, to a ripe old age. This puts you in the driver's seat—and that's where you should be in designing and carrying out your financial plan.

A life insurance company with whose principles I agree states its policy as follows:

1 · We write life insurance policies to protect investors.

2 · We encourage policyholders to continue to accumulate investments outside life insurance policies.

3 · We offer life insurance to the investing public through licensed life insurance agents who are also registered for the sale of investments.

4 · Due to the economic quality of our market and the specialized nature of our representative, we are able to offer life insurance policies at costs considerably lower than ordinarily encountered in the life insurance industry.

5 · We do not write complicated policies nor do we encourage expensive devices. We simply write maximum coverage for a minimum price.

• WHICH LIFE INSURANCE AGENT?

From which agent should you buy your protection? Certainly one of the prerequisites is that he not be a member of a captive sales force —meaning he can only write for the one company to whom he is beholden. He cannot be impartial under these conditions. His company will not let him. Too, his company may not even have a policy that fits your needs, and if it does have one hidden away, his supervisor may severely reprimand him for not selling you the kind that makes him and the company the most profit.

In my opinion, you should plan your life insurance needs with a person knowledgeable in investments to help you build a living estate and in life insurance to help you buy the time to build the estate. These two areas of financial planning are inseparable since you don't know how long your life span will be. Your financial planner should be dually licensed to recommend both investments and life insurance.

Being dually licensed allows the professional to balance your financial program. I should warn you, however, that it does not make him impartial. In fact, some life insurance agents have obtained a securties license as a tool for selling more high-cost, low-protection policies. They maintain that it will not make any difference to them whether you invest in securities or put your investment dollar into your policy. Actually, it makes a whale of a difference in his compensation. If he sells you a whole life policy at a cost of $1,000, he may receive as high as 110 percent of that premium (or $1,100 over a two-year period) plus some trail commission from the policy in the future. If he sells you "term" and invests the balance for you in a mutual fund, he would receive only a fraction of this amount that first year.

• HOW TO ANALYZE YOUR POLICIES

Let's discuss how to take the first step in analyzing your own policies. First, you'll need to get them out of the safety deposit box or wherever you have them stored. Now read them. After you have finished, look on the front of the policy. There you will find the date the policy was acquired. That's its birthdate. Take today's date less its birthdate and this gives you the age of the policy. For example, if you acquired your policy in April 1965, and it is now November 1975, it is 10 years old. Look toward the back of the policy, if you have the "permanent" variety. Go down to the tenth year of the nonforfeiture section. Go across and you will find a "cash surrender" or "loan value." This amount will be for either the face amount or per thousand. It will state one or the other at the top of the chart. For example, if it's a $10,000 policy and your cash value table shows $350 opposite 10 years, and the table shows "per $1,000," you would have a cash value of $3,500.

To give you a better picture of your policy, you'll find the form on page 214 helpful for listing your policies.

• HOW MUCH LIFE INSURANCE?

How do you calculate the amount of life insurance you should carry? First, take your present monthly salary. Let's assume it is $2,000. Multiply this amount by 70 percent, which is about what your family would need to maintain them at their present standard of living if you were not here to provide for them. Therefore, $1,400 would be needed. Let's assume you are under maximum Social Security. Your wife would receive around $530 per month until your child reaches 18 (until age 22 if a full-time unmarried student). Thus, $1,400 less $530 = $870. How much capital is required to provide $870 per month at 6 percent? Just multiply by 200, which gives you $174,000. Let's assume you have accumulated $20,000. Subtract this from the $174,000, leaving $154,000 capital needed. Assuming you are a male of age 30, your rate for deposit annual renewable term would be $2.30 per thousand this year (and gradually increase in subsequent years) or $354.20 per annum premium plus a one-time deposit of $3 per thousand or $462 which will be returned to the beneficiary if death occurs, or if you keep the policy 10 years, you will receive back an amount double your deposit—$924.

You should calculate the amount you need using this method (adding other appropriate expenses such as college costs, etc.); then determine if it can be fit into your budget. If it can, fine; if it cannot, you must reduce the coverage to fit your budget.

• WILL YOU LOSE IF YOU CHANGE YOUR POLICIES?

No more than my family did! The belief that you will lose if you change your insurance policies may have "scared" you away from the common-sense program of pure protection based on need. Your concern

INSURANCE RECORD AND ANALYSIS

Name _____

Address _____

Telephone _____

Date _____

Date of Birth _____

Age at Issue	Date of Issue	Company	Type of Policy	Mor-tality Table	Face Amount	Cash Value	Net Insurance	Annual Prem.	Last Year's Div.	Net Premium	Other Features
Totals											

should not be how much you will lose by dropping an existing savings policy. This money has already been lost. A large portion of total commissions and other acquisition costs were taken out in the early years of your policy, and this money never comes back. Your real question is "How much will I lose in the future by keeping my high-cost, low-protection policy?"

Look at it this way. Assume you are an airline pilot going to Miami. After an hour or so you calculate your location and find that you have overshot Miami and are out over the Atlantic Ocean. If you keep going, you'll run out of fuel and drop into the ocean. If you turn around now, you'll have enough fuel to get back to Miami. Would you bury your error or rationalize it? No! You would change your course and head toward your destination as soon as possible, for every minute wasted could be costly and catastrophic. Successful financial planning is based on the same principle. If you are heading in the wrong direction, alter your course as soon as possible.

Costly Friendship • Not changing a poor policy can be a very expensive error. I remember a young man of age 25 who was paying $130 per year for a $5,000 whole life insurance policy he did not need. His employer provided in excess of the amount of protection he needed under a company group term insurance policy. I suggested that he might want to consider using this $130 more profitably in the form of a savings plan or investments.

The policy had been sold to him by a good friend whom he felt had his best interest at heart. He did not want to upset his friend and decided to continue the policy. He felt, after all, that he had an above-average income and was not financially inconvenienced by paying a $130 per year premium. He told me he felt anyone could always use a little extra protection. He reasoned he had $5,000 of insurance in case he died, and he would get back $6,000 in cash when he was 65, if he lived, and that to him was a pretty good return on $130 per year.

He obviously did not know how to measure what money must do, or he would not have been so complacent.

Here is what $130 per year for 40 years will become (exclusive of taxes) at various rates of return:

$130 per year for 40 years at 15% = $265,973.50

$130 per year for 40 years at 12% = $111,688.20

$130 per year for 40 years at 10% = $ 63,290.50

$130 per year for 40 years at 8% = $ 36,371.40

$130 per year for 40 years at 6% = $ 21,329.10

This particular young man did not need the protection, but had he converted his whole life to level term to age 65, he would have had $80 difference per year ($130 − $50) to invest with these results (exclusive of taxes):

$80 per year for 40 years at 15% = $163,676.00

$80 per year for 40 years at 12% = $ 68,731.20

$80 per year for 40 years at 10% = $ 38,948.00

$80 per year for 40 years at 8% = $ 22,382.40

$80 per year for 40 years at 6% = $ 13,125.60

Remember this in your own planning.

• PAYING MORE WHILE YOU'RE YOUNG

Unfortunately, a family's need for protection is greatest at the time in their life cycle when their income has not reached its prime. Despite the fact that their mortality risk is low, most policies are designed so that the young are overcharged at the time they need maximum coverage so they can "underpay" when they are older and have little or no need for coverage.

Figure 12 is a diagram of the level premium method. Note how the policy is designed for coverage far beyond life expectancy.

• DOUBLE AND TRIPLE INDEMNITIES

The question often arises about the amount of accidental death insurance a young family should carry. In our financial planning we do not count his accidental death policies when calculating his need for protection. Even though he is convinced that if he dies, that's the way he'll go, it's not too likely—that's why the rates are low. It's more likely he'll die from a heart attack while mowing his lawn. It doesn't really matter how one dies: You are just as dead—and the family needs are

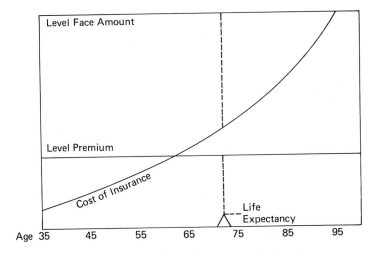

FIGURE 12.   Level Premium Method

going to remain the same. Buy sufficient life insurance to cover full needs and don't worry about how you may die.

• A GOOD COMPULSORY SAVING PLAN?

Is insurance, in fact, a good compulsory savings plan? The previous analysis of this aspect of "permanent" insurance should indicate that you are much wiser to put savings in a bank or an investment.

If you must have your savings guaranteed all you need to do is to buy term and place the difference in Series E bonds. There are more productive ways to save, but you don't have to worry about safety of principal, just safety of purchasing power.

• AN INEXPENSIVE WAY TO BORROW MONEY?

Sometimes a couple will proudly point out to me how very bright they have been to have figured out that they can borrow on their policy for 5 or 6 percent interest instead of from the bank at 8½ percent. If you are doing this, you are paying to borrow your "own" money. If your savings were in the bank, you would not have to pay the bank to take it out. You are also reducing your life insurance coverage when you borrow against your policy for they subtract the loan from the face amount if it is outstanding at the time of death. You have, therefore, increased your cost per thousand for life insurance because you now have an additional interest expense.

• LIFE INSURANCE
FOR CHILDREN?

I'm amazed at the amount of money wasted on premiums each year on life insurance for children.

Let's reexamine the purpose of life insurance. It's purpose is to protect those dependent upon the policyholder in the event he does not live long enough to build a living estate. If you have a policy on the life of your child, ask yourself, "Who is dependent on my child for a livelihood?" Is the answer, "No one"? You should not make a practice of protecting your liabilities, but of protecting your assets. As much as you love your child or children, they are a financial liability until they are old enough and well enough prepared to leave your nest.

Should you have enough for burial? You can if you want to, but I don't recommend that you do. There are limited dollars in the family budget for life insurance, and every dollar spent on life insurance for the children means a dollar was taken away from purchasing life insurance for the breadwinner. You may shun such a somber thought, but a child's funeral expenses will be defrayed by the decrease in cost of caring for the child, while the loss of a wage earner may be a near economic disaster for the family.

If you would feel more comfortable with a bit of insurance on the kids, you can obtain $1,000 on each child, regardless of how many children you have, for about $8 per year total (not $8 for each) by putting this coverage as a rider on your policy. You can usually carry five of these units, meaning you can have $5,000 of insurance on each of your children, for a total of $40 per year. You can carry this coverage on each child until they are 25 years of age. At that time they have the privilege of obtaining five times this coverage without evidence of insurability. In other words, when your child reaches 25, he has the privilege of carrying $25,000 of coverage without having to take a physical to prove his insurability, and at the rate of his attained age and on a current mortality table.

• COLLEGE
POLICIES

To me, one of the great hoaxes of the century has been endowment policies for college education. I've seen many of them that had been taken out at the time of the child's birth, with glowing descriptions of providing for four years of college, which did not even cover the first semester of expenses.

Although you certainly want to plan for your children's education, a college endowment policy is not an effective way. Planning for this expense is covered in a later chapter.

• UNDOING THE INDOCTRINATION

When we study insurance policies and sales presentations analytically under a bright light, we wonder how this misrepresentation has been able to continue. The insurance industry maintains an "educational" institution called the Life Insurance Institute to educate, or perhaps we should say indoctrinate, the public. The Institute has been so successful that it is often difficult to help clients change their thinking.

The very agent who sold you the wrong life insurance policy may have done so in good faith, not knowing any better.

Consumer News, in its February 1973, edition reporting on the congressional hearing on life insurance company abuses, states in issue #72, dated February 26, 1973, "History's first Congressional investigation into life insurance brought a succession of witnesses last week charging the industry with deceptive selling techniques on such a massive scale that even many agents themselves are unaware of what they are doing to American consumers." I recommend this issue to you. (It can be purchased by writing to *Consumer Newsweek*, 813 National Press Building, Washington, D.C. 20004.)

This same issue quotes Professor Joseph Belth, a professor at Indiana University, as calling our life insurance industry a "national scandal."

Ralph Nader, the fire-breathing crusader, called the life insurance industry "a smug, sacred cow feeding the public a steady line of sacred bull." He called "cash value" a "consumer fraud." I'm still puzzled why it took him so long to pluck this plum.

In my own case, I have been aware of how life insurance policies were constructed since 1958, and I was aware of the disasterous results of poor insurance advice in investment programs. Despite this, I conducted my seminars from 1962 until 1970 without mentioning the problem. Why? The insurance lobbies are extremely strong, and I was fearful of them. Also, I was concerned that if I attacked an idea that those attending had held to be true for so long and in which they had invested their hard-earned dollars, they might distrust my investment advice. (It's hard to admit to yourself that you've been unwise.)

However, in the interview to which each person attending a seminar is entitled, I would discuss any problems I detected in the design of their insurance program and would suggest how they might correct them by applying for a policy that fit their needs. Time after time, the agent they would go to for insurance after our visit would sell them a high-cost, low-protection policy.

Finally, it happened once too often. A young man of modest means came to my office to set up an investment program. He was married to a lovely woman with no vocational training, and they had five young children. When I learned he had no life insurance, I suggested that the first thing they needed before setting up an investment program was life insurance to protect their family. I recommended they obtain a $100,000 decreasing term to 65 on the husband. I then set up a monthly investment program for them.

Later I discovered that when he went to an agent for the coverage, instead of providing the amount and kind of insurance my client needed, the agent sold him a $10,000, 20 year pay life for approximately the same premium he could have obtained the $100,000 decreasing term policy. Had the man died, his family would have been destitute.

This intentional disservice infuriated me, and I swore that I would never again send out a client and subject him to the risk of this happening to him.

I set up a life insurance general agency and began to boldly speak about life insurance in my seminars. I truly believe that we are often doing a greater service in the area of life insurance than in the area of investments.

Let me re-emphasize—life insurance is a necessary keystone of a good investment program, provided that insurance is purchased as an intricate part of the overall program. It should be purchased with the following eight points in mind:

1 · Buy your life insurance as if you were going to die tomorrow.

2 · Life insurance is based on a mortality table; therefore, it should cost you more each year because you are more likely to die each year.

3 · Every time the insurance companies are forced to go on a new mortality table, apply for a new policy. If you pass the physical and are granted a new policy at a lower rate, redeem or cancel the old one. A life insurance policy is no more sacred than an automobile insurance policy.

4 · The purpose of life insurance is to protect those dependent on you in the event you do not live long enough to accumulate a living estate. Your goal is to become self insured by age

65 or sooner. You've either made it by then, or you'll probably never make it. Life insurance is to protect an economic
potential. After 65 your economic potential has greatly di-
minished. Yes, I know insurance proceeds can be used to pay
estate taxes. If your heirs are in that enviable position, hurrah
for you! Here we are speaking of bread on the table in the
event you are not here to provide for it. We can obtain pure
protection to age 100, and that should take care of most situations even including federal estate taxes.

5 · Life insurance is for dying. Investments are for living.

6 · All life insurance is pure protection (term), or pure protection
plus banking. There are no other kinds.

7 · Do not bank with an insurance company under conditions you
would not bank with your bank.

8 · Be sure that your policies are renewable and convertible at
your option without evidence of insurability. You should also
consider waiver of premium provisions.

My wish for you is that you will live a long and happy life and
that all the premiums you'll ever pay will be pure waste!

Application

*How much income would your family need to enable them to continue
at their present standard of living if you were not here to provide for
them? How much capital would this require? How much living estate
have you acquired? How much life insurance should you now have to
make up the deficiency in the total estate required? What would your
premiums be? Will this amount fit your budget? Which investments
should enable you to continue to substitute a living estate for a death
estate? How will you keep informed on newer and better policies and
rates that become available?*

{ 14 }

Investing
in
Energy

In previous chapters we have studied the investment potential of securities and real estate. In this chapter we will consider the potential of investing in energy. Energy is a broad category and not all areas will be viable considerations for you if your investment funds are limited.

- **BACKGROUND OF THE
  ENERGY CRISIS**

In 1974 the average man on the street came face to face with the fact that energy was not a magical manna that dropped from heaven and ran into his electric light switch and into the tank of his automobile. With the Arab oil embargo he discovered that he could no longer drive into the corner gas station; say, "Fill'er up"; receive a sheet of green trading stamps (double on Tuesdays) plus a drinking glass with the insignia of his local football team; and be merrily on his way in a few minutes.

The "energy crisis" did not just suddenly arrive on the scene, although it may have appeared to from listening to and reading the news media. In 1967, I interviewed Michael T. Halbouty, a highly respected independent oil producer, on my CBS affiliate television program, "Successful Texans." He warned then, as he had been doing since 1960, of the impending energy crisis if steps were not taken to allow a reasonable return on capital invested in the oil industry. At that time he was making warning speeches across the nation, and he has continued to do so. Two years later, I interviewed J. Hugh Liedtke, Chairman of the Board of Pennzoil. He also warned of the problems that were imminent if proper action was not taken. He quoted extensively from comprehensive government studies on the subject.

I also interviewed George Mitchell, Chairman of the Board and President of Mitchell Energy and Development. He gave the same warning and continues to do so.

He and others pointed out over and over again that the flow of new oil could not possibly meet the new and increasing demands.

The need to encourage production seemed obvious to those who were in production, but the opposite view was taken by those who controlled the legislation to fulfill the need.

The Federal Power Commission continued to hold down the price of natural gas to the $.17 per cubic foot price to which they had arbitrarily rolled it back, despite the continuous plea of the oilmen. The Commission took the pose of the three little monkeys, and put their hands over their eyes and said, "Hear no evil, see no evil, speak no evil," and all these bad, bad predictions will "fade away." Of course, the big bad wolf, called energy shortage, did not fade away.

The attitudes of the eastern congressmen also aggravated the picture as they took the attitude, "How dare you talk of raising the price of the natural gas used to bake the bread for the dear families residing in my state?" And then they added, "And don't you muss our scenic coast lines with refineries either; keep them down in Texas and Louisiana where they belong."

They also insisted that the federal government allow massive amounts of foreign oil to be imported into the United States at prices so low that domestic producers could not compete.

At this time a shortage of risk capital to be used to drill oil wells also occurred.

In the 1950s the corporate tax rate was 60 percent to 70 percent, and the individual rate could go as high as 90 percent. At these confiscatory levels there was a tremendous incentive to search for ways of turning tax liabilities into potential capital assets. Oil drilling programs fit this possibility because of the 100 percent write-off potential of intangible drilling costs. Large amounts of risk capital, therefore, were made available.

But in the 1960s, the maximum corporate tax level was reduced to around 48 percent and the individual's to the 50 percent to 70 percent level. This greatly reduced the tax incentive.

All of these factors combined to reduce the profitability of producing oil and gas.

The number of independent oil operators dwindled from 35,000 to 5,000 and the number of rig operators from 3,500 to around 900.

As the supply of oil and gas was decreasing, the demand was increasing. Collision course was already in the making when the Arabian bloc discovered our great vulnerability and decided their best bargaining tool against Israel was the U.S.'s dependence on their oil.

• TURNING LEMONS INTO LEMONADE

If the Arabian embargo had come just two years earlier, the United States could have absorbed the consequent cutbacks fairly easily and would not have become disturbed enough to do anything about its impending future shortage. If, on the other hand, the situation had developed two or three years later, it would have been catastrophic. It was a blessing that it happened late enough to make us aware of the problem facing us and early enough for us to take corrective steps.

There is no question in my mind that the government's ostrich-like policy created the "energy crisis of 1973-75." But instead of wasting our energies condemning their actions, let's examine ways that you might benefit from this situation by viewing it as an "Energy Opportunity" rather than an "Energy Crisis."

How can you best avail yourself of these opportunities? There are three areas that you should consider: investing in energy-related securities, investing in oil- and gas-producing wells, and investing in oil and gas exploration.

• ENERGY STOCKS

I believe we may be beginning a new Sputnik-like era. Our reaction to the Sputnik shock in 1957 caused a big boom in technical

equipment. Fortunes were made in semiconductors. Looking ahead, the President has set 1980, unrealistically perhaps, as the target year for self-sufficiency. Oil men tell me it will be nearer to 1985. This will take massive capital expenditures. But that should not discourage us. A nation that can put a man on the moon can surely solve her energy problems, especially in view of the fact that we are blessed with an abundance of two great energy sources, coal and uranium, in addition to oil and gas.

The current trend is toward more electrification and toward nuclear reactors as the source of power. It looks as if the trend will continue. It appears that nuclear power makes one of the cheapest, as well as the best, use of resources. Some of the processes involved in nuclear power have not yet hit the large scale. The fabrication of nuclear fuels is a tiny industry, but an industry that has the potential of tremendous savings from mass production.

The U.S. has enough uranium for the production of nuclear energy. Companies like Kerr-McGee and Anaconda are top producers. A large number of the oil companies are also entering the field. Uranium may some day overshadow oil as a source of energy. Another energy source is the manufacture of crude oil from coal. This should be no more expensive than importing oil. We still have untapped sources of hydroelectricity, and there is the possibility of solar energy.

The industries that will benefit from the new push to be self-sufficient in energy will offer a vast range of investment opportunities. Study each carefully, and pick the leader in the industries you choose.

I believe the "energy crisis" has set up one of those rare investment opportunities that comes along maybe only once every ten years.

You should use the same basic criteria that we've outlined earlier in the selection of your energy stocks. Some of the older, more heavily capitalized companies should fit the income category if this is your financial objective. The smaller, more aggressive companies, which may have more venturesome drilling programs, may fit the growth and speculative categories.

Many companies will broaden their base and engage in exploration, production, refining, and distribution. They may even go into the manufacture of products that use petrocarbons as their base.

You should consider not only these companies but also those who build offshore drilling rigs and those who build refineries. Oil without refineries is of no use. We faced a refinery bottleneck long before the Middle East war disturbed our international oil supply.

Management skills, company's assets, and consumer demand are vital areas for study, whether you are selecting an oil company or a company in a related field.

• ENERGY PRODUCTION

We have been examining investing in oil and gas and other energy through the stock market. This is a legitimate consideration for your investment dollars. But let's look at other ways. One way that I feel is worthy of your consideration is participation in energy through investing in oil and gas income-limited partnerships.

To compare investing in energy through stocks with investing through partnerships, let's look at the characteristics of each. First, let's look at the numbers using our largest oil company, Exxon. Here are the figures for 1972:

EXXON

1972 Figures per Share

22.39	Earnings before depreciation and taxes
4.72	Depletion and depreciation
17.66	Pretax earnings
10.83	Corp. taxes (including minority interest expenses and excise taxes)
6.83	After-tax earnings
3.80	Dividend (taxable to the shareholder, thus double taxation)
3.30	Retaining earnings (corp. decides how they will be used)

As you can see, if you owned a share of Exxon, only $6.83 of cash flow was left after taxes; $3.80 of this was paid out to you as a dividend, on which you probably paid federal income taxes, therefore suffering double taxation; and $3.03 was retained by the company. The company did not ask you whether you would like to have these funds reinvested. This was decided for you by the board of directors. You do hope, however, that these funds will be used to find more oil and gas, which will increase the profitability of the company and eventually be reflected in the price of the stock.

Exxon is a corporation; therefore, as an investor, your liability is limited to the amount of your investment. If you have invested $10,000, that is all you could lose, even if their stock became nonexistent. It is also readily salable since it is listed on the New York Stock Exchange. Its value may fluctuate, but it is a liquid investment.

Is there a way that you can obtain the same limited liability while avoiding some of the double taxation, get the benefits of the depreciation and depletion allowance, and avoid the worry of market fluctuation, in exchange for giving up daily liquidity?

Yes, there is, through the investment medium of oil and gas income-limited partnerships.

• OIL AND GAS INCOME-LIMITED PARTNERSHIPS

In making any investment decisions, you should attempt to find a vehicle that will supply a product that everyone wants, that everyone needs, and that is in short supply. Oil and gas income-limited partnerships can fit these criteria.

Oil and gas drilling programs have been offered to high-tax-bracket investors for many years, but it has only been in recent years that you have had the opportunity to invest in production without the drilling risks, through a product designed for the smaller, lower-tax-bracket investor.

As in real estate limited partnerships, the limited partner has limited his liability to the amount of his investment. The general partner takes the risk and is the key man. In exchange for his fee, he is to secure the proper producing properties and to operate them on a profitable basis.

Despite the oil business' reputation for riskiness, a well-managed oil income program probably has less short-term risk than most common stocks or mutual funds. That is so because oil income programs are not particularly subject to market fluctuations. The value of an oil income program depends upon the level of income that it produces.

When an oil company drills a discovery well, it will normally drill additional development wells since the oil or gas reservoir usually cannot be fully drained by only one well. Drilling of these development wells can take several years.

After sufficient time has passed, oil reservoirs will have enough production history and reservoir data so that reasonably accurate estimates of reserves can be made. Once those estimates are ascertainable, producing properties can be evaluated within an acceptable margin for error. It is at that stage that oil income programs become buyers of producing properties.

In these limited partnerships, the major portion of the oil and gas proceeds flow directly to you—you receive the depletion and depreciation allowance, and pay taxes once on the remainder as ordinary income.

These were our original anticipations when we first recommended a particular limited partnership in March of 1971. On a $10,000 investment we hoped to obtain a $1,000 write-off in the year the investment was made; 13–14 percent cash flow (including depreciation and depletion), which could give 40 percent of the income-tax sheltered; a 5.3 year pay-out (meaning you would hope to have your $10,000 back through cash flow by then—this is called restored liquidity). And we hoped that after you had recovered your $10,000 in quarterly checks, you would still have a cash flow for 15 or more years. The results through the second quarter of 1974 were:

	$10,000 investment quarterly distributions	Accumulative distributions
1971	44.00	44.00
	400.00	444.00
	400.00	844.00
	650.00	1,494.00
1972	400.00	1,894.00
	400.00	2,294.00
	400.00	2,694.00
	800.00	3,494.00
1973	450.00	3,944.00
	500.00	4,444.00
	500.00	4,944.00
	800.00	5,744.00
1974	1,600.00	7,344.00
	2,100.00	9,444.00
	1,930.00	11,374.00
	1,840.00	13,214.00

At the end of the second quarter of 1974, you could have had $9,444 of your investment restored with $556 to go. By the third quarter 113 percent had been restored. Reserve estimates as of February 1, 1974, were $29,960.

Should you expect to do this well if you were to invest in an oil and gas income-limited partnership today? I really don't know. I do know the 1971 timing was exceptionally good, and that this was and still is an excellent management team. They did, however, reap the advantages of greatly accelerated oil prices for which they cannot claim credit.

Another client who made a $10,000 investment in an oil and gas limited partnership with another company in 1973 received back a year later over $16,000. Amoco bought one of the fields in the fund. If you decide that this investment fits your needs, I hope you will be as fortunate.

Leveraged and Nonleveraged Programs • Oil income programs can be of two types: leveraged and nonleveraged. Leveraged oil income programs use production loans to finance a portion of the purchase price. Of course, as the properties produce revenue, some portion must be dedicated to principal and interest payments. Nonleveraged income programs do not use debt financing and are able to distribute all of a property's revenue to the limited partners.

Leveraged income programs are the more risky of the two types. Leveraging tends to magnify your profits or losses; and, therefore, you have more potential for success or failure. Nonleveraged income programs give you greater safety and, in turn, offer you less opportunity for larger profits.

I have never recommended the leverage partnership to my clients.

Return on Invested Capital • Computation of the rate of return on an income program is complicated because of depletion. The key indicator is return on invested capital (ROIC). Let's assume that an income program you have invested in is distributing income at the rate of $1,600 per year, per $10,000 invested. Let's also assume that 50 percent of that $1,600 is return *of* capital and 50 percent is return *on* capital.

With the above assumptions, the ROIC in the first years is 8 percent. This is so because $800 of the $10,000 invested in the first year is return *on* capital. In the second year, however, the ROIC would go up to 9.5 percent. This increase in ROIC happens because invested capital is decreasing. At the end of the first year, you have $800 of your money back, in addition to an $800 return on your money. After two years, you have $1,600 of your money back. Consequently, your invested capital reduced from $10,000 to $9,200 to $8,400. If return on capital is constant while invested capital decreases, the return on invested capital is automatically rising.

Restored Liquidity • Restored liquidity is a difficult concept to understand. This means how much of your original investment has been "restored" to you. For example, if you invested $10,000, and the first 10 months you received a cash flow of $1,437, your restored liquidity would be 14.4 percent. Let's assume the following on a $10,000 investment:

Year	Cash flow	Restored liquidity (%)
1st (10 mo.)	$1,437	14.4%
2nd	1,729	31.7
3rd	2,239	54.1
4th	2,330	77.4
5th	1,966	97.0
6th	1,577	100.0

Liquidity was restored in five years and three months. The liquidity of an investment you might make may be restored sooner than this, or it may take longer, if it is restored at all.

Building a Second Income • Since a portion of the quarterly checks you may receive are a return of your original investment, you may want to reinvest or deposit back into a savings account that which is considered depletion and depreciation (return of capital). Let's assume you moved $10,000 out of a savings account into an oil and gas income program. Let's further assume you spent that which you received from the program that was classified as ordinary income and that you moved back into the savings accounts that which was nontaxable because it had been classified as a return of capital.

Let's assume your results were as follows:

Year	Spendable income	Depletion and depreciation	Capital at work	Capital returned to savings
1st	$ 517	$ 920	$9,080	$ 920
2nd	738	991	8,089	1,911
3rd	1,159	1,080	7,009	2,991
4th	1,125	1,114	5,895	4,105
5th	1,002	964	4,931	5,069
TOTAL	$4,541	$5,069	$4,931	$5,069

SUMMARY

Capital		Income
Capital at work	$ 4,931	$4,591
Returned to savings	5,069	748
TOTAL	$10,000	$5,339

Average Return: 10.6% per year

Your investment may not do this well, or it may do better. Although oil income programs are still a new investment vehicle, the performance of well-selected programs has been good to date.

Depreciation and Depletion • Depreciation in an oil and gas program is similar to that which you obtain in a real estate investment. The depreciation schedule for each piece of equipment depends on its expected life.

Depletion allowances are unique to natural resources and are allowed because the resource is being depleted; therefore, that portion is considered to be a return of capital.

Presently the oil and gas depletion allowance is 22 percent of gross. This is constantly under attack by some members of Congress, mostly by those who do not have a large supply of oil and gas in their states. If this allowance should be discontinued, you should anticipate paying more at the gas pump.

Most of the oil and gas income funds use cost depletion instead of statutory depletion, so their tax shelter should not be greatly affected. Cost depletion works similarly to a depreciation schedule. Statutory depletion is illustrated under the drilling section of this chapter.

In the meantime the depletion allowance explains why an oil income program seems to have such a high rate of income coming back to you. After the funds placed in the program are invested in properties, the company may begin to send checks at the rate of 12 percent to 25 percent per year based on the original investment. However, you should realize that a portion of this money is a return of your own capital.

It is important to distinguish between return *of* capital and return *on* capital. Both are represented in the income returned to limited partners. Obviously, if a program returns only 20 percent per year for five years and then stops, it would not be a good investment.

A good rule of thumb is that a successful oil income program should return at least double the original investment over the life of the partnership.

Oil and gas limited partnerships are sold in units, and each unit is usually $1,000. In many states, the minimum investment is 5 units or $5,000. Most companies offer a new partnership every quarter, and the minimum must be invested in each new one. There will ordinarily be between 200 and 300 wells in each partnership. These wells are selected for a broad blend of pay-outs. Some wells should have a high cash flow and deplete more rapidly. Others should deplete over a much longer period.

Disadvantages of Oil and Gas Income Programs • There are two disadvantages to oil income programs of which you should be aware. These are investment lag time and liquidity.

Oil income programs ordinarily raise all of their money before they identify the properties that they intend to buy. After the partnership is organized, funds are usually invested in Treasury bills or certificates of deposit. The program manager then goes out to try to find suitable purchases. He may be able to find high-quality properties immediately, or it may take as long as a year. During that year you do not have oil income—you have interest income at a level lower than what you could expect from oil and gas properties, but usually higher than you can obtain from a bank on your own, unless you have over $100,000 for a certificate of deposit.

A more important disadvantage of oil income programs is their lack of liquidity. There is no ready market for limited partnership interests, and the limited partner should really look for his money back only as the properties produce income. Some program managers try to provide buyout values once a year; however, you should only plan to avail yourself of these if you truly need the funds.

• OIL AND GAS EXPLORATION LIMITED PARTNERSHIPS

Historically, oil drilling programs have raised far more money than income programs. In recent years, public and private drilling programs have attracted $1 billion per year, while the newer income programs attract only around $100 million per year.

Oil drilling programs were left relatively untouched by Congress in their last go around of pot shots at tax shelters—the reason being, of course, the country's great need for energy.

If you are in the 50 percent tax bracket or above, you should consider investing in drilling programs. You may ask, "But aren't they risky?" The answer is "Yes, they are!" Searching for oil does involve considerable risk. However, paying taxes is risky, too. (Your chances of getting those tax dollars back are quite slim.) The oil companies attempt to reduce your risk by drilling a large number of holes spaced over wide geographic areas on which vast geologic study has been done.

A drilling limited partnership I use for my own funds, and recommend to my clients, uses the following way of distributing its drilling dollars in an attempt to reduce risks.

They divide each program's capital into three parts. One-third goes into development wells where they feel the odds on finding reserves are

1:2, with the value of the reserves ranging from 5:1 to 20:1 and return on risk on invested dollars ranging from 1:1 to 2:1. Another third is invested in controlled wildcats where they feel the odds on finding reserves are 1:4, value of reserves 5:1 to 30:1, and return on risk on invested dollars 1:1 to 3:1. The last third is invested in wildcats, with odds on finding reserves moving up to 1:15, value of reserves 5:1 to 50:1, and return on risk on invested dollars 1:1 to 5:1.

If all their odds worked perfectly, they would drill a minimum of 21 wells and find 3 producers and 18 dry holes. However, it would have been worth the risk they took, for the 3 producers should return to them one to three times their investment.

As you can see from the above, it should greatly enhance your potential if each drilling program in which you invest has sufficient capital to drill a large number of wells. Drilling for oil and gas not only takes skillful geologic research, but also your chances are greatly increased as you increase the number of wells drilled.

Structure of a Drilling Program • There are many ways to structure a program regarding who bears the cost, who receives the tax advantages, and who receives the income.

In the program described above, the General Partner trades the limited partners (which would be you if you chose this medium) all of the tax advantages and 60 percent of the revenues for a free look at the bottom of the hole.

Let's use an example of a successful well drilled at a cost to the partnership of $100,000. The limited partner would provide $60,000, deduct all the intangible drilling costs, and receive 60 percent of all revenues. The General Partner would bear all the tangible costs of $40,000 that are capitalized over the life of the assets and receive 40 percent of all the revenues.

Many oil and gas managements offer four to five drilling programs per year. Others will offer larger but fewer programs.

In no sooner than 18 months to 2½ years after the initial investment has been made in a drilling program, the company has had time to complete a cycle that consists of the following: (1) drilling the wells in each prospect, (2) arranging outside financing for any subsequent drilling, (3) carrying out subsequent drilling, (4) being evaluated and (5) offering to exchange for stock or a buy-out at a stated amount. Some programs exchange for stock that did not previously exist; hence there is no way of establishing a true market value for it. If this course is used, no taxable gain is made at the time of exchange. Another way is for the limited partners to be offered registered stock in exchange for partnership interests.

When this is done, a capital gains tax is realized, and you would have a tax liability unless you again invest in another drilling program a sufficient amount to offset the gain. When the latter course is followed, the price is determined by the average of the bid and asked prices of the stock for two months previous to the exchange. There is no question of true value of the stock for which it is exchanged, while in the case of new stock this can certainly be a factor. In the past, this has been a very definite shortcoming with too ambitious pricing on the new stock.

You must usually decide within a specified period of time whether to make the exchange for stock. If you do not, you will continue to receive the oil income, but you will not have an opportunity to exchange at a later date.

A third choice may be offered and that is for the general partner to buy your production. The value will be based on the evaluation placed on the reserves by an independent geological engineering firm and discounted back to give credit for the earning power of money.

Your choice will probably be dependent on your income needs at the particular time and your tax considerations.

The program described above is only one of the ways a drilling program can be structured by a sponsor. There are six different ways commonly in use.

Let's first look at the one described above, and then look at five other ways:

Tangible–Intangible Sharing · For income tax purpose, the IRS refers to two basic types of costs in connection with drilling for oil and gas. These are tangible costs and intangible costs. Tangible costs are expenditures for items that can be salvaged. The intangibles, the nonsalvageable costs, may be deducted from current income as a business expense by the investor. In the tangible–intangible sharing, the General Partner bears the tangible expenses, and the limited partners bear the intangible expenses.

Working Interests · In this structuring, the General Partner shares in the operating expenses and net profits of the producing wells. This formula may or may not entail investment by the General Partner. If the General Partner pays no part of further costs, it is called a "carried working interest."

Net Profits Interests · This formula entails no expenses on the part of the General Partner. The investor pays all drilling costs and bears all ex-

penses of operating the wells. The General Partner receives a stated percentage of net profits.

Carried Interests · In this case, the investor carries the General Partner, usually to the casing point, at which time the General Partner is
permitted to buy into the partnership at the original price.

Disproportionate Sharing · This is a common feature. The investor
bears $\frac{1}{3}$ of the total cost of a program and in return receives $\frac{1}{4}$ of any
profits.

Overriding Royalty Interests · Under this formula the investor pays
the cost of drilling and completing wells, and the sponsor receives a percentage of gross revenues.

Tax Considerations in Drilling Programs · The Internal Revenue Service holds that many of the costs of seeking oil and gas, such as expenditures for contract drilling labor and other nonsalvageable costs, are
business expenses that are deductible against current income for tax
purposes. These expenses are called intangible drilling costs. The Tax
Reform Act of 1969 left these cost deductions untouched, while considerably reducing the tax shelter benefits available in real estate, cattle breed-
ing, equipment leasing, farming, and citrus groves. The Act did reduce
the depletion allowance on oil and gas income from $27\frac{1}{2}$ percent to 22
percent, but this is relatively minor. The most important deduction, intangible drilling costs, was left untouched.

I'm often surprised to find clients who feel that it is illegal or at least
immoral to reduce their tax burden. Such is not true, and you should not
feel this way if you do. Once Congress adopts a policy, then you have
the right to avail yourself of that policy. You are entitled to every tax
break the law allows, and oil and gas still comprise the kingpin of all
tax shelters.

Should you consider investing in exploration? The answer to this
question is dependent on your temperament and your tax bracket.

Let's examine various possibilities that may fit your category. Here
we will use an example of a program using a balanced approach. This
program consists of exploratory drilling (high risk, high potential),
semiproven acreage (lower risk, lower potential return) and proven
acreage (lowest risk, lowest potential return). Since only 25 percent of
the funds in this partnership are to be used for exploratory prospects,

your write-off may be less (as will your potential and risk) than those doing only exploration.

Let's take a look at the tax considerations in drilling programs for a married couple filing jointly, a single person, a person with a long-term capital gain, and a corporation.

Married Couple · I am making the following assumptions: $10,000 investment, 95 percent write-off, $54,000 taxable income, married individual filing jointly, and no state and local taxes; federal taxes are based on 1973 rates.

	Without program	*With program*
Taxable income	$54,000	$54,000
Less estimated deductible expenses	0	(9,500)
Revised taxable income	$54,000	$44,500
Federal tax	19,120	14,310
Reduction of tax		$ 4,810

If you fit these criteria, your net out-of-pocket cost remaining from $10,000 is $5,190. If your taxable income is greater than $54,000, the percentage savings may increase.

Single Person · If you are a single person, you pay a greater tax on taxable income. Taxable income in excess of $32,000 is taxed around 50 percent.

Let's make the same assumptions as before with the exception that you are single and have a taxable income of $42,000.

Your picture could look like this:

	Without program	*With program*
Taxable income	$42,000	$42,000
Deductions	0	(9,500)
	$42,000	$32,500
Federal tax	15,490	10,540
Reduction of tax		$ 4,950

Your net out-of-pocket cost for the $10,000 investment equals $5,050.

To aid you in making an intelligent decision about whether you should invest in oil and gas exploration, here is a simple worksheet:

Tax Savings Worksheet
for an
Oil and Gas Exploration Program

	Without investment	With investment
Taxable income	$_____	$_____
Deduction:		
Investment $_____x		
Deductibility _____%	$_____	$__(____)_
Taxable income	$_____	$_____
Federal tax due	$_____	$_____
% rate at top	_____%	_____%
Tax savings		$_____

Summary:

Investment	$_____
Less tax saved	$_____
Out-of-pocket cost	$_____

Long-Term Capital Gains · Perhaps you have sold some property on which you have a long-term capital gain. Even though capital gains are taxed at a lower rate than ordinary income, you may find it worthwhile to consider the possibility of reducing your taxes by investing in a program.

Let's assume you have realized a net long-term capital gain of $100,000, have $54,000 other net taxable income, are married filing a joint return, and are making a $10,000 investment in the program:

	Without investment	With investment
Long-term capital gains	$100,000	$100,000
Other net taxable income	54,000	54,000
Less:		
Capital gains deduction	(50,000)	(50,000)
Deduction from $10,000 investment	0	(9,500)
Taxable income	$104,000	$ 94,000
	$ 45,260	$ 39,945
Reduction of tax payable		$ 5,315

Your net out-of-pocket cost remaining from a $10,000 investment is $4,685.

If you have incurred a large capital gain within the past three years, the tax law permits you to carry net operating losses as far back as three years and receive refunds of taxes paid.

I won't give an example of this possibility, but it is well to discuss it with your CPA.

Another possible way of using oil and gas programs is when you have a large unrealized capital gain in a particular stock and you desire diversification, but you are reluctant to subject yourself to a large capital gain. Sell a portion each year, and use an investment in the program to reduce the tax and also leave funds over for investing in other areas.

Corporations · If you have a profitable corporation, it pays federal taxes each year on its earnings. Corporate earnings in excess of $25,000 are taxed at a 48 percent rate (below that at approximately 22 percent).

Let's look at the numbers, but this time we'll assume an investment of $50,000:

	Without investment	With investment
Taxable income	$100,000	$100,000
Deductions from $50,000 investment	0	47,500
Revised taxable income	$100,000	$ 52,500
Federal tax		
First $25,000 @ 22%	$ 5,500	$ 5,500
Excess @ 48%	36,000	13,200
	$ 41,500	$ 18,700
Reduction in taxes		$ 22,800

Out-of-pocket cost to the corporation from a $50,000 investment is $27,200.

Use Your Tax Shelter Early · Drilling limited partnerships can also reduce or eliminate estimated taxes. I usually recommend investing smaller amounts in several partnerships rather than a large amount in one. This allows you to spread your risk over a larger number of wells. It also gives you the additional benefit of having your annual investment deductible in advance against your estimated tax liability.

This time let's assume you will have a taxable income of $100,000, and that your taxes will be approximately $45,180. Instead of paying an estimated quarterly tax of $11,295, you could invest $5,000 in each of four drilling partnerships. Your tax picture may look like this, assuming 100 percent deductibility:

	Quarterly	Yearly
Taxable income	$	$100,000
Taxes due		45,000
Investment in four drilling partnerships	5,000	20,000
Instead of paying estimated taxes of	11,295	45,180
Reduce your taxable income to		80,000
Pay estimated tax of	8,335	33,340
Tax savings of	2,960	11,840
Cost of investment	5,000	20,000
Less tax savings	(2,960)	(11,840)
Your net cost	$ 2,040	$ 8,160

As you can see, there is a wide range of possible tax savings circumstances during the first year of your investment.

If the oil program you choose also borrows funds for additional development, there may be deductions in excess of your original investment in the year the investment is made and to some degree in following years.

If production is found in your drilling program, then another possible tax advantage occurs that we call depletion allowance.

Depletion Allowance • In addition to your write-off of intangible drilling costs, as previously discussed, the first 22 percent of the gross income each year from oil and gas is tax free, thanks to the depletion allowance.

To illustrate, let's break down the income into $1.00 units, and assume that your program generates $1.00 of gross income and that the operating expenses involved in lifting this oil and gas to the surface total $0.30 (assuming no depreciation). This would leave you a net income of $0.70. The tax depletion allowance would be 22 percent of gross income or $0.22 (but it cannot exceed 50 percent of net income—in this case $0.22 is less than 50 percent of $0.70 minus $0.22), leaving tax due of $0.24 in your 50 percent tax bracket, as well as after-tax cash flow of $0.46 ($0.24 plus $0.22). In this case, 22¢ of every dollar you receive, as long as the wells produce, will be tax free.

To give you a clearer picture of this possible advantage, let's compare your keepable income from one dollar of oil and gas income over one dollar of ordinary income, assuming a 50 percent tax bracket:

	Ordinary income	Oil and gas income
Gross income	$1.00	$1.00
Less: operating expenses	(.25)	(.25)
Net income	.75	.75
Tax depletion allowance (22%)	–	(.22)
Taxable income	.75	.53
Tax @ 50%	(.38)	(.27)
After tax cash received	$ .37	$ .48

Depletion allowance has been given over the years because the asset is being depleted. This same principle is also applied to other areas. However, Congress seems to get emotional when this same principle is applied to oil and gas and constantly talks of eliminating the allowance for oil and gas.

I do not know whether this will occur. Suffice it to say that I have found that any time Congress is in session my money is in "jeopardy."

If depletion is eliminated, the price of oil and gas will have to rise accordingly for the depletion allowance acts as a subsidy.

The law of supply and demand can never be repealed, regardless of how hard politicians try and how ignorant they may be of this basic principle of economics.

If it is profitable to produce a product, it will be produced. If it is not profitable, it will not be produced. Lack of potential profits commensurate with potential gains is the reason for our present shortage of energy.

What Is the Risk of Total Loss? • In the event of total loss—meaning you were so unfortunate as to pick a drilling program that drilled all dry holes—the tax laws do help soften your blow. Dry hole losses are deductible from current income for tax purposes, reducing your out-of-pocket cost.

For example, let's assume you have a pretax income of $50,000 and invest $10,000 in a drilling program that bombs completely. Here would be your picture:

Pretax income	$50,000
Dry hole losses	10,000
Taxable income	40,000
Taxes due	12,000
Taxes without dry hole write-off	17,000
Tax savings	$5,000

Your dry hole loss of $10,000 was reduced to $5,000 because of the $5,000 tax savings.

What is your risk of total loss? How often can you expect that the drilling program you choose will drill only dry holes? Unless the program is very small or management assumes unbusinesslike risks, in my opinion your chances are virtually nil. Statistically a large, well-diversified program operated by competent geologists should find some oil.

If Your Program Breaks Even • If your program breaks even on a dollar-for-dollar basis, you're ahead after taxes. In your 50 percent tax bracket if you have made a $10,000 investment that returns exactly $10,000 over its productive life, you would have approximately a 25 percent after-tax profit despite the fact that the pretax amounts invested and returned were equal.

These numbers in this example would look like this:

Investment	$10,000
Tax deduction	$10,000
Tax savings	$ 5,000
Net cost of investment	$ 5,000
Repurchase price	$10,000
Capital gains tax	(2,500)
Balance on sale	$ 7,500
Net cost	$(5,000)
Net profit	$ 2,500

Upside Potential • The industry is too young to have developed meaningful statistics as to what your chances are of getting your money back.

On the upside what can you hope for? The best drilling program I know of is one that discovered a major gas field in California in 1962. With a $58,000 investment in the program it is estimated that by 1983, the return will be roughly $3 million, based on old oil prices—a 51 to 1 return. Obviously the possibility of your being so lucky is remote.

Importance of Management • As in any business venture, management is the single most important consideration. Determine before you invest if the General Partner has substantial assets, a good reputation in the industry and an excellent past performance record.

You will find drilling program management difficult to evaluate because future performance cannot be directly related to past success. Management's drilling success ratio does not lend itself to making a judgment regarding profitability potential. A company that drills successful wells 90 percent of the time, for example, may not have any profitable wells; but a company with a 10 percent record of success can be profitable.

I try to avoid both high and low success ratios. (Not that I consider this overly scientific, but it has been effective.) A balanced drilling program that consistently achieves a success ratio of 85 percent to 95 percent may be concentrating on low-risk/low-return prospects. On the other hand, if the company has a success ratio below 60 percent, it may indicate that they are drilling too many high-risk prospects or that they are not successful oil finders.

Even this approach does not lend itself to accurate selectivity. The majority of drilling programs now in existence were started since 1968. This means that few of the programs have been in operation long enough for you to judge their success. Drilling programs take time before all prospects have been developed and transportation channels worked out, to permit production of the reserves discovered.

Too, the Securities and Exchange Commission does not permit drilling programs to publish reserve estimates for past programs in their prospectuses. Cash pay-out tables can often be very misleading, especially if the program is a nonassessable one that relies heavily on bank borrowings to finance their development work. This could mean that a large portion of the initial revenues have been used to repay loans; therefore, the investor has not yet realized large returns.

Should You Invest in Exploration? • Not everyone should invest in drilling programs. You should look at your personal finances very critically before reaching a decision. Factors you should consider are:

1 • *Do you have a stable high-level income taxed in the 50 percent or above tax bracket?* I would recommend that you should anticipate this high income for at least three years. This income can come from earned income, unearned income (income from investments) or substantial capital gains. Your tax savings may be greater than 50 percent and may go as high as 70 percent.

The reason I recommend that you should have a high income for at least three years is the fact that even good program managements will have bad years. You should plan to diversify your drilling program investments over several years with the same company. Consistent investment with the same company increases your chances of overall success.

2 · *Do you have substantial assets?* You should not consider investing unless you have assets of $50,000 plus a 50 percent tax bracket or, in the absence of the latter, a net worth of over $300,000. You should also probably have equity in a home, adequate life and medical insurance, and cash reserves.

3 · *Are you temperamentally suited to investing in exploration?* That is, are you willing to assume the risks involved, and do you have the patience to wait for the exploration to be done? If you should draw a blank in your drilling program, will it cause you to lose sleep? You should invest in anticipation of gains, but you must be prepared to accept losses.

Drilling programs are relatively illiquid, and if you were forced to sell your interest in a hurry, you may have to do so at a substantial discount.

You should anticipate being locked in for a period of time sufficient to allow the completion and development of most of the drilling prospects. Otherwise, until drilling is completed, the program's value cannot be accurately determined.

Before investing in any tax shelter, discuss the matter with your CPA, but do find one who has tax savings for you as his chief concern, not just tax tallying.

I have a doctor client in a very high tax bracket who has needed some tax-sheltered investments every year I've had him for a client. Whenever I would suggest a particular shelter to him, he would ask that I submit it to his CPA, which I was happy to do. Unfortunately, his CPA was an uncreative soul who could tell him to the penny how much taxes he owed at the end of the year, but he could not imagine taking any "risks" to prevent paying taxes. So the CPA always turned down each proposal. Finally, I told the doctor, "By saying 'no' to all my proposals, your CPA will never be wrong, but he'll never be right either." The doctor admitted this was true and joined with me in investing in the oil and gas drilling program that discovered a gas field in Louisiana.

Investing in oil and gas exploration is attractive today because the demand has drastically outstripped supply. Oil and gas account for three-fourths of all the energy we consume, and the demand is growing at an unprecedented rate, both here and in foreign countries. It is estimated that on a worldwide basis, there will be more oil consumed during the decade of the 1970s than has been consumed during the entire previous 110 years since petroleum was discovered.

An intelligent approach to financial planning cannot ignore the potential rewards of investing in energy.

Application

Which method of investing in energy best fits your financial objective, your investable funds, your tax bracket, and your need for liquidity? If you have $5,000 to invest in this category and your tax bracket is below 50%, should you invest in energy stocks or income limited partnerships? If your tax bracket is 50% or above, are you temperamentally suited to investing in drilling limited partnerships? If so, which type of sharing arrangement should you use?

15

HOW
To Become
a
Millionaire

It is only fair to tell you I've never helped anyone become wealthy overnight. I've never helped someone with $10,000 turn it quickly into a million. The only people I've ever helped make a million dollars are those who brought me a million dollars to invest. Before you become too impressed, remember that it only takes an average return of 10 percent to double your money in 7.2 years.

I remember calling the office of Percy Foreman, the nationally known and brilliant criminal lawyer. I was calling to invite him to be my guest on my weekly television program, "Successful Texans."

When I asked to speak to him, the receptionist blurted out "He's in jail." After chuckling over this literal response, I left word for him to call me when he "got out of jail." Later that afternoon he called, and I invited him to be our guest. He accepted my invitation; and just as I was about to say my good-bye, he said, "Aren't you that lady stock-broker? Can you make me rich?" I answered, "Mr. Foreman, I understand you are already rich; but I believe I can make you richer."

Let's assume you do not have the elusive million with which to start your high adventure. Is it still possible for you to become a millionaire? The answer is probably Yes, if you have the discipline to save, the inclination to study, and a lifespan of sufficient length.

First, let me say that there are more desirable goals in life than becoming a millionaire. But if this is your desire, there are some very practical ways to approach your objective. To reach any goal, the first step is to divide it into its component parts so that it can be approached one step at a time.

• COMPONENT PARTS
OF A MILLION DOLLARS

What are the component parts of a million dollars? It's $1,000 multiplied by 1,000 isn't it? Trying to reach a million dollars in your lifetime may not be all that difficult to do.

How do you obtain the first $1,000? The most obvious beginning is to save from current income. If you save slightly under $20 per week, you should have your $1,000 in a year. Or if you do not want to wait until you have saved the $1,000, you can start investing as you earn on a weekly or monthly basis from your current income. Another possibility is to borrow the $1,000 from the bank at the beginning and pay the bank back on a monthly basis. This could give you a head start toward your goal.

Therefore, the first requirement for reaching your goal is the ability to set aside the relatively small amount of $20 per week.

• MONEY,
YIELD, TIME

The second requirement is to obtain a high return produced by adherence to aggressive but sound investment practices. These can be readily learned if your desire is strong enough.

Third, a life span of sufficient length.

So you see, the two most important things are time and yield. If you set your sights on a million dollars, you must keep these two factors in mind. Time is something over which you have very little control. But yield is different. I personally feel that anyone of good intelligence has the potential of earning a high return on his investment, and high returns are an absolute must if you ever expect to attain the million dollars. When we speak of "yield," we ordinarily think of income (dividends or interest) as an annual return on the sum invested, expressed in the form of a percentage. For instance, if you receive $5 at the end of a year on a $100 investment, your yield is 5 percent. However, we will broaden this definition for the purpose of this chapter and use "yield" to describe any distribution, plus any growth in market value. For example, if $100 grows to $318 in 10 years, we would say its yield is 12 percent.

One thing I think you must be fully aware of is the magic that comes from compounding the rate of return. This means that you are never to treat any income as spendable income in this endeavor to become a millionaire, but only as something to be reinvested to increase your accumulation. In other words, don't eat your children. Let them produce more children to build your army of little coppers that will be working for you.

LITTLE COPPERS

In thinking of reaching the million dollars, rate of return should include appreciation of the value of your investment, plus the reinvestment of any interest or dividends that you might receive, plus any realized capital gains. For the purpose of our calculations, any taxes you must pay on your investments are deemed as having come from another source.

One of the most important things you must remember is how important the rate of return you receive on your investment is to your compounding. For instance, if you can put to work $1,000 each year and average a compound rate of 10 percent per annum, you will be able to reach your goal in 48.7 years. However, if you can increase this compound rate to 20 percent per annum, you can reach your goal in 29.2 years. So you see, it does make a great deal of difference what return you obtain on your money.

• DIVERSIFICATION AND DOLLAR-COST-AVERAGING

Risk in investing can be reduced by following some basic investment principles. As you have already become aware, two of the most important principles are diversification and dollar-cost-averaging.

Dollar-cost-averaging was discussed in detail previously. As you will remember, it's the ability to invest over a long period of time the same amount of money in the same security at the same interval, with the assumption that the market eventually goes up.

• THE BLUE CHIP SYNDROME

As we have seen, there are those who have the mistaken idea that all one has to do to make money in the market is to buy "blue chips" and throw them in the drawer and forget about them. In my opinion, this can be riskier than buying more aggressive stocks and watching them like a hawk. The "blue chips" of today may become the "red chips" or "white chips" or "buffalo chips" of tomorrow. We live in a dynamic, throbbing, changing economy.

Just think back a few years. What car did the "man of distinction" drive? A Packard. I would have had difficulty convincing my father that only a few years later the manufacturers of the Packard automobile would be out of business. At the same time, what was the chief family home entertainment medium before television? It was radio, wasn't it? And who was the chief manufacturer of that half-egg-shaped wooden box in every home? Atwater-Kent. As you know, the Atwater-Kent Company no longer exists. We live in a world of constant change, and we must always be alert and ahead of this change if we want to become millionaires through our investment know-how. We must sharpen our talents to predict trends before they happen, buy these stocks, and move out of them before the trend has run its course.

If you possess the three "T"s and the "M" we have discussed, you may want to select and constantly supervise your investments yourself. If not, let the pros do it for you.

Let's assume that you are not willing to put forth the effort or take the higher risk to obtain a 20 percent return on your investment, and you decide to take a less-active, aggressive course and only average 15 percent. What investments have yielded near this return?

1 · Carefully managed family businesses have often brought such a return.

2 · Well-located real estate: raw land, commercial income properties.

3 · Some quality growth common stocks. For example, the combined annual return from dividends and capital appreciation on common stocks in Standard and Poor's Industrial Stock Average has been over 15 percent for many periods. Stocks in some industry groups have done even better, and others, of course, have not done this well.

4 · Some growth mutual funds.

Of course, no one can be sure that any of these methods will continue to equal this performance.

• REACHING A MILLION DOLLARS

Let's assume that you are 25 years of age, have saved $1,000, can save $50 per month, can maintain an average of 15 percent performance on your investments, and can pay income taxes from another source. Your progress report should then look something like this:

Age 25	$1,000 + $50 per month
25	$ 1,000
30	8,663
35	18,054
40	40,967
45	87,052
50	179,745
55	466,185
60	741,183
65	1,495,435

If you are 30 years of age and fortunate enough to be able to make a lump sum investment of $10,000, and can obtain an average return of 15 percent compounded annually, and do not add new money to your investment, but do reinvest all distributions, your progress report should look something like this over a 35-year period:

Age 30	$ 10,000
35	20,113
40	40,456
45	81,371
50	163,670
55	329,190
60	662,120
65	1,331,800

• WORKING DOLLARS ARE A NECESSITY

Remember, we are not talking about "guarantees." All we are doing here is obtaining a visual picture of what compounding accomplishes over a period of years if you are able to maintain a 15 percent average.

We do not know what our future economy will be. Of one thing we can be certain, however—you will never reach the million dollars with this amount of savings using "guaranteed" dollars. If you hope to reach your goal of becoming a millionaire, you must save and let your money grow. Investing your money in well-managed American companies, real estate and natural resources will not guarantee growth of capital, but it certainly provides the opportunity for your money to work as hard for you as you had to work to get it. The working dollar is an absolute necessity if your goal is to become a millionaire.

Figure 13 shows how money compounds in a curve, not a straight line.

• SITTING TIGHT

Do not be tempted to rationalize that market conditions are unsettled now so you should postpone starting your investment program. When has the outlook been so obvious that you knew exactly what course to follow? If you take this attitude, you might as well dig a hole and bury your money. There is risk in any investment at any time. There is also a risk in a liquid position because of the steady erosion of fixed dollars due to inflation.

I'm indebted to *Brevits* for the graphic illustration in Figure 14, printed with their approval. As the illustration shows, there are always good reasons for investment inactivity and our "Sitting Tight" friend was expert in discovering them. In so doing he missed an entire lifetime of opportunities.

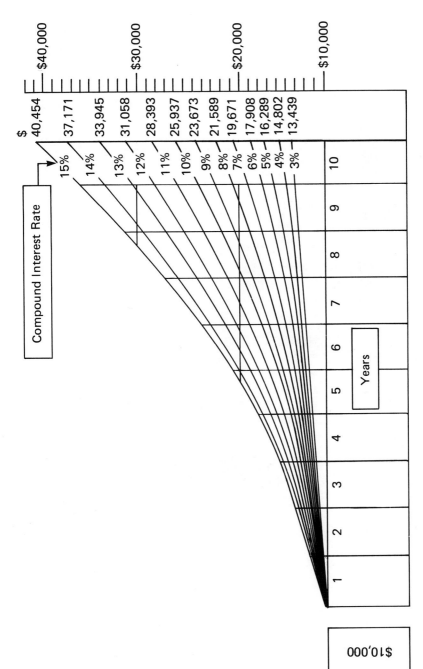

FIGURE 13. Potential $ Value of $10,000 Over a Ten-Year Period at Compound Interest

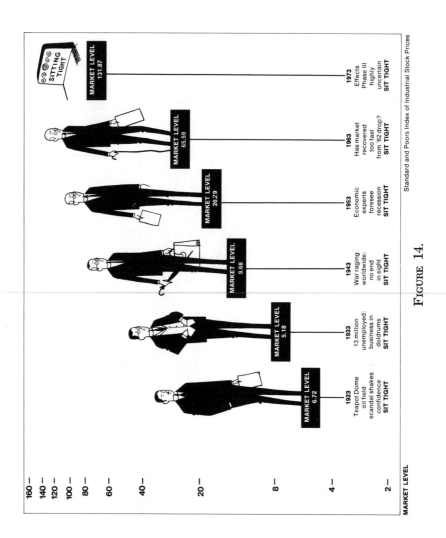

FIGURE 14.

• THE COMMON DENOMINATOR OF SUCCESS

During my 7 years as moderator of a television show, and my 15 years as a financial planner, I've searched for the common denominator of success. In my search one particular characteristic seems to run through each life. That characteristic is that the successful person has formed the habit of doing things that failures do not like to do.

Perhaps you feel that you have certain dislikes that are peculiar to you, and that successful people don't have these dislikes but like to do the very things that you don't like to do. This isn't true. They don't like to do them any more than you do. These successful people are doing these very things they don't like to do in order to accomplish the things they want to accomplish. Successful people are motivated by the desire for pleasing results. Failures search for pleasing methods and are satisfied with results that can be obtained by doing things they like to do.

Let's assume your purpose is to become a millionaire—that your purpose is strong enough to make you form the habit of doing things you don't like to do in order to accomplish this purpose.

To have maximum creativity, your body needs to have pure air, wholesome food, and creative thoughts. When you get home from work, do you grab a can of beer, light up a cigar, and sit in front of the tube to watch a wrestling match or the solving of one of the three to four murders that occur on television each night? Or do you jog, ride a bicycle, or walk a distance; eat a light nutritious dinner, sans large amounts of carbohydrates and saturated fats, but high in proteins, vitamins, and minerals; and then study *Barrons, The Wall Street Journal,* and *Forbes?* The successful investor does these things not because he wants to but because he must to accomplish his goal.

You must, too, if you desire to become knowledgeable. Then you must learn to act upon that knowledge. Failures avoid decision making. Successful people know they must act whether or not they want to in order to accomplish their goal.

Time plus Money plus American Free Enterprise may make you a millionaire. If it does, fine. If it makes you financially independent, that will be a major accomplishment for which you can be justly proud.

Application

Do you really and truly want to become a millionaire? Are you willing to do things you don't enjoy in order to accomplish this goal? What pro-

gram of physical fitness are you planning to follow in order to keep your mind creative and alert? How much of your funds do you want to dedicate to this goal? How much are you willing to invest systematically? How will you invest these funds? Where will you obtain funds to pay your tax liabilities on the earnings as they accumulate? What courses of study do you plan to pursue to help you make decisions quickly and intelligently?

$$\left\{ \begin{array}{c} 16 \end{array} \right\}$$

Avoiding
the One-Way
Trip
to Washington

Learning to keep your hard-earned dollars from taking a one-way trip to Washington may become an all-consuming passion with you as it has with many of our citizens.

This is understandable when you consider that if you were in the 30 percent tax bracket last year, you did not start working for yourself until well into the month of April. If you were "blessed" with a 50 percent tax bracket, you quit working for the government after the middle of the year. I do say "blessed" because it is a blessing to live in a country where you can earn a high income. Of course, you would feel twice as "blessed" if you could keep more of it.

Tax avoidance is using your intelligence. Tax evasion is illegal, and the consequences are unpleasant. It is essential to observe the line of demarcation between the two. How much you can earn is not as important as how much you are allowed to keep. That is what adds to your net worth and buys your daily groceries. If there are legitimate ways of lowering your tax bite, it behooves you to find out what they are and to take advantage of them.

Congress periodically has enacted laws to encourage the shift of funds from taxable sectors of our economy to areas of public need or good by creating tax-free, tax-sheltered, or tax-deferred investments.

There are those who delight in referring to these incentives as loopholes, inferring that Congress was not intelligent enough to design a proper tax bill. They fail to recognize that without the incentives of a potential gain, no funds would be risked in areas when money is much needed for the welfare of our citizens.

Judge Learned Hand, the famous New York State jurist said:

Anyone may so arrange his affairs that his taxes shall be as low as possible: He is not bound to choose that pattern which best pays the treasury. Everyone does it, rich and poor alike, and all do right; for nobody owes any public duty to pay more than the law demands.

Senator Harrison of Mississippi, former Chairman of the Senate Finance Committee, expressed the matter in this way: "There's nothing that says a man has to take a toll bridge across a river when there is a free bridge nearby."

Unfortunately, over the years our tax laws have become so complicated that it takes a great deal of study to avail ourselves of some of their benefits. Jerome Kurtz, a Philadelphia lawyer who specializes in tax matters, has told Congress that, "The existing estate and gift tax system could well be characterized as a government levy on poor advice."

So that you will not suffer any more than is absolutely necessary from the government levy, I will point out a few of the ways you may legitimately use to turn some of your tax liabilities to potential net worth.

But before we do, let's determine your tax bracket. I find that most people do not know their bracket. They assume, for instance, that if they earn $50,000 and do not pay $25,000 in taxes, they are not in the 50 percent tax bracket. Your bracket refers to the amount you will lose to taxes for each additional taxable dollar you add. For example, if you are filing a joint return and have taxable income of $44,000, your federal income tax would be $14,060, your bracket would be 50 percent, and you will lose one-half of any dollar you receive until you reach $52,000; then you begin the 53 per cent level.

Let's now make a distinction among tax free, tax sheltered, and tax deferred.

Tax free means that you will never pay a tax on the income received. Tax sheltered and tax deferred mean you will pay a tax at a later date, and hopefully at a lower rate than if it were taxed now. Tax

shelter usually occurs when the income is classified as a return of principal, thereby reducing your cost basis on the asset that is producing the income. When the asset is sold at a later date, the difference between your remaining cost and your sale price will then be taxed on a capital gains basis. Tax deferred means the taxes are not paid as the income is accrued, but are to be paid at a later date. In a tax-exempt and a ,tax-sheltered investment there is current income. There is no current income with a tax-deferred investment.

- ## TAX-FREE INCOME

Tax-exempt bonds are commonly known as municipal bonds because these securities are issued by local governments, public authorities, and special agencies to finance various needs of the people in their communities. Such services as water and sewer systems, bridges, airports, and schools have been financed in this manner.

Their tax-exempt status comes from a Supreme Court decision that created reciprocal immunity from taxation between the federal and local government. By this ruling, the interest on municipal bonds is exempt from taxation by the federal government, and the converse is true for federal government securities.

If your state has a state income tax, there may be an added advantage to buying municipal bonds issued in your state for such bonds are usually exempt from state taxes as well.

Most municipal bonds are issued in serial form, meaning that a portion matures in fixed amounts at regular intervals ranging from 1 year to 50 years. As a result of this feature there is a vast supply of bonds available maturing in virtually any year you may choose.

Tax exemption can provide you with more spendable income. For example, if you are in the 40 percent tax bracket (you probably should not consider municipals if you are not), only 60 percent of your pretax income is available after taxes. An 8 percent taxable yield provides an after-tax return of only 4.8 percent. Therefore, a tax-free municipal providing a return in excess of 4.8 percent would provide more spendable income.

There has been talk from time to time about Congress' eliminating the tax-exempt privilege inherent in municipal bonds. This speculation has existed for some time, and each attack has been unsuccessful. If such a change should be legislated, it will not, in all probability, have an effect on those bonds issued prior to the legislation. If a change should occur, the scarcity of bonds could easily enhance their value.

Another important feature of municipal bonds is their safety. Next to U.S. government bonds, municipal bonds are considered the safest of all securities. The total number outstanding is around $150 billion, and only a fraction of 1 percent has ever defaulted and that occurred during the Depression years of the 1930s. (The New York and Puerto Rican situation may now pose a problem.)

However, you can select the quality of bond you desire. Moody's Investor Service and Standard and Poor each rate municipal bond obligations according to relative investment qualities.

Here are the rating systems used by each service for the most prominent categories:

Moody's	Standard and Poor's
Aaa	AAA
Aa	AA
A	A
Baa	BBB
Ba	BB
B	B

Using the Standard and Poor's notation system, the following rough definitions can be given to the more prominent categories for corporate bonds, with similar logic applying to municipal bonds:

AAA · Prime or highest-grade obligations, possessing the ultimate degree of protection as to principal and interest.

AA · High-grade obligations, differing from AAA issues only in small degree.

A · Upper-medium grade with considerable investment strength, but not entirely free from adverse effects of changes in economic and trade conditions.

BBB · Medium-grade category bonds on the borderline between definitely sound obligations and those in which the speculative element begins to predominate. These bonds have adequate asset coverage and normally are protected by satisfactory earnings. This is the lowest category that qualifies for commercial bank investment.

BB · Lower-medium grade, possessing only minor investment characteristics.

B · Speculative, with payment of interest not assured under difficult economic conditions.

Types of Municipal Bonds · Municipal bonds fall into three main categories:
Full faith and credit bonds of a state or political subdivision of the state have the full taxing power of the issuing local government available to pay both the principal and the interest.
Special tax bonds have a designated tax (gasoline, liquor, cigarettes) specifically pledged to pay the interest and principal.
Revenue bonds are backed by the earnings generated in a particular facility and do not have the taxing power of a local government upon which to draw. Many of these bonds are of a very high quality and are often rated equal to or higher than some bonds backed by taxes.
There are also a limited number of hybrid bonds that are paid from both taxes and revenues. Industrial revenue bonds have also appeared in recent years. These bonds generally are secured by a corporation that has entered into a lease agreement with a community. The bond issuer is normally a public authority that issues the bonds under its municipal title but receives annual installments from the corporation that is using the facility sufficient to pay the principal and interest on the bonds.

Municipal Bond Trust Funds · If tax-free income fits your financial plans, yet you do not have the expertise to select, the time to supervise, or sufficient funds to diversify, you should consider investing in a municipal bond trust fund. There are a large number of excellent funds offered regularly. They are usually sold in units of $1,000, plus accrued interest to settlement date. Most of them contain a well-selected diversified portfolio of municipal bonds selected from the top four categories. They provide a tax-exempt yield between 6 and 8 percent which they will pay to you on a monthly basis. The funds are closed-end and self liquidating, and usually do not carry a management fee, though a nominal sales charge of around 3½ percent is charged when they are purchased. Although the sponsors are usually not required to do so, they do make a secondary market in the trusts, thereby giving you liquidity if you should so desire.

Should You Invest in Municipal Bonds? • When I am asked that question, my answer is, "It depends on what you are going to do with the money if you do not." If you are planning to put it into a savings account at 6 percent or a corporate bond at 8 percent, and you are in a 39 percent bracket, you obviously would receive more keepable income from municipal bonds. As you will note from the tax equivalent table (Table 21), you would have to receive an income of 9.84 percent to equate a 6 percent tax-exempt income. If you are in a 55 percent bracket, you would need to receive a 13.33 percent yield to be equivalent to 6 percent tax exempt.

Tax-Free vs. Taxable Income • Table 21 is based on federal income tax rates effective during 1974. It gives the approximate yields that taxable securities must earn in various income brackets to produce after-tax yields equal to those on tax-free bonds yielding from 5 percent to 6.9 percent.

The table is computed on the theory that your highest bracket tax rate is applicable to the entire amount of any increase or decrease in your taxable income resulting from a switch from taxable to tax-free securities, or vice versa.

When you are considering tax-exempt income, you should also include your first $200 of dividends from American corporations if you are filing a joint return or $100 on a single return. If you are not receiving at least these amounts in dividends, you are missing some tax-free income.

• TAX-SHELTERED INVESTMENTS

An investment to be sound must be a good investment first and a tax shelter second. However, I find many that are potentially good invest-

Table 21. Yields from Taxable Securities to Equal Savings from Tax-Free Bonds (Taxable Income in Thousands)

Joint Return	$8 to $12	$12 to $16	$16 to $20	$20 to $24	$24 to $28	$28 to $32	$32 to $36	$36 to $40	$40 to $44	$44 to $52	$52 to $64	$64 to $76	$76 to $88	$88 to $100	$100 to $120	$120 to $140	$140 to $160
% Bracket	22	25	28	32	36	39	42	45	48	50	53	55	58	60	62	64	66
5.00%	6.41	6.67	6.94	7.35	7.81	8.20	8.62	9.09	9.62	10.00	10.64	11.11	11.90	12.50	13.16	13.89	14.71
5.10	6.54	6.80	7.08	7.50	7.97	8.36	8.79	9.27	9.81	10.20	10.85	11.33	12.14	12.75	13.42	14.17	15.00
5.20	6.67	6.93	7.22	7.65	8.13	8.52	8.97	9.45	10.00	10.40	11.06	11.56	12.38	13.00	13.68	14.44	15.29
5.30	6.79	7.07	7.36	7.79	8.28	8.69	9.14	9.64	10.19	10.60	11.28	11.78	12.62	13.25	13.95	14.72	15.59
5.40	6.92	7.20	7.50	7.94	8.44	8.85	9.31	9.82	10.38	10.80	11.49	12.00	12.86	13.50	14.21	15.00	15.88
5.50	7.05	7.33	7.64	8.09	8.59	9.02	9.48	10.00	10.58	11.00	11.70	12.22	13.10	13.75	14.47	15.28	16.18
5.60	7.18	7.47	7.78	8.24	8.75	9.18	9.66	10.18	10.77	11.20	11.91	12.44	13.33	14.00	14.74	15.56	16.47
5.70	7.31	7.60	7.92	8.38	8.91	9.34	9.83	10.36	10.96	11.40	12.13	12.67	13.57	14.25	15.00	15.83	16.76
5.80	7.44	7.73	8.06	8.53	9.06	9.51	10.00	10.55	11.15	11.60	12.34	12.89	13.81	14.50	15.26	16.11	17.06
5.90	7.56	7.87	8.19	8.68	9.22	9.67	10.17	10.73	11.35	11.80	12.55	13.11	14.05	14.75	15.53	16.39	17.35
6.00	7.69	8.00	8.33	8.82	9.38	9.84	10.34	10.91	11.54	12.00	12.77	13.33	14.29	15.00	15.79	16.67	17.65
6.10	7.82	8.13	8.47	8.97	9.53	10.00	10.52	11.09	11.73	12.20	12.98	13.56	14.52	15.25	16.05	16.94	17.94
6.20	7.95	8.27	8.61	9.12	9.69	10.16	10.69	11.27	11.92	12.40	13.19	13.78	14.76	15.50	16.32	17.22	18.24
6.30	8.08	8.40	8.75	9.26	9.84	10.33	10.86	11.45	12.12	12.60	13.40	14.00	15.00	15.75	16.58	17.50	18.53
6.40	8.21	8.53	8.89	9.41	10.00	10.49	11.03	11.64	12.31	12.80	13.62	14.22	15.24	16.00	16.84	17.78	18.82
6.50	8.33	8.67	9.03	9.56	10.16	10.66	11.21	11.82	12.50	13.00	13.83	14.44	15.48	16.25	17.11	18.06	19.12
6.60	8.46	8.80	9.17	9.71	10.31	10.82	11.38	12.00	12.69	13.20	14.04	14.67	15.71	16.50	17.37	18.33	19.41
6.70	8.59	8.93	9.31	9.85	10.47	10.98	11.55	12.18	12.88	13.40	14.26	14.89	15.95	16.75	17.63	18.61	19.71
6.80	8.72	9.07	9.44	10.00	10.63	11.15	11.72	12.36	13.08	13.60	14.47	15.11	16.19	17.00	17.89	18.89	20.00
6.90	8.85	9.20	9.58	10.15	10.78	11.31	11.90	12.55	13.27	13.80	14.68	15.33	16.43	17.25	18.16	19.17	20.29

Tax Exempt Yield

ments only with the tax shelter. Before making any investment that attracts you because of its tax-sheltered features, consult with your certified public accountant, who should be thoroughly familiar with your tax situation. If he is not or does not become so, change to one who is knowledgeable and creative.

Always remember that tax shelters involve risk and are usually difficult to sell in a hurry. Funds committed to this type of investment should not be a part of your emergency reserves. You should also be willing to wait for results. The sponsors must have time to put your money to work. Your waiting period for tangible results will probably be at least six months and could be two years or longer.

In the section on real estate, I discussed the commercial real estate investment trust, the commercial real estate limited partnership, and raw land. Let's review their tax characteristics in this section.

Real Estate Investment Trusts • There are two basic kinds of real estate investment trusts. One invests only in mortgages, receiving interest on loans. This provides little or no tax shelter because interest is fully taxable. I do not recommend this type of REIT because of its lack of tax shelter and its volatility caused by fluctuating interest rates.

The second type invests in income-producing commercial real estate and, if properly chosen, can provide good appreciation and good tax shelter. The kinds of properties in which these REITs invest are usually office buildings, hospitals, shopping centers, apartment complexes, warehouses, and motel–hotels.

For example, the trust I have used since 1971 was purchased by my clients at $10 per share. The income last year was $1,200: 21.4 percent was taxed as ordinary income and 5.2 percent as capital gains, leaving 73.4 percent tax sheltered. If you had owned these shares and were in a 30 percent tax bracket, your results would have been as follows:

	Before taxes	*After taxes*
Ordinary income	$256.80	$ 179.76
Capital gains	62.40	33.04
Return of principal (depreciation)	880.80	880.80
		$1,113.60

As you can see, the total cash flow was 12 percent, 76 percent of which was tax sheltered.

Commercial Real Estate Limited Partnerships • If you are in a higher tax bracket and liquidity is not a concern, you may want to consider a limited partnership investment for it usually offers greater tax advantages since deductions pass through to you.

The term "limited partnership," as you will remember, refers to an association between a General Partner who has the expertise to operate in a certain industry and a group of limited partners who have capital to invest. The General Partner manages the business and generally assumes unlimited liability for partnership losses in return for reimbursement of specified expenses and a share of the profits. As a limited partner you and your co-investors would supply most of the money and receive most of the profits, if any. You also trade the right to manage the property for protection against personal liability and partnership debts beyond your original investment.

Limited partnerships and tax-sheltered investments go hand-in-hand. The partnership itself pays no taxes; instead, as a limited partner, you report your pro-rata share of the partnership's profits or losses on your own tax return.

When a limited partnership is publicly registered, the Securities and Exchange Commission has reviewed the sponsor's prospectus. Remember, however, that their guiding principle is full disclosure of all material facts concerning the venture. They do not pass on its investment merit.

In a trust you will know before an investment is made the properties in which they have invested up to the time of the offering. In a limited partnership you will not know. This is called a "blind pool," and properties are selected after the funds are received.

On a real estate limited partnership you should receive a write-off going in. A management team we have been using has provided between 20.5 percent and 31 percent write-off the first year. In addition, they have consistently paid 8 percent a year (2 percent per quarter) completely tax sheltered. Using the minimum write-off and assuming you are in a 50 percent tax bracket, on a $10,000 investment, you would write off $2,000 and save 1,000 in taxes. During the life of the partnership you could receive $800 per year, nontaxable due to the depreciation and so forth, passed on to you. (if properties are held a long period, cash distributions could become partially taxable.)

These would be your current benefits—tax write-off going in and tax-sheltered income currently. Your other two potentials for gain or loss would come at a later time when the properties are sold. Most partnerships plan to sell their properties in 4 to 10 years. When the sales are made, they do not reinvest these funds, but pay them out to the investor. (In the trust they are reinvested.) Upon sale you, as an investor, could benefit from the equity build-up and the appreciation.

Equity build-up comes from the repayment of the mortgages. Management pays the monthly mortgage payments from the rents collected from the tenants. This reduces the debt and thereby increases your equity. When the property is sold, you then benefit from this equity build-up if the sales price is sufficient.

Let's assume the equity build-up is 4 percent per year—on $10,000 this would amount to $400 per year.

Also, commercial property, well selected and maintained in growth areas of the United States, has been appreciating over the past 10 years at approximately 6 percent per year. If this property does as well and if the property is leveraged 3 to 1 (if the partnership has used mortgages), this would give you an 18 percent (6% × 3) appreciation based on your original investment.

At the time the sale is made, any income you have received and have not been taxed on must then be deducted from your cost basis. The remaining profit, if any, would then come out as a capital gain.

New Improved Real Estate • If you want to take more risk, you can participate in partnerships that build on raw land, replace existing buildings, or purchase newly constructed "first owner" properties. These programs utilize leverage, management fees, prepaid interest, and maximum depreciation, thus producing write-offs that may be very high. If you invest in this manner, your goal would be investment recovery through tax savings within five to seven years. Because of the leverage used, you should not expect a cash flow for the first several years.

Most new property programs concentrate on residential development, principally apartments, because more favorable 200 percent "double-declining balance" depreciation is available. Remember, however, that high write-offs, high leverage, and new untried properties create a high-risk investment while they are offering the potential for rapid investment recovery (getting your original investment back) and capital gains (with its favorable tax status).

Income-producing commercial real estate is probably the least risky of the tax shelters you may be considering, but there definitely is risk. Your profitability depends on many things including interest rates, occupancy, operating costs, location, competition, and, above all, management. Quality of the management is the key factor. They must have the ability to conduct successful operations before your partnership can succeed.

Raw Land • Raw land syndications can offer you tax shelter and should be considered if you are in the higher tax brackets. Your interest payments can be deducted, and you may even prepay interest for maximum tax advantage in the year in which you invest, though caution should certainly be used. Real estate taxes on the property are also tax deductible, but be sure you have either sufficient income from the property (through pasture leases, etc.) or sufficient personal income to service the debt.

When you sell your property, if it has been held for over six months, your gain will be taxed at the capital gains rate.

Oil and Gas Income-Limited Partnerships • I have previously discussed the potential of investing in oil and gas production, and you should probably consider this potential through a limited partnership if you are below the 50 percent tax bracket or if exploration disturbs your peace of mind. Let's look at some possible numbers with these assumptions: $10,000 investment; 15 percent cash flow of which 40 percent is depletion and depreciation, 60 percent ordinary income; 40 percent federal income tax bracket.

$$
\begin{array}{rl}
\$10,000 & \\
\times\ 15\% & \\
\hline
\$\ 1,500 & -\ \text{Cash flow} \\
\times\ 40\% & -\ \text{Depletion and depreciation} \\
\hline
\$\ \ \ 600 & -\ \text{Tax sheltered} \\
\textit{Net results} \qquad 900 & -\ \text{Taxed as ordinary income} \\
? & -\ \text{Growth potential}
\end{array}
$$

Here you have the tax shelter of 6 percent (formerly comparable to a municipal bond, now they can be obtained with rates over 7 percent). And you have $900 in ordinary income (less 40 percent federal income tax or $540 net), plus growth potential if the price of petroleum products should continue to escalate. As you can see, the amount you could have to buy groceries can be greatly increased by deriving your income from the proper source. (However, keep in mind that you do have a depleting asset.)

Oil and Gas Exploration Limited Partnerships • I have covered the tax savings potential so thoroughly in the energy chapter, I will not repeat it here except to remind you that if you have taxable income in excess of $44,000, are married, and are filing a joint return (if single $32,000, if a corporation $25,000), you should be considering this type of an investment. I believe the petroleum economics are ripe for potential profits in this area.

In a 50 percent tax bracket you must earn $2 to have $1 to invest if you are planning to invest in stocks or municipal bonds. You need to earn only $1 to invest $1 in an exploration program with 100 percent of your funds spent on intangible drilling costs.

For example, let's assume you have earned $10,000 and invest $5,000 in a stock. You must also send the government $5,000. Your stock must then grow to $11,666 for you to regain your $10,000 net after paying out a capital gains tax of 25 percent on the $6,666 profit you have made.

Varied Uses of Drilling Investments • There are many ways oil drilling investments can be used to eliminate or lower taxes for the individual and for corporations. They can be used to lower corporate taxable income, to eliminate corporate accumulated earnings taxes, to fund contributions to retirement plans, for deferred compensation and stock redemption plans, and to reduce passive income for personal holding companies.

Here are three interesting adaptations that you may find helpful.

Obtaining a Double Deduction • I hope you contribute regularly to your church and to other charities that make a worthwhile contribution toward reducing the pain and grief some must bear. So that you may make an even larger contribution, you may want to consider the possibility of a double deduction if you invest in an oil and gas drilling program that is successful.

Perhaps in the past you have made your charitable contributions in cash or appreciated property such as stocks. The latter allows you to avoid paying the long-term capital gains tax while giving the charity the benefit of the total market value of the stock. You also get to deduct the total value of the contribution.

You may want to consider this possibility. You have invested $10,000 in an oil and gas drilling limited partnership and have taken a 100 percent deduction. Two years have passed, and you have been informed that your investment has a cash-in value of $8,000. You donate your limited partnership certificate to the charity. Your tax picture on this investment might be as follows.

Tax bracket	50%	60%	70%
Investment	$10,000	$10,000	$10,000
Tax deduction	10,000	10,000	10,000
Tax savings	5,000	6,000	7,000
Cost to investor	5,000	4,000	3,000

Charitable contribution:

	$8,000	$8,000	$8,000
Tax deduction	8,000	8,000	8,000
Tax savings	4,000	4,800	5,600
Original cost	5,000	4,000	3,000
New cost or savings	(1,000)	800	2,600

If you were in a 50 percent tax bracket, with the above conditions, your $8,000 contribution would have cost you $1,000. If you were in a 60 percent bracket, you would have come out $800 ahead, and with a 70 percent bracket, the amount would be $2,600.

Elimination of Long-Term Capital Gains · Let's assume you have sold a parcel of raw land, which you have owned for five years, for $150,000 and you have a cost basis of $50,000. You are now faced with a capital gains tax on $100,000. Let's also assume this same year you have a taxable income from your earnings of $50,000 and are filing a joint return. Here is an option you may want to consider.

Invest $50,000 or 50 percent of your gain in a 100 percent tax deductible oil drilling limited partnership. Your numbers could look like this:

Taxable income from earnings	$ 50,000
50% of realized capital gains	50,000
Total taxable income	$100,000
Tax deduction from drilling	50,000
Taxable income	$ 50,000
Taxes due	$ 17,060
Taxes due without investment (alternative method)	$ 45,180
Taxes due with $50,000 investment	17,060
Tax savings	$ 28,120
Summary:	
Investment in drilling	50,000
Tax savings	28,120
Cost of investment	$ 21,880

Using Long-Term Capital Losses · You may have a long-term capital loss. Under our present tax laws you can only charge off $2,000 of loss against $1,000 of ordinary income per year. If you have a sizable loss, it may take you years at this rate to use up your loss.

Let's look at some possibilities of using this loss by investing in a 100 percent tax-deductible drilling limited partnership, creating a long-term capital gain sufficient to offset your loss in one taxable year. Let's assume for our illustration that you have a long-term capital loss of $40,000 and taxable income of $100,000, file a joint return and make a $50,000 investment in a 100 percent tax-deductible drilling limited partnership:

	Without investment	*With investment*
Taxable income	$100,000	$100,000
Deduction	—	50,000
Taxable income	$100,000	$ 50,000
Federal income tax	45,180	17,060
Tax savings		$ 28,120
Investment		$ 50,000
Less tax saved		28,120
Out-of-pocket cost		$ 21,880
Assume 80% repurchase price on $50,000 investment		$ 40,000

This is a long-term capital gain of $40,000 which you can apply against your $40,000 capital loss without paying taxes on the gain:

Repurchase price	$ 40,000
Net cost	21,880
Net profit	$ 18,120

• CABLE TELEVISION

While cable television is a relatively new and small industry ($600 million), it exhibits a consistent growth profile, at approximately 11 per-cent annually, and a remarkable record of stability. There are approxi-mately 3,400 operating cable organizations, and there have been only six recorded business failures since the beginning in late 1948. Penetration into the major television market cities with new communications services offers substantial growth opportunity for cable television for the future.

Some innovative companies in the industry have shown excellent growth through equity acquisition, utilizing private placement through limited partnership. The tax advantages and equity position attendant to this type investment method can be attractive to the high tax bracket investor.

The tax shelter the first year usually runs in excess of 100 percent and amounts to around 210 percent over the first eight years. An approxi-mate 6 percent cash flow, tax sheltered, usually occurs after the first 12 months. If these properties are held beyond eight years, the income anticipation will be higher, but the tax shelter will have run out. If you are still in a high bracket, you would probably encourage the partnership to sell the system, take your capital gains, if appreciated, and invest the proceeds into another system to again obtain tax shelter.

• COMPUTER LEASING

A limited partnership which some of our clients have used is one that engages in the leasing of IBM 370 computers and peripheral equipment. This shelter provided a 150 percent write-off the first year and an additional 20 percent the third (if the client was filing a joint return and had not used his maximum $4,000 bonus depreciation). We anticipate a cash flow beginning the fifth year, and liquidation the eighth, with both the cash flow and the liquidation value, if any, being taxed as ordinary income at that time.

• CATTLE FEEDING PROGRAMS

Cattle feeding program tax objectives can be summarized in two words: "tax deferral" (postponing a tax liability until a later, more convenient time, or usually to give you time to figure out a way to avoid the tax altogether). There's no write-off or depreciation on the cattle, but feed costs, prepaid interest, and management fees are deductible in the year you invest. Because of leverage, first-year write-offs range up to 150 percent.

When the cattle are sold the following year, your net profit, if any, after loan repayment, sponsor's compensation, and other expenses, is taxed as ordinary income. This allows you to shift taxable income from one year to the next, giving you the flexibility of paying the tax or reinvesting in another cattle feeding fund and, thereby, deferring the tax another year.

Most cattle feeding programs employ borrowed funds. If you are a limited partner your funds become a part of the down payment for feeder cattle. The General Partner then borrows additional funds to finance further cattle purchases, plus the cost of feed to be fed during the period. Feeder cattle are purchased and placed in feedlot pens of 100 to 200 animals. Buyers for the lots buy cattle weighing between 400 and 600 pounds. The feed lot operators then feed them a scientifically designed diet in order to maximize their weight gain at the lower cost. In about four to six months they reach a level referred to as "finished" where they weigh between 900 and 1100 pounds. Finished cattle are sold quickly at prevailing market prices since feed costs make it uneconomical to hold them after they reach their optimum weight.

The price the General Partner must pay to obtain feeder cattle, the cost of feed, and the price of finished cattle fluctuates with supply and demand. An investment in only a single feeding program, therefore, can generate for you a significant profit or a significant loss. This will depend on timing of purchases and sales. Price changes are the major cattle feeding risk. However, disease and natural disasters can also greatly affect your profit.

If you feel that cattle feeding fits your tax picture, let me recommend that you diversify. Pick out a sponsor with a good success record and plan to make a small investment in each of his programs for a period of time, depending on your tax picture. This should help to smooth out the peaks and valleys you are likely to encounter, but does not assure a profit. Cattle feeding is an extremely high risk investment as those who were feeding in 1974 discovered.

• CHICKEN AND EGGS

Another program for tax deferral that, in my opinion, has less risk is the chicken and egg operation. The demand for eggs remains more constant than for many products. If you are a two-egg person for breakfast, you will probably continue to be so. If eggs become very cheap, you will probably not eat three instead of two, and, on the other hand, if they become more expensive, you probably will not cut your consumption to one.

There are times when the number of laying hens drops below the level necessary to furnish the desired level of egg production. This may offer an investment opportunity. Some partnerships are structured so they can provide you with a 200 percent write-off in the year the investment is made. This comes about due to the fact that if a laying hen is sold within 13 months of its purchase, the partnership is allowed to expense it in a 12-month period. Feed for the laying hens will also be bought, delivered, and paid for (usually through a non-recourse loan). This is also deductible in the year purchased. Studies have found that in a five-year cycle, the dips and valleys may be smoothed allowing for a profit potential from producing shell eggs. Therefore, most programs are designed to keep rolling over the investment with no interim cash flow and a pay out in five years. This pay out will then be taxed as ordinary income.

If you are in a 50 percent bracket and receive a 200 percent deduction, you have none of your funds invested. (You are investing with what is referred to as soft dollars.) In five years your gain plus your deduction will be taxed at ordinary income rates.

• CAPITAL GAINS ON STOCK TRANSACTIONS

Captial gains, for the most part, unless you receive a large amount in one year, are half tax free.

What is a capital gain? It is any asset that you have held for six months and one day, and then sold at a profit. For example, let's assume you bought 100 shares of a stock for $50 a share or $5,000, and three years later sold it for $100 a share, or $10,000. You would realize a $5,000 capital gain. Our tax laws allow you to divide this amount in half, put $2,500 in your pocket without taxes, and pay on the other $2,500 at your regular tax bracket.

If you are in a 50 percent bracket or above, your maximum tax is 25 percent of the gain, unless you have received extraordinarily high income and capital gains in that year. Look at capital gains as one of the golden ways to receive cash flow.

• PROFIT-SHARING AND PENSION PLANS

If you work for a corporation with a profit-sharing and/or pension plan, you may also be avoiding the one-way trip to Washington, at least for the present. Your company's contribution, and yours, and the compounding return it produces are tax sheltered. When you retire, money that was allocated to service prior to December 31, 1974, will come to you as capital gains, and that contributed since that date will be taxed as ordinary income.

There are several ways to reduce the tax bite at that time. First, since you'll be retired, you'll probably be in a lower tax bracket. Second, you can income average over a period of time. Third, most retirement programs permit you to draw income in several optional ways, in one lump sum, or at a per annum rate. You can select whichever option you wish and whichever serves your purpose best. You may also convert into an annuity. There is one that allows you to select your own investments. Do hire a good certified public accountant that particular year. He should be able to save you taxes, and his fees are tax deductible.

If you are the president of your own small corporation, you may want to consider setting up a profit-sharing and/or pension plan. It allows you to get before-tax dollars into a retirement program and lets them compound tax free. Since you are no doubt calling the shots, you can have a skilled specialist design a plan that will give you the maximum benefit both now and when you retire, while keeping within the IRS guidelines.

Technically, profit-sharing and pension plans are designed to attract and hold good employees, which they do if employees are kept adequately informed. However, since your pay is probably higher than most of your employees', the greatest advantage will usually accrue to you.

Qualified pension and profit-sharing plans are undoubtedly the most attractive of all corporate fringe benefits. Specific details are beyond the scope of this book. Suffice it to say that more and more Americans will be receiving retirement benefits, and these benefits will become a more significant percentage of the average person's accumulated wealth. The impact this will have can be better seen when we realize that total pension/profit-sharing assets now have a value of over $154 billion.

There are many variations of qualified pension and/or profit-sharing plans that can be tailored to the individual employer. However, the basic concept is simple.

1 · The employer contributes dollars in a special account, taking a current tax deduction.

2 · The employee is not taxed at the time of contribution, and assets are allowed to grow without taxation until retirement.

3 · Death benefits paid to a named beneficiary or intervivos trust are estate-tax free. All such proceeds, however, must be attributable to the corporation's contributions.

4 · Lump-sum distributions paid to an employee or beneficiary can enjoy a long-term capital gains tax treatment.

• COMPOUNDING WITH TAX SHELTER

In both pension and profit-sharing plans the income from the investments made under the plans is permitted to compound tax sheltered.

Let's look at the difference this can make to *you* if your employer contributes $1,000 per year and you are in a 35 percent tax bracket.

Without tax shelter		With tax shelter
5 yrs.	$ 3,560	$ 5,751
10 yrs.	$ 8,006	$13,817
15 yrs.	$13,560	$25,130
20 yrs.	$20,499	$40,996

If your company had invested in the Seminar Fund $1,000 each year for your benefit, Table 22 is a summary of past results for 40 years (during the next 40 years, as in the past 40 years, there will probably be periods of escalating stock prices, as well as periods of severe market corrections).

Since this is a book on investments, I will not detail the requirements, tax status, advantages, or disadvantages of a pension versus a profit-sharing plan or a combination of both.

• NONQUALIFIED DEFERRED COMPENSATION PLANS

A nonqualified deferred compensation plan is a commitment by an employer to pay an employee a predetermined amount of money for a specified period of years upon his retirement or termination of employment.

Let's assume you are a highly paid executive. You could choose to have your income reduced and have the amount of the reduction become the substance of a deferred compensation plan. You could also have additional amounts deferred in lieu of a salary increase. This would allow you to reduce your current income tax and have an investment compounding under a tax shelter.

When you reach retirement, you would begin to pay income taxes on your withdrawals. At that time, you will no doubt be eligible for additional tax exemptions as a retiree, and you will probably be in a lower tax bracket.

The nonqualified plan can be installed without prior approval of the IRS. The rules for adoption and maintenance are few, and the plan can be discriminatory. You may have a deferred plan in addition to a qualified profit-sharing or pension plan.

Your corporation, however, cannot deduct from its federal income tax its contributions. As your taxes on this money come due, then the corporation begins to enjoy a corresponding tax deduction.

• SELF EMPLOYED, NOT INCORPORATED

If you are self employed and not incorporated, you should consider a Keogh Plan, a tax-sheltered retirement plan established by Congress in 1962, which we will cover later. The Keogh Plan allows you to contribute 15 percent of your earned income from self employment to your own retirement plan, up to a maximum of $7,500, and to deduct this contribution as an expense of doing business. Also, all earnings compound tax

Table 22. $1,000 Annual Investment
in the Seminar Fund for 40 Years

If you had invested $1,000 per year for this many years ↓		Your annual investments would total ↓	The dividends, which you would have automatically reinvested, would total ↓	Adding your annual investments to these dividends, your total cost would be ↓	And the value of your investment would be ↓
Number of Years	Period Jan. 1 - Dec. 31	Total Annual Investments	Income Dividends Reinvested	Total Cost (including dividends reinvested)	Total Value of Shares December 31, 1973
40	1934 - 1973	$40,000	$214,728	$254,728	$695,518
39	1935 - 1973	39,000	184,249	223,249	599,941
38	1936 - 1973	38,000	159,930	197,930	523,669
37	1937 - 1973	37,000	146,656	183,656	482,031
36	1938 - 1973	36,000	137,246	173,246	452,490
35	1939 - 1973	35,000	122,018	157,018	404,530
34	1940 - 1973	34,000	110,075	144,075	366,879
33	1941 - 1973	33,000	98,236	131,236	329,510
32	1942 - 1973	32,000	86,156	118,156	291,275
31	1943 - 1973	31,000	73,132	104,132	249,881
30	1944 - 1973	30,000	62,020	92,020	214,434
29	1945 - 1973	29,000	53,676	82,676	187,715
28	1946 - 1973	28,000	46,924	74,924	166,024
27	1947 - 1973	27,000	42,016	69,016	150,175
26	1948 - 1973	26,000	37,014	63,014	133,950
25	1949 - 1973	25,000	32,094	57,094	117,859
24	1950 - 1973	24,000	27,245	51,245	101,866
23	1951 - 1973	23,000	22,841	45,841	87,229
22	1952 - 1973	22,000	19,208	41,208	75,012
21	1953 - 1973	21,000	16,157	37,157	64,647
20	1954 - 1973	20,000	13,468	33,468	55,394
19	1955 - 1973	19,000	10,827	29,827	46,188
18	1956 - 1973	18,000	9,159	27,159	40,288
17	1957 - 1973	17,000	7,853	24,853	35,586
16	1958 - 1973	16,000	6,696	22,696	31,341
15	1959 - 1973	15,000	5,415	20,415	26,519
14	1960 - 1973	14,000	4,547	18,547	23,188
13	1961 - 1973	13,000	3,810	16,810	20,273
12	1962 - 1973	12,000	3,127	15,127	17,483
11	1963 - 1973	11,000	2,591	13,591	15,217
10	1964 - 1973	10,000	1,995	11,995	12,605
9	1965 - 1973	9,000	1,530	10,530	10,480
8	1966 - 1973	8,000	1,151	9,151	8,652
7	1967 - 1973	7,000	867	7,867	7,212
6	1968 - 1973	6,000	609	6,609	5,786
5	1969 - 1973	5,000	427	5,427	4,680
4	1970 - 1973	4,000	295	4,295	3,734
3	1971 - 1973	3,000	172	3,172	2,675
2	1972 - 1973	2,000	80	2,080	1,643
1	1973	1,000	25	1,025	762

sheltered until you begin to draw from it. The details of this are covered in the chapter entitled "Are You Self Employed?"

• TAX-SHELTERED ANNUITIES FOR
  EMPLOYEES OF NONPROFIT INSTITUTIONS

If you work for a nonprofit institution such as a school, city, or hospital, you may also qualify for a tax-deferred retirement plan.

Let's assume you are a school teacher. You may request that the school reduce your salary up to 16⅔ percent and have them place the funds into a qualified annuity program through a life insurance company. You thereby avoid paying current taxes on the amount of the reduction. This may also reduce your income sufficiently to reduce the taxes on the remainder.

There are three types of annuities: (1) the fixed, (2) the variable, and (3) the self-directed investment annuity.

Fixed Annuities • I cannot recommend most fixed annuities I have studied. They usually compound at a dismally low rate of return—many as low as 3 percent annually. Even with tax shelter that is not progress at our present rate of inflation.

Figures from the U.S. Bureau of Labor Statistics indicate that an individual would have to earn over $15,000 in 1972 to duplicate the purchasing power of $5,000 in 1940. No economist would suggest that there is even a remote possibility that we will ever return to the 10 percent income tax of 1940 or regain the purchasing power of the 1940 dollar. Whether one considers inflation a destructive force, real or pseudoprosperity, or merely a normal way of life, he must recognize that it will forever be a part of the nation's economic environment.

Despite the foregoing, many people still feel that conservative investment requires a "riskless" savings device such as a fixed annuity, and that any nonguaranteed equity investment is automatically speculative. This attitude is dedicated to the proposition that the long-range economy will be deflationary rather than inflationary, and that the world's economy will stand still awaiting one's retirement.

History, however, has proved beyond any doubt that basing one's financial security on fixed-guaranteed savings vehicles is the ultimate in absurd speculation.

Variable Annuities • Another choice you will have is to use a variable annuity. I have examined a large number and find them discouraging.

They can offer some hedge against inflation if properly managed. However, I find that most of them are managed by a life insurance company and have had lackluster performance. Too, they are usually middle-of-the-road, which may not fit your needs. You may be relatively young and are interested in growth, but your money may be pooled with a person who is about ready to retire and whose objective is income.

Self-Directed Investment Annuity • An annuity you may want to consider is the self-directed investment annuity. Here you have the opportunity to direct the investment of your funds in accordance with your financial objective and temperament. You may select from a wide variety of investments, such as corporate bonds, common and preferred stocks, certificates of deposit, mutual funds, and so forth.

• INVESTMENT ANNUITY

You do not have to work for a nonprofit institution to set up an investment annuity that allows you to defer taxation. By becoming a policyholder of a company offering an investment annuity, you may place various assets into the account and avoid current taxation of their income. Other features that may be important to you are as follows.

You pay no taxes on this account until after you have been returned all of your investment tax free.

Although you will pay taxes on the interest when you withdraw it, you decide which years to withdraw the interest.

Your money is not tied up. You can withdraw it at any time, or you can borrow against it at favorable rates if you prefer.

You don't have to sell your present holdings to get the tax advantages because the account can shelter taxes on presently held bonds, savings accounts or certificates of deposit.

Age 75 is the latest age you can let the funds compound tax deferred without taking complete withdrawal or regular monthly withdrawals. If you die before age 75, your family and heirs will be able to take the investment and the interest in cash and never pay any income taxes on them.

This account passes to your heirs outside of probate. Thus it avoids the expense, delay, headaches, and publicity of passing through the courts.

Let's take an example of the difference this might make in your tax picture. Let's assume you live in California, are married, and file a joint return on $24,000 of net taxable earned income. You would pay a combined state and federal income tax of 44 percent on all dividends and interest income over $24,000.

Let's assume you own a certificate of deposit yielding 7¼ percent. In your bracket your certificate really earns 4.06 percent net after taxes. If the same 7¼ percent yield was generated by a deferred annuity, it would be free from current taxation.

The following shows the difference with and without tax shelter, assuming a fixed return of 8 percent and a 50 percent tax bracket on a $100,000 investment:

Years	Without	With
5	$118,769	$130,213
10	141,060	176,620
20	198,979	324,948
30	280,679	597,841

If you feel this type of tax shelter may be of interest, you should carefully study its costs and potential benefit.

• DO-IT-YOURSELF RETIREMENT PLANS

With the signing of the Employee Benefit Security Act of 1974, if you are not covered under any of the other tax sheltered retirement plans other than Social Security, you may now set up one for yourself, tax deductible.

You may create an Individual Retirement Account, commonly referred to as an "IRA." You may invest as much as 15 percent of your pay into an IRA, up to $1,500 a year, and take a tax deduction for that amount. You may take the deduction even if you take only the "standard" deduction rather than itemizing when you file your income tax return.

You may invest your funds in one of three ways:

1 · You may buy a special annuity that will not begin to pay off until age 59½.

2 · You may invest in a special type U.S. Treasury bond.

3 · You may place the funds in trust to be administered by a bank or other approved institution.

An excellent way to accomplish this would be to select a well-managed mutual fund. Each fund uses as its custodian a national bank, thereby qualifying them to administer the plan. This method can make available the possible advantage of dollar-cost-averaging, as explained in the chapter "Is There an Infallible Way to Invest?"

Your annual earnings on your investment will compound tax free. When you withdraw your funds at age 59½ or later, they may be fully taxable income, though usually at a lower rate than you would have paid during your working years.

The Family Installment Sale • You may own stocks or other assets that have greatly appreciated in value. These may no longer fit your financial objective of more income, or you may desire to lower your risks through better diversification. However, if you sell the asset, you will incur capital gains taxes. This leaves you with that locked-in feeling. Is there a way to postpone a portion of the taxes, obtain diversification, increase your income, and possibly decrease future inheritance taxes?

Yes, there is through the use of an installment sale.

To illustrate the possible advantages of this approach, let's consider the options open to you.

First, you can hold onto your present investments. By taking no action you remain locked in. To avoid capital gains taxes, you would have to keep these investments for the rest of your life. Also, any additional appreciation will further increase the value of your estate for federal tax purposes, as well as your potential capital gains tax.

Second, you can sell your investment for cash and reinvest the proceeds. This creates an immediate capital gains tax (unless you invested half of the proceeds in a 100 percent deductible investment such as an oil and gas drilling fund). Assume you have a cost basis of $20,000 on assets that now have a value of $100,000. Upon sale you realize an $80,000 capital gain. However, your reinvestable proceeds are not $100,000. After the capital gains taxes for most people in the 30 percent to 50 percent income tax bracket, this would range somewhere between $17,000 and $22,000, thereby reducing the amount available for investing.

Third, you can make an installment sale. Under this plan you would sell your asset to a buyer at its full market value. The buyer would give you an interest-bearing installment note. In this way you incur capital gains liability only as you actually receive payments from this note. The provisions of the note establish the amount of money you will receive at specified intervals and the period of years over which the periodic payments will be made.

Advantage to the Seller • There can be advantages to you, the seller, and to the buyer. Let's examine some of them, and for the purpose of our discussion let's assume the buyer is your son.

First, you can unlock your gains and spread your tax liability over a period of years, possibly putting you into a lower tax bracket. Second, you can increase your income over the term of the note. Third, the payments you receive are taxable as capital gains. Fourth, as the note is repaid and the payments spent, the value of your estate decreases for federal estate tax purposes. Any growth in assets you have sold now belongs to the buyer and will not be reflected in your estate. Fifth, it protects your estate against possible increases in estate taxes on the future appreciation of your investments.

Advantages to the Buyer · The installment sale allows your son to become the owner of substantial assets, without making any large and immediate cash outlay. He can now sell his newly acquired stocks or other assets without the payment of substantial income gift or estate taxes and put the proceeds into a more appropriate investment. He may also receive an annual tax deduction for the interest he is paying on the note. In the meantime, all future growth belongs to him.

How To Fund the Installment Sale · One of the best ways, in my opinion, to provide the necessary funds for the monthly payments your son will need to make to you is for him to invest the proceeds from the sale of the assets in shares of a high-quality, middle-of-the-road mutual fund and begin a systematic withdrawal program. In this way the investment would be diversified in a quality cross-section of stocks and be professionally managed, and the custodian bank would send a monthly check to you.

The proper legal instruments to accomplish an installment sale should be prepared by your attorney and should be coordinated with the advice of your CPA. Remind them that the note should be carried at interest. The interest may be stated or unstated. If stated (which I recommend), it must be at least 4 percent per year. In the event the interest stated is less than 4 percent, or if no interest is stated at all, Uncle Sam will impute a 5 percent interest rate.

A summary of the advantages of the installment sale are:

1 · Avoids some of the cost of probate (balance of the note is in the estate).

2 · Saves on the costs of federal estate taxes (since only the balance of the note is in the estate).

3 · Saves on state inheritance taxes (since only the balance of the note is in the estate).

4 · Spreads the long-term capital gains tax over a number of years.

5 · Eliminates or drastically reduces the preference tax.

6 · The transfer is not a gift.

7 · No future appreciation to increase estate valuation.

Private Annuity • Another tool which may fit your financial objective is the private annuity. This type of an annuity involves the transfer of your property to a transferee—an individual, a partnership, or a corporation—in exchange for an unsecured promise to make periodic payments to you in fixed amounts for a designated period of time. In most cases, this will be for your lifetime.

The assets you may use for this are real property, stocks, bonds, mutual funds, limited partnerships and so forth.

The advantage to you in using this method is that it can usually increase your cash flow from your assets without substantially increasing your income tax liability. Capital gains taxation will be spread over the life of your agreement. This should serve to reduce and probably eliminate any minimum preference tax that otherwise might accrue on the sale of your assets.

The transfer can be a gift. If you choose not to make the annuity a gift, the three-year contemplation of death rule should not apply. Since these assets are generally not includable for estate tax purposes, there could be a savings on estate taxes in the event of your premature death. The private annuity can be partially taxable under the estate under certain conditions which your attorney can detail for you. This transaction does not have to show a gain as in the case of an installment sale.

There are some disadvantages to the private annuity. If you should die prior to completion of the agreement, your son would have a low basis in the property. If your son holds the property for more than six months the gain is subject to treatment as a long-term capital gain. If you live longer than the life expectancy table indicates, the payments may be greater than the original value, but the tax savings and appreciation could more than make up for this. Also, there is no tax deduction accruing to your son for interest paid to you. Too, another disadvantage is the provision that you are unable to secure the annuity payments by collateratizing through a trust or by mortgage.

The installment sale and private annuity can be funded in various ways. Some that you should consider are oil and gas limited partnerships, mutual funds, real estate limited partnerships, tax-free bonds, and quality stocks with generous dividends.

In summary, the advantages of the private annuity are:

1 · Avoids all the costs of probate.

2 · Saves on federal estate taxes in premature death and after the transferor's mortality.

3 · Saves on state inheritance taxes.

4 · Spreads the long-term capital gains tax over a number of years.

5 · Eliminates or reduces the preference tax.

6 · The transfer can be a gift or not a gift.

7 · No future appreciation to increase estate valuation.

The Living Trust • The proper use of the living trust (also referred to as the revocable or the intervivos trust) can reduce the cost of passing your assets to your heirs.

With the living trust a pour-over will should be drawn to cover all assets you have not registered to the trust. You should have the trust drawn in the state you reside.

Your trust can be written so as to pass your assets as you would do in a will. Some states will allow you to be your own trustee. Some require co-trustees. You may also use a bank or corporate trustee. All of the assets you want to place in the trust should be listed. As changes are made the list should be changed.

The trust can offer the following benefits:

1 · The cost of probate and administration fees saved because the trust assets are not probated through the courts.

2 · The prolonged probate time can be saved as the assets can be passed immediately. All creditors must be paid, and the federal estate taxes and the state taxes can be put into an escrow account with the trustee liable.

3 · The problem of incapacity is lessened. Generally, under the will method the individual has no document while he is alive, and, should incapacity occur, the court must be petitioned to declare him incapacitated in order to sell any property. The document can state that three doctors can declare the individual incapacitated and the co-trustee or successor trustee assume the trustee role.

4 · The trust can afford privacy in death as to the amount of the assets held in the estate since it does not go through the probate court. No listing of assets is required, which usually ends up in the local papers.

5 · A trust can keep the estate under family control. Since assets such as stock, property, or closely held corporations or businesses are not under court control, these can be sold to raise cash for costs and fees and for state and federal estate taxes.

6 · The savings of federal and state inheritance and estate taxes may be achieved by splitting the assets between husband and wife into two trusts. Since spouses can gift each other and 50 percent of the gift is gift-tax free, and there is a $30,000 lifetime exemption plus $3,000 per year, you can divide an estate with little or no cost as the federal gift tax is generally much less than estate taxes at the higher levels.

There are some assets you should avoid placing in the living trust. Some of these are cars, jewelry, furs, and furnishings. You also should not place in the trust professional corporation stock since most states require that the stockholder be of the same profession as the original stockholder.

Also, you cannot place in the trust tax option corporations and subchapter "S" corporations—since a trust cannot be the owner of such stock as it would terminate the election.

The transfer of assets into a living trust is not a taxable consequence. (Gift taxes can occur when assets are placed into short-term or irrevocable trusts.)

• SUMMARY

If you are in the 50 percent tax bracket or realize a large capital gains in a particular year, you should consider investing in oil and gas drilling programs, real estate with high tax deductions, and perhaps cattle feeding programs when under time limitations.

These càn be in the form of limited partnerships, joint ventures, or private placements. You may want to restrict yourself to limited partnerships registered with the SEC unless you or your respected advisor has considerable sophistication in the particular field under consideration and has personal knowledge of the joint venture and private placements.

Effective June 10, 1974, the SEC issued a "Notice of Adoption of Rule 146 Under the Securities Act of 1933—Transactions By an Issuer Deemed Not to Involve Any Public Offering." This ruling exempted certain offerings with less than 35 investors. The burden of determining who is eligible to qualify as an investor was shifted to the financial planner selling the partnership.

My interpretation of the rule boils down simply to this: To be eligible to make the investment in an exempt partnership, you must be rich and smart, or be rich and have a smart friend (technically called the "offeree representative").

With the increased scarcity of venture capital, Rule 146 may be the salvation of the capitalistic system in the United States.

If your tax bracket is below 50 percent, you should consider such investments as oil and gas income-limited partnerships and real estate income-limited partnerships with smaller deductions and less tax shelter.

In all of these, you should look for a capable management team with an excellent past record. You should not try to make a killing on any one of your investments. Keep in mind that your goal is to take ordinary income and convert it into long-term capital gains or to delay the income to a lower tax year. Remember that income from shelters is not usually earned income which receives the more favorable 50 percent maximum tax consideration. It is other income which may be taxed up to 70 percent. Purchase your shelters early in the year. Drilling rigs are usually less expensive, and drilling prospects may offer greater profit potential. Cattle and feed may be lower priced. At the end of the year, everyone is looking for shelters, and the competition is fierce. Pressure to save your tax dollars may cause you to invest without proper investigation.

The operation, taxation, and investment characteristics of the various tax shelters vary greatly; however, most of them have certain aspects in common: They are complex, involve risk, and are illiquid. But then the alternative involves considerable risk too—that of paying taxes—and sending those hard-earned dollars on their one-way trip to Washington.

Application

What will be your taxable income this year? What federal tax bracket is this? What state and county income tax percentages must you pay? In which potential tax-sheltered investment areas do you have the greatest interest and expertise? What steps are you going to take to search out and study limited partnerships that offer tax shelters? How can you best employ these "soft" tax dollars.

$$\left\{ \begin{array}{c} 17 \end{array} \right\}$$

Are
You
Self Employed?

- **MR. KEOGH**

Are you self employed as a professional person or a proprietor of an unincorporated business? If so, you probably work longer hours than your friend who works for a corporation; but you probably enjoy your freedom and independence. However, when you sit down at the beginning of each year to assess your financial progress and begin to make plans for the new year, you may become painfully aware that the tax bite left you very little to invest for the golden years of retirement.

At that time you may look with envy at your friend who works for a corporation with a pension and profit-sharing plan or who has incorporated his business and set up such a plan. Contributions have been made for his benefit in a retirement plan with "before-tax" dollars while you, if you are in a 30 percent tax bracket, had to earn $1.36 to have $1.00 left to set aside to invest for your retirement.

Congressman Keogh felt this was an inequitable arrangement, so in 1962 he was successful in getting Congress to enact the Self-Employed Individuals Tax Retirement Act, HR-10. With the passage of this legislation and later amendements, it became possible for you, if you are self employed, to establish a Keogh Plan for your retirement.

• YOUR CONTRIBUTIONS

The plan allows you as a self-employed individual to set aside 15 percent of your earned income (after expenses and before income taxes) or $7,500, whichever is the smaller of the two.

If you have employees, you must also include all full-time employees who have been in your employ for three years. Full-time employee is defined as one who works for you at least 1000 hours per year (but may drop below this number without elimination).

If you have had your self-employed status less than three years and are setting up a plan for yourself, you must also do the same for each employee who has worked for you the same period of time. Here is a rule that may help you to answer questions you may have with regard to contributions you must also make for employees: "You must do for your employees what you are doing for yourself, if all conditions are the same."

HR-10 Calculations • As an example: if your earned income from self employment is $25,000 for the year, you have been in business two years, you have an employee who has worked for you for those two years, and you pay him $6,000 per year, you must include him. Your Keogh contribution would be:

$25,000 × 15% = $3,750 contribution for yourself

$ 6,000 × 15% = $ 900 contribution for your employee
$4,650

In a 36 percent tax bracket, you are saving a tax on $3,750 × 36 percent, or $1,350 on your contribution. You may also deduct 36 percent of your $900 contribution to your employee's retirement program. This would amount to $324, making your cost for the employee $576 ($900 − $324 = $576). You saved $1,350 on your taxes, less the $576 it cost for your employee, giving you a net savings of $774. You, therefore, have been privileged to buy $3,750 of securities at an actual cost to you of $2,976.

The Higher Your Income, the Greater Your Advantage • If, however, you are netting $50,000 annually, and have one employee who you pay $6,000, you are still limited to a $7,500 contribution on your own behalf. Since $7,500 is 15 percent of your income, you must contribute 15 percent of the employees' income or $900. Your net gains would be as follows:

Contribution for your Keogh	$7,500
Contribution for employee	900
Total contribution deductible	8,400
Your after tax cost ($8,400 × 50%) =	$4,200
Tax savings	4,200
Securities purchased	7,500
Net gain in year contribution was made	3,300

If your income is above $100,000, you will not be permitted to count more than $100,000 of earnings in figuring the amount you may set aside. Therefore, you would use a set-aside factor of 7½ percent to invest the maximum of $7,500. To meet the nondiscrimination rules, you must also contribute 7½ percent of your employees' pay.

Do You Have a Large Payroll? • Not all self-employed persons, of course, can benefit equally from the law. Take the case of Dr. Williams, age 35, who has a taxable income of $22,000 and an eligible payroll of $12,000.

The law allows Dr. Williams to invest $3,300 or 15 percent of his income. His tax saving on this amount would be $1,056 in a 32 percent tax bracket. But he must also contribute 15 percent of his payroll or $1,800. This, of course, is classified as a business expense and gives him a further tax savings of $576. By adding the $1,056 to the $576, we have a total tax saving of $1,632. That means that the cost of the Keogh Plan to Dr. Williams is $168 a year ($1,800 less $1,632).

Remember, though, that's not the end of the story because of the tax-free accumulation feature. Over the years this could overshadow the small annual cost since no taxes are payable until retirement.

If Dr. Williams did not want to contribute to his employees' retirement program, he could set up his own individual retirement account (covered more fully in the chapter "Avoiding the One-Way Trip to Washington") and set aside $1,500 tax deductible. The same provision was established for those who do not qualify for Keogh or are not under a qualified pension or profit-sharing plan.

Voluntary Contributions • If you have at least one employee under a Keogh plan, you may also make a $2,500 voluntary contribution (or 10 percent, whichever is the smaller). This must be made with after-tax dollars; but, again, the dividends and capital gains compound tax sheltered during the time they are in the plan.

Your employees may also make voluntary contributions up to 10 percent of their salary.

The principal in this account may be withdrawn without penalty. If you are in this position and have children whom you plan to send to college, this may be a good way to accumulate funds for this purpose. For example, let's assume you have placed $2,500 per year into your voluntary account. In ten years it's college time. You may withdraw the $25,000, leaving the earnings to continue compounding tax free.

• INVESTING YOUR RETIREMENT FUNDS

Once you have decided to adopt the Keogh Plan, you are then faced with a decision as how to invest your contributions. The law permits alternatives: a bank-administered plan, annuities, a special savings and loan account, a special government bond, or a mutual fund. Of these, in my opinion, none compares with the mutual fund from the standpoint of flexibility and potential for growth to offset the inroads of inflation.

They also publish their past performance records which may be of help to you in programming possible future benefits (with no guarantee, of course).

Assuming you have chosen the mutual fund route, you may want to consider investing monthly as you earn. This gives you the possible benefits of dollar-cost-averaging. For example, if you are contributing $7,500 to the plan, you might invest $625 per month.

You may also consider a lump sum investment at the begining of the year so your dividends and capital gains, if any, could be compounding throughout the year. Market conditions each year will determine which approach would have been best.

I find that most of my clients wait until we call to remind them that it's time to make their yearly Keogh contributions. We do this at the end of November.

• UNDERSTANDING YOUR BENEFITS

In my opinion, if you are self employed, do not have too many employees, and do not have a Keogh plan, you just do not understand the situation. (An exception might be if you are in a 50 percent tax bracket or above and are willing to use these dollars in over 100 percent tax-deductible investments.)

First, it allows you to buy securities or savings accounts at a discount. Uncle Sam is paying part of the cost of your retirement program. (At least he is not taking this amount away from you so you can have some to set aside.)

Second, the earnings compound tax sheltered. We are so accustomed to paying taxes we've forgotten what tax shelter can mean. You may begin withdrawing retirement benefits at 59½ years of age and must begin withdrawals at 70½.

Some self-employed professionals will not set up a Keogh Plan because they can't withdraw these funds until they are 59½ years of age without some penalties. It is usually a blessing that the funds cannot be withdrawn or pledged at the bank for collateral. You would be amazed at the number of professionals who arrive at what was supposed to be their golden years and find themselves scrimping to eke out an existence that is not so golden.

The Magic of Tax-Sheltered Compounding • When you add to the benefit of tax shelter the phenomenon of compounding, you have double forces working for you.

Let's assume you can afford to set aside $2,500 per year. If you have a tendency to dismiss this as just insignificant, let's take a look at what this can mean to you.

If you contribute $2,500 per year from age 35 to age 65, you will have contributed $75,000. (And remember, these are before-tax dollars.) If you average 6 percent on your funds, this will grow to $209,504. If you move up to 10 percent, this amount will grow to $452,356. If you do as well as our Seminar Fund has in the past (with no guarantee of the future), your funds would have averaged $675,731. If you could have contributed $7,500, your results would be tripled, or $2,027,193.

These funds are "tax sheltered" instead of "tax free" because at retirement you will have several choices as to how you will receive your benefits, and your tax will vary accordingly. These conditions seem to be changing so rapidly it's difficult to give you any estimates about what will be your tax status in the future. However, after retirement, you are usually in a lower tax bracket. Also, there is presently an income-averaging formula the IRS allows. Even if the funds were taxed as ordinary income, which can usually be avoided, just the privilege of compounding without taxes for 30 years will make a tremendous difference in your results.

It Does Make a Difference • Here is an example using the Seminar Fund with and without Keogh:

A • Without tax-sheltered benefits (assumed 50 percent tax bracket)

B • With tax-sheltered benefits

Tables 23 and 24 cover the period from January 1, 1957, through September 30, 1972. I chose this period because it is about an average 15-year period. There were thirteen 15-year periods that did better, and thirteen that did not do as well since the fund was formed. This period, on the whole, was one of generally rising common stock prices, but it also includes some interim periods of substantial market declines. Results shown should not be considered as a representation of the dividend income or capital gain or loss that may be realized from an investment made in the fund today. A program of the type illustrated does not insure a profit or protect against depreciation in declining markets.

The illustrations assume an investment in the Seminar Fund by a self-employed individual who is in a 50 percent bracket each year and who invested $2,500.

Example A—Without Tax Shelter • In example A, without tax shelter (Table 23), only 50 percent, or $1,250, is available for investment after taxes; also, 50 percent of the income dividends and 25 percent of the capital gain distributions received go for taxes each year.

An initial investment of $1,250 was made on January 1, 1957, and additional investments of $1,250 were made annually each January 1. Income dividends were reinvested, and capital gain distributions were taken in additional shares. Shares were purchased at offering price that included a sales charge.

Example B—With Tax Shelter · Example B (Table 24) is an illustration of an assumed investment program in which the entire $2,500 is available for investment since the Act permits a full deduction for all contributions made by an employer after December 31, 1967. All income dividends and capital gain distributions are also figured as reinvested since they are free from federal income tax until they are withdrawn from the plan. A decreasing sales charge (starting with 8½ percent on the initial purchase and falling to 4½ percent on the most recent purchase) was included in the price of shares purchased since purchases of the fund are eligible for a reduced charge under the right of accumulation.

Summary

Potential Tax Savings on $2,500

	Example A Without tax shelter	Example B With tax shelter
Total invested since January 1, 1957	$20,000	$40,000
Income dividends reinvested	3,349	16,167
Total cost (including dividends reinvested)	23,349	56,167
Value of investment on September 30, 1972	$37,869 *	$98,311 *

* Includes value of shares acquired through capital gain distributions.

The above figures summarize the following tables which show two assumed investment programs in The Seminar Fund and are based on an assumed tax bracket of 50 percent. Investors in other tax categories would have proportionately larger or smaller savings.

Over the 15¾ year period during which the program was in effect, Example B would have produced $98,311 (before taxes), or nearly three

Table 23. Illustration of a 15-3/4-Year Assumed
Retirement Program—Without Tax Shelter

| Year Ended Dec. 31 | Cost of Shares | | | Value of Shares | | | | Dollar Amount of Capital Gain Distributions Taken in Shares§ |
| | Total Annual Investments (cumulative) | Income Dividends Reinvested† | | Acquired through Annual Investments | Acquired as Capital Gain Distributions (cumulative) | Sub-Total | Acquired through Reinvestment of Income Dividends (cumulative) | |
		Annually	Cumulative					
1957	$ 1,250	$ 16	$ 16	$ 919	$ 44	$ 963	$ 14	$ 46
1958	2,500	35	51	2,796	146	2,941	60	79
1959	3,750	51	102	4,101	385	4,486	114	231
1960	5,000	72	174	5,039	621	5,660	183	241
1961	6,250	86	260	7,050	1,046	8,096	298	332
1962	7,500	104	364	6,640	1,095	7,735	347	277
1963	8,750	123	487	8,941	1,616	10,556	527	347
1964	10,000	148	635	10,806	2,341	13,147	711	605
1965	11,250	176	811	13,939	3,608	17,546	1,017	852
1966	12,500	232	1,043	13,798	4,361	18,158	1,157	1,126
1967	13,750	284	1,327	17,911	6,178	24,089	1,675	927
1968	15,000	355	1,682	20,790	7,777	28,567	2,204	854
1969	16,250	401	2,083	17,877	7,633	25,510	2,184	1,447
1970	17,500	439	2,522	18,072	8,202	26,273	2,546	951
1971	18,750	469	2,991	21,489	9,637	31,126	3,323	472
1972‡	20,000	358	3,349	23,864	10,146	34,010	3,859	—
							Total	$ 8,787

‡to September 30
†Income dividends reinvested after assumed withholding of 50% of each distribution for Federal income taxes
§capital gain distributions taken in shares after assumed withholding of 25% of each distribution for Federal income taxes

Table 24. Illustration of a 15-3/4-Year Assumed Retirement Program—With Tax Shelter

Year Ended Dec. 31	Cost of Shares			Value of Shares				Dollar Amount of Capital Gain Distributions Taken in Shares
	Total Annual Investments (cumulative)	Income Dividends Reinvested		Acquired through Annual Investments	Acquired as Capital Gain Distributions (cumulative)	Sub-Total	Acquired through Reinvestment of Income Dividends (cumulative)	
		Annually	Cumulative					
1957	$ 2,500	$ 65	$ 65	$ 1,838	$ 119	$ 1,957	$ 58	$ 124
1958	5,000	145	210	5,591	395	5,986	244	215
1959	7,500	212	422	8,202	1,058	9,260	467	639
1960	10,000	304	726	10,078	1,721	11,799	761	676
1961	12,500	371	1,097	14,128	2,928	17,056	1,250	949
1962	15,000	455	1,552	13,324	3,089	16,413	1,477	802
1963	17,500	542	2,094	17,959	4,603	22,562	2,262	1,023
1964	20,000	660	2,754	21,762	6,755	28,517	3,075	1,809
1965	22,500	802	3,556	28,095	10,545	38,640	4,445	2,590
1966	25,000	1,083	4,639	27,827	12,929	40,756	5,125	3,484
1967	27,500	1,348	5,987	36,146	18,511	54,657	7,511	2,935
1968	30,000	1,725	7,712	41,973	23,512	65,485	10,023	2,730
1969	32,500	1,991	9,703	36,107	23,372	59,479	10,097	4,704
1970	35,000	2,221	11,924	36,513	25,365	61,877	11,972	3,160
1971	37,500	2,398	14,322	43,433	29,962	73,395	15,826	1,615
1972‡	40,000	1,845	16,167	48,244	31,547	79,790	18,521	—

Total $27,455

‡ to September 30

times the amount produced by Example A (after taxes). Three basic factors accounted for this result:

1 · The investor was able to invest $20,000 more under Example B because he did not have to use this money to make tax payments.

2 · $16,167 in nontaxable dividends was reinvested instead of the $3,349 left after taxes in Example A.

3 · Shares were received for the full $27,455 of capital gain distributions instead of the $8,787 left after taxes in Example A.

The $98,311 (79,790 + 18,521)) produced by Example B, however, would be subject to income taxes when distributed from the retirement plan. Assuming a joint return, the net amount received as a lump sum from Example B after taxes would have been $77,726, if there was no outside income in the year of distribution. Thus, it may be seen that the results obtained from an investment in Example B were greatly increased by the postponement of taxes until after retirement.

• COMMONLY ASKED QUESTIONS ABOUT KEOGH

Here is a list of the most commonly asked questions about Keogh plans. I have given the answers as I interpret the Keogh provisions. If you have a question not answered here, I suggest you call the IRS. You'll find them most helpful.

1 · *Q: How much can I contribute to a Keogh plan?*
A: You can contribute up to 15 percent of your earned income with a maximum of $7,500.

2 · *Q: Do I save federal taxes by contributing to a Keogh plan?*
A: Yes, you are allowed to deduct from your pretax earnings the total contribution made on behalf of yourself and your employees during the taxable year.

3 · *Q: Are there other tax benefits for the Keogh plan?*
A: Yes, all interest and all dividends and capital gains earned by your Keogh plan are accumulated free from current taxation.

4 · *Q: Is a "silent partner" eligible for a Keogh plan?*
A: No. To be eligible for a Keogh plan your income must be derived from personal services and be considered "earned

income." An individual who has merely contributed capital to an enterprise, but not his time, is not considered eligible for Keogh.

5 · *Q: Can I be covered under a corporation or government retired plan and also have a Keogh plan?*
A: Yes, if you have earned income from personal services, as well as corporate or government income, you are eligible for a Keogh plan.

6 · *Q: What if my partners refuse to join the Keogh plan—may I have one?*
A: Yes, a partnership can establish a Keogh plan covering only those partners who consent to participate.

7 · *Q: Do I have to include my employees?*
A: Yes, but you may exclude all part-timers who work less than 1000 hours per year and employees with less than three years of service (with some exceptions).

8 · *Q: Do I have to contribute 15 percent of my employees' pay?*
A: No, not necessarily—the " minimum" percentage that you may contribute is determined by what percentage of your personal income you are contributing to the plan. For instance, an individual earning $50,000 a year and contributing $2,500 to a Keogh plan is actually contributing 5 percent of his pay to the plan. He may apply that same 5 percent figure to all of his employees.

9 · *Q: Are there other tax advantages for my employees?*
A: Yes, your employees have the same advantage of employees covered by corporate retirement plans. For instance, they are not taxed currently on the plan contribution made in their behalf, and their earnings under the plan compound for them tax free.

10 · *Q: Can I put my wife on the payroll so that she can qualify for Keogh benefits?*
A: Yes, if your wife is now an employee of yours, she'll be covered under the Keogh plan. If she works for you but is not formally recorded as an employee, you may place her on the payroll and she becomes qualified for Keogh coverage.

11 · *Q: Can my employees and I make voluntary contributions that are not tax deductible but have the same tax shelter on earnings?*
A: Yes, if you have at least *one employee* who is covered and you permit him to have voluntary contributions, you and

your employee can contribute up to 10 percent of your compensation. Though you receive no tax deductions for these contributions, the money does compound tax free in the plan. You may withdraw from the plan, at any time, up to the amount you have contributed voluntarily without incurring any tax liability.

12 · *Q: When may I receive distributions from my plan?*
A: Your retirement benefits may not ordinarily be withdrawn from the plan until you reach the age of 59½ years, and you must start withdrawing at age 70½ years. You may select any age within this range as your retirement age.

13 · *Q: How are my distributions taxed at retirement?*
A: You are entitled to treat as capital gains that portion of your taxable contribution which reflects your participation in the plan measured by the number of calendar years before 1974. You may elect to apply a ten-year averaging rule to that portion of your lump sum distribution which reflects your participation in the plan for years beginning after 1973, and which is treated as the ordinary income portion of the distribution. If you choose an annuity, payments received over a period of time are taxed in the years received as ordinary income.

14 · *Q: I have a Keogh plan with XYZ Fund. Is it possible to switch my plan to another fund?*
A: Yes, you have two possible choices: (1) Keep your Keogh plan with XYZ Fund and start a new Keogh plan with ABC Fund; (2) Establish a new plan in ABC Fund and have the custodian of your XYZ Fund transfer your total assets to your new plan.

• A SLICE IS BETTER THAN NONE

Just because corporate executives can have a much larger amount than $7,500 set aside for their benefit is no reason to pass up the advantages that are offered to you. To pass up the $7,500 allowance now is like passing up the enjoyment of eating two slices of German chocolate cake just because your neighbor has a whole cake. If this bugs you too much, look into the pros and cons of incorporating. Many professionals are doing so under provisions for professional corporations. A very good booklet on this subject is one published by Prentice-Hall, Inc., entitled "Professional Corporations and Associations."

The Professional Corporation • In 1970 IRS threw in the sponge in its long fight to keep incorporating professionals from being treated as corporations for tax purposes. By 1973, one-third of the physicians in the U.S. had incorporated, and it is estimated that at least half will be incorporating their practices by 1977. These can be one-man corporations.

The main advantage you will have if you are self employed and incorporated is that you will then be considered an employee as well as an owner. As an employee of a corporation you may then participate in retirement and insurance programs on a tax-deductible basis.

Let's assume you are earning $50,000 as a physician and have incorporated. A comparison under Keogh and under a professional corporation would be as follows.

As a sole practitioner you may deduct $7,500 annually and put it in your Keogh plan.

As a principal of Doctor, Inc., you draw a salary of $50,000 and set up a combined profit-sharing and pension plan. You may now contribute $12,500 (25 percent of $50,000) on a tax-deductible basis to your retirement plan. The corporate retirement plan may also have estate tax benefits.

As you can see, the corporate plan would allow you to set aside $5,000 more than would a Keogh plan.

There are also insurance advantages under the corporate structure. You may also be eligible for substantial life, health, and disability insurance coverages, deductible to the corporation and not taxable as income to you.

Some of the extras you would be entitled to are:

1 • Group life insurance—up to $50,000 tax free. Above that you would pay a nominal tax on term cost of insurance.

2 • Group health insurance—hospital, surgical, major medical, and dental.

3 • Disability—you would be eligible for long-term disability for life or up to age 65.

4 • Key man insurance—the corporation could insure your life as a key employee.

5 • You also may elect to set up a nonqualified deferred compensation plan and a medical expense reimbursement plan. The plan also permits a $5,000 federal-income-tax-free death benefit.

You should weigh carefully the pros and cons of incorporation. Your attorney and certified public accountant should be consulted, and the financial and legal possibilities should be studied thoroughly before you take this step.

Do Get Started • While you are studying the pros and cons of incorporation, go ahead and start your Keogh plan. Even if you incorporate later, this money can be left in your Keogh plan to grow. If you skip this year, you can never make it up. When they blow the horn to signal a new year, you've passed up this year's tax savings forever.

Application

Are you self employed? If so, determine if you should have a Keogh Plan or if it would be more advantageous to you to set up an Individual Retirement Account. Does your income flow from self employment lend itself to monthly contributions or will lump-sum be better? Which of the available investments allowed best fits you?

{ 18 }

HOW
To Read
a
Prospectus

The first rule is—Don't! At least, don't try to read the prospectus cover to cover as you would a mystery novel. Use the prospectus as you would a handy reference guide. It can be horribly long, confusing, and worthless unless you know *beforehand* what to look for and who wrote the prospectus.

It is much too long and contains unnecessary detail. The Securities and Exchange Commission has many bright young men (some in training for top corporate or legal jobs) and many dedicated career servants, but the information it usually requires a company to transmit to potential investors can at times be misleading.

If a company wants to offer shares to you and the general public, it must submit a "registration statement" to the SEC, together with a copy to each state in which shares are to be sold. Nine-tenths of the information called for by the registration statement constitutes the "prospectus." It contains information required by a checklist compiled by the

SEC. There are about 15 different forms, each pertaining to a different kind of company. Each form is designed to cover every conceivable type of information about the company. And each time the checklist is revised it gets longer. This has been going on since 1934. By now, the average prospectus contains about 50 pages of fine print which may cause you to miss seeing the forest because of the many trees. I hope in the not-too-distant future the prospectus will be shortened to no more than ten pages. As it is now, it usually takes the proverbial Philadelphia lawyer to make heads or tails of all that mass of fine print, and I suspect he often has difficulty with it too.

- ## UNDULY LONG

The undue length of the prospectus does serve one very practical purpose, however. Past experience has shown that small enterprises have a much higher mortality rate than do the larger and older ones. It does cost a great deal of money to gather together all the financial data and other information required by the SEC for the prospectus. Small companies are often presented with insurmountable expense hurdles to overcome if they intend to offer their shares publicly. A few have actually gone bankrupt in the attempt. If the SEC wants the company to change the terms of its offering or if it believes the company to be weak, it can delay the offering, require new audits, and increase the burden of expenses. The final draft of the prospectus has, for all intents and purposes, been edited by an SEC examiner to such an extent that he might as well be the author.

The SEC rarely makes any field investigation of a company to check out the truth of the information supplied—hence, the disclaimer that appears in bold type on the face of every SEC prospectus:

THESE SECURITIES HAVE NOT BEEN APPROVED OR DISAPPROVED BY THE SECURITIES AND EXCHANGE COMMISSION NOR HAS THE COMMISSION PASSED UPON THE ACCURACY OF THIS PROSPECTUS. ANY REPRESENTATION TO THE CONTRARY IS A CRIMINAL OFFENSE.

This caption must be placed on every prospectus, regardless of the size or quality of the offering. If General Motors were making an offering of new shares, the same paragraph would be required. Even the most conservative of investment company trusts must have this caption in bold, frightening print on the front. I remember recommending to a prospective woman client a particular fund that has a portfolio of such high quality that every stock in it is taken from the Legal List of the Registry of Wills of the District of Columbia. In keeping with what registered representatives are legally required to do, I gave her the prospectus of the fund with the above in bold print on the front. She called me the next day absolutely incensed that I dared recommend to her something that the Securities and Exchange Commission had not approved. I explained the reason, but I was never able to really satisfy her, and she did not make the investment. This caption has frightened away a host of people who should be investors. I feel some of the blame for so many of our citizens' being flat broke at 65 must be placed on our present prospectus system.

I truly believe in having all my clients completely informed of the nature of the investment they are about to make, the risks involved, and what they may reasonably hope to accomplish if they do decide to invest, but the prospectus as it is presently required is a serious deterrent. My sincere hope is that the Securities and Exchange Commission will take the simplification of the prospectus they require as one of their most important projects for the near future.

• **INVESTOR LOSSES**

Most investors' losses occur from factors that never appear in the prospectus. The number one factor is the market system itself. It is a mechanism that favors the large institutional investor over the small investor. The reason is simple. Most small investors tend to buy when

everything looks great and common stocks are performing well. They
tend to sell when everything looks gloomy. Hence, the tendency for
small investors is to buy a stock near its peak price and sell it near its
low. It is the large investors who more often do just the opposite. Fortunes
were made in common stocks by those investors who bought in 1931 to
1933, not those who bought in 1929. The same story holds true for all
the peaks and valleys in share prices since then. Small investors have
their best chance by buying into the large investment funds or large
individual companies at a time when most people regard them with dis-
favor and when most people think the country is at an all-time economic
or political low. If history repeats itself, they will then participate in
their subsequent rise.

• MANAGEMENT IS THE KEY

The other major factor that doesn't appear in the prospectus is the
honesty, integrity, and ability of company management. One can be
sure that a company whose management is bent on defrauding its shareholders will show a beautiful prospectus. All the financial statements
will look great and so will company prospects. Dishonest corporate
officers will make dishonest reports to the SEC. Major company frauds
often are discovered after the fact—not beforehand. Most investors fail
to make any kind of independent investigation of the company in which
they are investing.

• MAKE A CHECKLIST

It is essential that you go beyond the prospectus in determining
whether to buy shares in a new offering. Your "checklist" for determining
whether a company is a good investment is short and simple. If your
timing is good (which is vastly important), then you should be able to
consistently make money on new stock issues by making these determina-
tions, in order of their importance:

1 · Who is really running the business? Find out which persons
are actually in day-to-day charge of company affairs. It is
usually no more than a handful. Separate the directors who
have been added as "window dressing." Then independently
check out in detail the reputation for honesty, integrity, and

ability of those persons who are in charge. You won't find this in the prospectus. But it is worth more than 10 prospectuses. Check on these corporate officers the same as if they were filling out an employment application. After all, if you buy shares in the company they run, they should be working for *you*. If you find any lack of good character, drop the company like a hot potato!

2 · Are shares owned by management? If they don't own any, why should you? If they own a bunch, you should make a serious study of the company. Be careful about "dilution." If management owns a lot of shares, that's great. But did they pay 20¢ two years ago for shares they are offering to you for $20? If so, this usually is picked up in the prospectus under a separate paragraph headed "Dilution." It will give you the details.

3 · Look at the *size* of the company. This appears in the balance sheet. The smaller the size, the more risk is involved. For every large company that fails a hundred small ones go under. You will find the size of the company in the balance sheet. If there are less than seven figures in assets, the company has a high risk. Of course, if you are looking for a long shot that could pay off handsomely, such a company might be for you. Otherwise, pass.

4 · Look at the *debt* of the company. This is also in the balance sheet. If shareholder equity is less than 30 percent of total assets, watch out!

5 · Age. Time often cures all. The first five years are the biggest risk. Over 10 is over the hump.

6 · Management take. Compare management compensation with other, similar companies. Often, as may be the case with your auto repairman, the best job is also the least expensive job. Think in terms of percentage of company income. The president of General Motors can be paid an enormous sum (which he is) without hurting the percentage. But when a small company pays an enormous sum, then doublecheck who runs the business and the number of shares they own.

7 · Preferred stock and debentures. The safest policy is to put your money in a company with little or no "senior" securities. This is just another form of debt. Take senior securities into account when figuring debt risk.

8 · Earnings. Why does this come last? Because nine times out of ten, management will think of every accounting trick pos-

sible to show high earnings during a stock offering. Go back over the past five years and see what the trend is. Most companies have to carry three sets of books: one under SEC accounting rules, one under Internal Revenue Service regulations, and one to know what is really going on in the business. If you could get the last set, that would be a big help. But you won't find it in the prospectus.

• THE "RED HERRING"

Most brokers mail to prospective investors a preliminary or "red herring" prospectus in advance of a company's offering. This prospectus is used to solicit preliminary orders, called "indications of interest." The "red herring" prospectus has not been finally reviewed by the SEC. Use the "red herring" to do your homework on the kind of people who are running the business and how many shares they own. On the basis of your preliminary investigation you may decide to place a preliminary "order." You are not obligated to pay for your "order" until you have received the final prospectus. Don't send in your check until you have reviewed the final prospectus carefully as to each of the above eight points.

It has not been my intent to be unduly critical of the Securities and Exchange Commission. They do an admirable job with dedicated and limited personnel. I am, however, keenly aware of the great need for a simpler, more understandable prospectus that the person who has not had the benefit of legal training can read and grasp in order to make an informed investment decision.

Application

Go to a financial planner and obtain a prospectus on a new offering. Using the above checklist, how well did the offering stand up?

How do you evaluate management? Are there conflicts of interest? If so, would this really work to your disadvantage if you were an investor?

{ 19 }

Planning
for
Your Children's
Education

If your son or daughter asked you for $14,000 to $30,000 for college expenses, would you be able to make the college of his or her choice a reality instead of a dream? Costs for a year of college today begin in the neighborhood of $4,000. Future costs are unknown; however, if the present trend of escalation continues, this cost could run as high as $9,600 per year by 1992.

- **BASIC
  COSTS**

Here's a graphic projection if costs continue to increase as they have in recent years.

Using these projected cost figures, let's assume you have two children. One will start to college in 1985 and the second in 1988. Their college cost picture might look something like this.

	Child No. 1	Child No. 2
1985	$ 7,400	
1986	7,700	
1987	8,000	
1988	8,300	$ 8,300
1989		8,700
1990		9,000
1991		9,300
	$31,400	$35,300
		$31,400
		$66,700

- ## COLLEGE
  ## FINANCING FORMULA

Let's now change our basic formula to read: Time plus Money plus American companies equals Opportunity for a college education.

Often I'm counseling a couple that has stated that their financial goal is to educate their children. After I have outlined a plan, one of them will ask, "Is it 'guaranteed'?"—meaning every hour of every day.

Of course, it's not "guaranteed" on a daily basis. Their goal is to have the necessary college funds in 10 to 15 years. They may not be able to afford a "guaranteed" investment.

For example, let's assume they can save $150 a month toward building a college fund to educate their two children. One will be going to college in ten years and the other in 14 years.

- ## THE GUARANTEED ROUTE
  ## vs. THE UNGUARANTEED

At 5 percent compounded annually $150 a month in 10 years will be $23,778. In 14 years it's $37,044. This brings them up short for Child No. 1, to say nothing of Child No. 2.

At 12 percent, on the other hand, $150 per month would be $35,370 in 10 years and $65,304 in 14 years. You may be concerned with the fact that if child No. 1 is taking from the kitty, funds will not be there to compound. This is true. However, Child No. 1 does not need the total amount of $31,400 the day he enters the vine-covered portals. He just needs the funds for one semester which allows the remainder to grow until it is needed.

A plan that I have used successfully to accomplish this objective has been a check-a-month withdrawal from a fund similar to the Seminar Fund. While the student has been taking out funds, American industry has been putting funds back in.

Don't worry about the short-term fluctuations of the market. If you want to have enough money in the college fund using the "guaranteed" route, you will have to increase your savings to such a huge amount that you will have to drastically reduce your present standard of living. The "guaranteed" dollar in many cases becomes an academic discussion rather than a workable plan.

• **DON'T FIGHT THE BATTLE ALONE**

Don't try to fight the battle for college funds alone. Give American industry a chance to help. You may find that American industry will contribute more to your child's educational funds than you do, if you'll give it a chance through proper investing.

On March 21, 1965, I was interviewed by Patricia Shelton, who was then a reporter in the women's department of *The Houston Chronicle*. She is now a well-known syndicated fashion writer. Her question to me in her interview was how to go about financing a college education. At that time we estimated that if parents had a child who would be entering college in 10 years, they would need to save $5,400 at $45 per month. If they had 15 years, they would need to save $3,600 at $20 per month. (See how important time is to the accomplishment of any financial objective?)

This would not be sufficient if they used the guaranteed route, but we found that it should be if they had used a specific local mutual fund. We arrived at these figures by working backward using the bank's computer. We wanted to be able to withdraw $3,000 a year or $250 per month each month for four years. Working backward, we found that if the account had $9,565 in it at registration time and $250 a month had been drawn out each month for four years, a total of $12,000 would have been withdrawn and there would have been $440 left.

Again, here is an example to encourage you not to fight the battle alone, but to let American industry help you. In this case American industry had contributed $7,040, and the parents had contributed $5,400 (at $45 per month). These parents had placed their money in a position to let American industry pay more of their child's college costs than they had contributed.

College costs have skyrocketed since this article was published, and stock market performance has been erratic; however, it seems evident that American industry can provide a very helpful hand to you if you are a parent desiring to send your child to college.

Figure 15 shows anticipated college costs.

- ## UNIFORM GIFTS TO MINORS

If you are in a fairly high tax bracket, you should consider setting up custodial accounts for each child and registering the stock in this manner:

> John E. Jones, Custodian for
> John E. Jones, Jr., under the
> _____ Uniform Gifts to
> State
> Minors Act.

This should allow most of the dividends and capital gains to compound tax free. You should use your child's Social Security number for the account. You will still be able to claim the child as a deduction if you supply over 50 percent of his support. I should caution that you may not use any of these funds for things you are legally obligated to do for your child—items such as food and clothing. But you can use the funds for college education.

If your estate is large you may want to name as custodian someone other than yourself. In the event of your death, the value of the account could be considered a part of your estate for estate tax purposes if you are the custodian.

- ## DON'T PROCRASTINATE

Time plus Money—both are essential to combine with American free enterprise. The sooner you start, the easier it will be to accomplish your goal. By starting five years earlier, you can usually reduce the amount you must invest by one-half. A college education can add a new dimension to a life. If you have children, help them to reach their maximum potential.

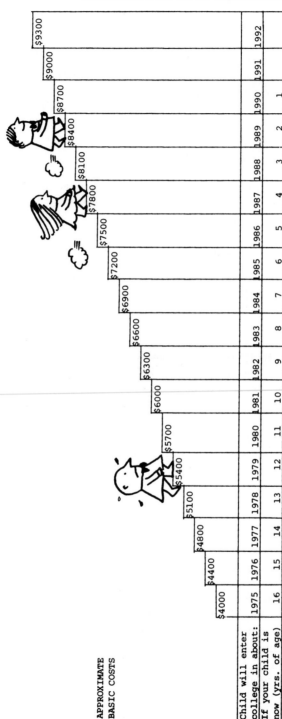

FIGURE 15. Anticipated College Annual Costs

Application

If you have small children, make out a worksheet showing how many years before college and what the anticipated costs will be for each year in college. What amount must you invest at 6 percent to arrive at your desired goal? At 12 percent? What immediate action will you take?

{20}

Financial
Planning
Is Like
Navigation

Financial planning is like navigation. If you know where you are and where you want to go, navigation isn't such a great problem. It's when you don't know the two points that it's difficult.

To find out where you are, take an in-depth financial inventory. Below is the personal planning data sheet I hand out at the first session of my three-session financial planning seminars.

I encourage each person in attendance to complete and return it to me before our consultation. This allows me sufficient time to map out tentative recommendations. If they do not return it or bring it with them, we complete one together. Without this information, I'm flying blind. If they do not choose to give me this information we usually do not accept them as clients. It would be as if they had gone to their family doctor in pain and refused to tell him where the pain was located.

Here is your personal planning data sheet. Please stop now and complete it.

PERSONAL PLANNING DATA SHEET

Name	Date

Address	

Telephone: Home	Office

Marital Status   Age   Do you have a current will?

MY FINANCIAL RESOURCES

I. *Loaned dollars:*

A. Checking account $_____

B. Savings at bank $_____

    Certificates of deposit $_____

C. Savings and loan $_____

    Certificates of deposit $_____

D. Government bonds
and instruments $_____

E. Corporate bonds $_____

F. Municipal bonds $_____

G. Credit union $_____

H. Mortgages receivable $_____

I. Loans receivable $_____

J. Cash value of insurance policies
(Worksheet follows) $_____

    TOTAL LOANED DOLLARS $_____(1)

Present Life Insurance and Annuities
(Worksheet to compute Item I.J)

Company	Type	Face amount	Cash value	Net insurance °	Annual premium
TOTAL:					

° Face Amount Less Cash Value = Net Insurance.

II. *Working dollars*

A. *Stocks*

No. of shares	Name of company	Date of purchase	Cost	Market value
			$	$
			$	

TOTAL MARKET VALUE $_____(2)

B. *Real estate*

Equity in home (market value less mortgage) $_____

Other real estate (net after mortgage):

_____ $_____

_____ $_____

_____ $_____

TOTAL REAL ESTATE .... $_____(3)

C. *Other investments*

Limited partnerships:

_____ $_____

_____ $_____

Commodities:

_____ $_____

Silver and gold:

_____ $_____

Art objects and antiques:

_____ $_____

    TOTAL .... $_____(4)
TOTAL WORKING DOLLARS
    (2, 3, and 4) .... $_____(5)
TOTAL LOANED AND WORKING
    DOLLARS (1 and 5) .... $_____
D. *Loans outstanding (other than mortgages above)* $_____

MY FINANCIAL OBJECTIVE

(Please number in order of importance)

_____ Income now
_____ Income at retirement
_____ Maximum tax advantage
_____ Educate children
_____ Travel

Present monthly income $_____
Amount I could save per month $_____
My tax bracket _____%

If retirement is your objective:

How many years before retirement? _____ yrs.
Desired monthly income at retirement $_____

SOURCES OF MONTHLY RETIREMENT INCOME:
Social Security $_____
Pensions $_____
Other $_____
    TOTAL $_____
    ADDITIONAL INCOME NEEDED
        PER MONTH $_____

If education of children is objective:

Name of child	Years before college	Estimated cost
_____	_____	$_____
_____	_____	$_____
_____	_____	$_____
_____	_____	$_____
_____		$_____
TOTAL COST		$_____
AMOUNT SET ASIDE		$_____
ADDITIONAL NEEDED		$_____

• YOUR WILL

You will note that I ask if you have a will. This is a very important part of your financial planning.

In reality, you and everyone have or will have a will. It will be the one that you have written to fit your own wishes or the one the state writes for you after your death. However, the state's will most likely will not bear any resemblance to the way you would have written it, had you done so during your lifetime.

I urge you to obtain a properly drawn will prepared by a competent lawyer in the state where you are living.

I won't go into details about all the will should contain. However, let me make this one suggestion as to what you should not do. Do not, for example, will so many shares of XYZ company to your daughter Sally, nor your credit union account to your son Johnny. If you do, every time you change your investments, which you may need to do often, you'll need to change your will. Plan for the disbursement of your assets by percentages. If you have four children and want your estate to be equally divided among them, specify in your will that 25 percent of your assets should go to each.

If you want a portion to go to charity, reduce these percentages so as to have some left for this purpose.

In making these suggestions, I'm not trying to practice law. A competent lawyer should prepare your will. I'm a financial planner, and I should and will stick to recommending financial plans that can fulfill your needs. How I've often wished that lawyers would do likewise and stick to their profession and let me practice mine.

The temptation to give financial advice seems at times to be just too great for them. So often they are the only strong man in the life of a widow at a time when she is very lonely and insecure. She naturally turns to them for advice. Unfortunately, many times they take the easy way out and tell her to just put her funds where they will be "safe," meaning a savings account. Here the ravages of inflation can destroy the only value the money has—purchasing power.

Many a large law firm will have very strong ties with a particular bank in its city. They secure clients for the bank's trust department by drawing up the will in such a way that the bank becomes the trustee. This may be a good arrangement if the heirs have a spendthrift nature and little or no knowledge of money management. It may be a very poor arrangement otherwise.

• LOANED DOLLARS

Under this section we have listed many of the ways you can loan money. I've covered these in detail in the chapter entitled "Lending Your Dollars" and will not repeat them here.

All of these ways of "lending" money offer you a reasonably good guarantee of return of principal and a stated rate of return with the exception of the cash value of life insurance policies. Technically, as you have seen, it belongs to the insurance company. You can obtain that portion designated as cash surrender value by borrowing it from them or surrendering your protection. If it is left with the insurance company and death occurs, the beneficiary only receives the face amount of the policy, regardless of how much you have "saved" using this method.

Included in the data sheet is a worksheet for the calculation of your cash surrender value. As you will remember, this is done by looking at the date of issue of the policy and subtracting that date from today's date. This gives the age of your policy. Look toward the back of the policy and find the nonforfeiture table, which will be either for the face amount or per $1,000. For example, let's assume you have a $10,000 whole life policy that you've had for 10 years, and the cash surrender value is per $1,000. You look down the table to 10 years and go across the chart to cash value column where it states a value of $365. You multiply the $365 × 10 which is $3,650. On your data sheet then write the name of the insurance company, type of policy, face amount of $10,000, cash value of $3,650, and net insurance of $6,440. Do this for each policy and then total them.

The net insurance is the face amount less the cash surrender value. The annual premium is next. List and then total.

At this point take time to calculate your present cost per thousand for life insurance protection.

This can be done very simply in this manner:

Face amount $_____

Less cash value $_____

Net insurance   _____

Present premium   _____

Less dividend   _____
   (last year)

Net premium   _____

Loss @ ____% on
   _____cash value   _____

Total cost   _____

$$\frac{\$_____}{(\text{Total cost})} \div \frac{\$_____}{\substack{(\text{Net thousands} \\ \text{of insurance})}} = \frac{\$_____}{(\text{Cost per thousand})}$$

Assuming a loss of earnings at 6 percent and a premium of $200 per annum on the above policy, you would calculate your total cost by multiplying $3650 times 6 percent ($219) and then add this total to the $200 ($419).

$419 ÷ 6.4 = $65.47 cost per thousand

• HOW MUCH IN CASH RESERVES?

As you make a total of your "loaned dollars" you may be asking, "How much should I keep in cash reserve?"

When I first started giving Investment Seminars, I suggested three months' expenses in cash reserve.

Now my answer is, "Leave as much money idle as it takes there to give you peace of mind, for peace of mind is a good investment."

I don't seem to have peace of mind with any of my money idle, with the exception of a checking account. You may not have any peace of mind without a lot in a "guaranteed" savings account where you can give it a comforting pat every now and then. I call that "patting money."

You may be asking what I do when I find myself needing cash. I have much of my funds invested in good stocks, mutual funds, and real estate partnerships. I can sell them any time I desire. However, it may not be the right time in the market, or I may not want to destroy the goose that is laying the golden eggs, so I take my stock certificates to the bank and use them for collateral for a loan.

I can rent a lot of time for a reasonable amount of rent (interest) and deduct the rent on my income tax.

Therefore, I don't feel I need to keep money idle working for someone else while waiting for an emergency. I have cash any time I need it.

• WORKING OR "OWNED" DOLLARS

The four main categories in this area are stocks, real estate through individual ownership or through limited partnerships, energy, and other commodities through the same form.

Stocks • Under stocks you should list your common stocks, preferred stocks, convertible bonds, and any warrants or rights you may own. List the number of shares, the cost basis, date of purchase, and today's market value.

Knowing your cost basis is very important in doing good financial planning for two reasons. First of all, you need to unemotionally take a good hard look at your performance in the market. For example, let's say you purchased 100 shares of XYZ Corporation five years ago for $10 per share. Today's market value is 14⅝. Your average gain per year has been 8 percent compounded. If the stock pays a significant dividend which you are reinvesting, add this to your return after adjusting for your tax loss.

Is 8 percent gain per year within your investment results guideline? If you have calculated that you must have a result of 12 percent a year to reach your goal and your investments are not reaching this objective, you will need to consider making some changes in your investment program.

Another important reason for knowing your cost basis is that you would need to know how much capital gains would be realized if you were to sell at a profit or capital loss if selling at a loss. You will need to weigh how much you will have to gain from another investment to overcome the tax loss if you are selling at a profit, to come out ahead. On the other hand, if you have a loss, you may need to know how much you could save on your income taxes by establishing the loss.

Many have difficulty figuring cost basis. This is because of poor record keeping or because they become confused by stock splits. It only takes a small amount of time to keep good records if done as the transactions are made. In the back of this book I have a stock record sheet you may want to consider using. I like to use this sheet in a looseleaf notebook, and then pull and file the sheets after the stock has been sold. Both the buy and sell confirmations that you receive from your broker should be kept in your permanent files.

Figuring the effect of stock splits and dividends is not difficult if done as they are made. Let's look at an example. You purchased 100 shares of XYZ Corp. at $50 per share, or $5,000, in 1970. You received a stock dividend of 2 percent or two shares in 1971, and a two for one stock split in 1972, which gives you a total of 204 shares. You have added no new money. Your cost basis is still $5,000. Your cost basis per share, however, has changed. You now have 204 shares. Your original 100 plus 2 = 102 × 2 = 204 shares. You paid $5,000, and you have 204 shares so your new cost basis per share is $24.51. If you should sell 50 shares, your cost basis would be 50 × $24.51, or $1,225.50, and the cost basis for your remaining shares would be $3,774.50.

Real Estate • Real estate can also be a good variable dollar investment. First, list your home (its current market value less the mortgage).

Then list your equity in other real estate holdings. Others: limited part-nerships in real estate and oil and gas, commodity accounts, silver bullion and coins, gold jewelry, art works, and antiques bought as investments. Now total your assets and subtract any liabilities. This should give you your net worth.

- ## YOUR FINANCIAL OBJECTIVES

The last section of the personal planning data sheet is designed to help you determine your financial objectives. Number these in the order of their priority to you.

   _____ Income now
   _____ Income at retirement
   _____ Maximum tax advantage
   _____ Educate children
   _____ Travel

- ## HOW MUCH CAN YOU SAVE?

"Present monthly income" is followed by "Amount I could save per month." Sit down with your family and determine how much you can comfortably save each month—not too comfortably, or you won't save anything. However, don't set the amount too high, but establish an amount you can actually save. If you set it too high, you may become discouraged, abandon the plan, and fail to reach your goal of financial independence.

- ## YOUR TAX BRACKET

Your tax bracket is a very important item for it should influence your selection of investments. If you are in the lower brackets, you can afford to invest for income that is taxable. The higher your bracket, the more you should consider tax-sheltered investments.

- ## IF RETIREMENT IS YOUR OBJECTIVE

Determine when you plan to retire and map your plan accordingly. Sometimes I'll be counseling a couple age 50 who solemnly tell me they plan to retire at age 55. When I look at their assets, I realize there is just no way. They are not being realistic. Regardless of how much they may "want to" retire in five years, they will not be able to do so with only the income from the assets they have accumulated.

Desired Monthly Income • Decide what you feel would be an adequate or desired monthly income and adjust for inflation. Use no less than 3½ percent for an inflation factor. You would probably be safer using 5 percent or more.

Sources of Monthly Income

Social Security • I had planned to include in the back of the book a table for your use in making this calculation; however, the amount seems to be changing so rapidly it is impossible to keep it current. I suggest you call your local Social Security office and request this information.

Pension • If your company has a pension and/or profit-sharing plan, find out how much your pension will be and what has been credited to your profit-sharing account. Also find out how much is vested (meaning how much you could take with you if you should leave).

• COLLEGE
FINANCING NEEDS

The chapter on college education will be helpful in calculating how much you are going to need for college expenses.

• HOW DID
YOU DO?

You've now completed your personal planning data sheet. You have, haven't you?

How did you do? How many years have you worked? How much have you earned? How much have you saved? How many years before retirement? What do you plan to do about your financial situation beginning today? Write down specific steps you are going to take to accomplish your goal. Have a family council and plan your attack.

Financial planning should be a joint endeavor if a couple is involved

and a family matter if there are children. When it comes to financial planning, I find that love is not so much looking into each other's eyes as looking in the same direction. If both have the financial vision, the chances for accomplishing their financial goal are vastly improved.

• FINANCIAL ADVICE

For advice on a legal question, go to a competent lawyer; for advice on taxes, go to a CPA; for advice on banking, go to a banker—but don't expect good money management advice from any of them. Yes, I did intend to include the banker. Many bankers are trained to be money changers, money counters, and money lenders, but few are trained to be money managers.

Seek out a financial planner who has an excellent reputation and in whom you truly have confidence. Then follow his advice. Don't make the mistake of going from person to person asking their opinions. This will only serve to confuse you, causing you to make poor decisions. You'll always find those eager to give free advice about your money. Often the more readily they give advice, the more miserable the job they have done with their own money.

Your financial planner should be experienced in investments, life insurance, tax shelters, and estate planning, and have a close working relationship with a creative CPA and a competent attorney.

All of these areas must be skillfully meshed together in the complex money arena you will find yourself in today.

Application

Complete the financial data sheet. Examine how many dollars you have idle. Do you really need that many there, or should you have more cash reserves? What yearly rate of increase are you averaging on your fixed dollar investments? What rate are you averaging on your variable dollars? What date each year will you set aside to update your analysis and consider alternative courses?

{ 21 }

To Win
the
Money Game

My dear investor, it is now time to summarize my years of observations of why so many are failing to win the money game and what you must do to become a winner.

• WHY SO MANY FAIL

Lack of a Well-Defined Goal • The greatest cause for failure is the lack of a well-defined goal and a step-by-step plan to accomplish that goal. I have never interviewed anyone who has said to me, "I plan to fail." Unfortunately, I have visited with many who were well down the road to failure because they had "failed to plan."

Lack of Self-Discipline • Another cause of failure is lack of self-discipline. The secret of financial independence is not brilliance or luck, but the discipline to save a part of all you earn and to put it to work in shares of American industry, real estate, and natural resources.

Procrastination • Procrastination is a deadly enemy to success. Time is a tremendous asset. If you have a sufficient amount of time, you do not need as large an amount of money to combine with American industry or the other two major areas of investing. Do not waste this precious commodity—a commodity that is distributed to each of us equally.

Procrastination always stands in the shadows, awaiting his opportunity to spoil your chance for success. You will probably go through life as a failure if you wait for the "time to be right" to start doing something worthwhile. Do not wait; the time will never be "just right" to start your journey down the road to financial independence. Remember our illustration of "Mr. Sitting Tight."

Lack of Persistence • Don't be a good "starter" and a poor "finisher," as is true with so many. Each year we must close our reservations early for our January financial planning seminars because we cannot seat all who want to come. It's obvious that many have made good New Year's Resolutions to "get organized" and do something about their finances. We rarely have to turn down reservations for our fall sessions.

If you experience a temporary setback, do not give up at the first sign of defeat. I've often observed this in a monthly investment program. If the market goes up after they start their program, they'll happily put in their investment each month, but if it goes down, they'll abandon the program, regardless of how I've tried to explain that dollar-cost-averaging results can benefit from stock market fluctuations. There is no substitute for persistence. If you make persistence your watchword, you'll discover that "old man failure" will finally become weary of you and make his exit. Failure cannot cope with persistence.

Lack of Ability To Make a Decision • I have found over and over again that men who succeed reach decisions promptly and change them, if at all, very slowly. I have found that men who fail reach decisions, if at all, very slowly and change them frequently and quickly. Procrastination and indecision are twins. Pluck this grim pair out of your life before they bind you to the treadmill of financial failure.

Making a decision is a privilege. No one can make your decisions for you. You will find that free advice about your money is always available. It's usually those who lean back and give you the most "positive" advice whose finances are bordering on catastrophy. They are often wrong, but never in doubt.

There are times when I have counseled a couple who have attended all three sessions of our investment seminar and thus have listened to me for at least 4½ hours. They have asked for an appointment, and I have spent an hour and a half in an uninterrupted personal conference. When it comes time to apply this information to their own personal finances, they will say, "This sounds fine, but let us go home and think it over." On the surface this sounds like a prudent, sensible thing to do, doesn't it? However, I find that it usually is not. They already have all the information they need. They will not be "thinking it over" after they leave. Dozens of other matters will require their attention. They are trying to avoid making a decision, not realizing that no decision is a decision. They are deciding that where their money is now is the best place for it to be—for that is the result brought about by their lack of a decision.

Overcaution · The person who takes no chances generally must take whatever is left over after others have finished choosing. Overcaution is as bad, if not worse, than lack of caution. Both should be avoided. Life will always contain the elements of chance.

If you proudly tell me you've never had a loss in the stock market, don't expect me to be impressed. The opposite will be my reaction. If you've never missed, you've not been in there trying or you've been holding your losers far too long for maximum profits. Play the money game well, but never safely.

Avoid a life of no hits, no runs, no errors.

Prejudice · We all have prejudices, but we should continually work to rid ourselves of them. In counseling, I sometimes encounter a couple who seem to be saying to me, "Please don't confuse us with facts." They do not want to know the truth. The truth will not make them free.

Lack of Concentrated Efforts · To become a good investor you must seriously apply your intelligence, use your ability to acquire knowledge, and give your attention to details and timing. If you cannot, will not, or do not have the ability to do these things successfully for yourself, do not take a distorted ego trip, but put the professionals to work for you.

Desiring Something for Nothing · If I were to distill all the wisdom I've ever learned into nine words it would be: "There is no such thing as a free lunch." I've observed this in two opposite ways. One is the gambling instinct, which has driven many to failure in the market. Investing, properly approached, is, in my opinion, the safest thing that can be done with money. Speculation, on the other hand, can be the riskiest.

This desire for a "free lunch" is often seen in the opposite manner by those who will leave their funds in a savings institution because they refuse to pay a brokerage commission to get their funds invested. This obsession with what something "costs" rather than what it "pays" may also lead them into investing in a lower performance mutual fund that does not charge a commission rather than in a better performing one that does. (There are some that do not charge that perform well.) The money they often "save" is very costly. In making an investment decision the important factor is not what it "costs." You do not care what it costs, but you are truly concerned about what it "pays."

Lack of Enthusiasm • I do believe I can forgive almost any short-coming other than lack of enthusiasm. It is essential in the acquisition of money. Enthusiasm is contagious; and if you have it in sufficient quantities, others will welcome you into their group. You will be more in touch with the needs and thinking of the people around you, and you can profit from the investment opportunities that will become obvious to you.

Guessing Instead of Thinking • Information is available about almost any subject you need. Don't let indifference or plain laziness keep you from acquiring the facts essential to making good judgments. Acquire the major points of information you need—you'll never have "all" the information. If you wait that long, you'll probably make your decision too late for maximum profit. I find most decisions are made too late rather than too soon.

Lack of Capital • Build up your nest egg, and do it while you are young. Don't spend the nest egg, but use it for collateral to leverage for a larger egg and then a larger one. Remember again, money gives you options.

Being Overly Influenced by the Opinions of Others • I have observed that those who fail to accumulate sufficient amounts of money are easily influenced by the opinions of other people. Opinions are cheap commodities. You will find them everywhere. There are always those who are just waiting to foist their opinions on anyone who will accept them. If you let others overly influence you when you are reaching decisions about your money, you will not succeed.

You have a good brain and mind of your own. Use these in reaching your own decisions.

I find that those who have only a smattering of knowledge try to give the impression that they have much knowledge. I also find they do too much talking and too little listening. Keep your eyes and ears wide open and your mouth closed if you wish to acquire the habit of prompt decision making. I find those who talk too much do little else. If you talk more than you listen, you'll deprive yourself of many opportunities to accumulate useful knowledge. God has given each of us two ears and only one mouth.

Indiscriminate Spending • If you are a spendthrift you cannot succeed, mainly because you will always be worried about poverty. Form the habit of systematic saving by putting aside a definite percentage of your income and then putting your money to work for yourself as hard as you had to work to get and save it. You will never be "free," regardless of your race, creed, or color, until you are financially independent because you will have no options. Financial independence provides you the freedom to choose if you'll get out of bed in the morning and go to work. Without it, you don't have much of a choice. It's a lot more fun doing something by choice rather than from economic necessity. Money gives you a feeling of courage when bargaining for the sale of your services. Without it you must take what is offered, and be glad to accept it.

Now let's take a look at the positive side of the coin.

• WHY SOME SUCCEED

The Plan • Success in money management is not a will-o'-the wisp that comes to some and not to others because of fate, chance, or luck. If you've held this idea in the past, do get rid of it now. Success in money management can be predicted, but you must have a plan and follow that plan.

If you give a blueprint to a skillful builder, do you think it will be a matter of chance, or luck, that he will complete the structure successfully? Of course not. He merely begins at the beginning and follows the plan step by step to its completion.

This book is your blueprint for success. If you follow it, financial independence can be yours.

Attitude • There is a "magic" word you must place not only in your vocabulary but also in your sense of being if you are to be successful in money or any other area of life. That magic work is ATTITUDE!

Everything in life operates on the law of cause and effect. You must produce the causes—the rewards will take care of themselves. Good attitude—good results. Fair attitude—fair results. Bad attitude—bad results.

You will shape your own financial life by the attitudes you hold each day. If you have a poor attitude toward learning about money management, you will not learn very much until you change your attitude. If you have an attitude of failure, you are whipped before you start.

Often a prospective client will say, "If I invest, the market will go down." "I've never made any money in the market." Until they can change their attitude, they probably will not become a successful investor. Optimists make money. Pessimists rarely do.

If your present attitude is not a winning one, don't let that discourage you. The brilliant William James of Harvard University put it this way: "The greatest discovery of my generation is that human beings can alter their lives by altering their attitude of mind."

You see, this is an area over which you have control. You have control over what's going to happen to your money and to you.

Look around you. Study successful people. How privileged I have been over these past seven years to visit with at least one successful man or woman each week on my television program "Successful Texans."

They go sailing through life from one success to another, and when they occasionally fail at something, they shrug it off and head right out again. These people take the attitude toward themselves that they can accomplish what they set out to accomplish. Because of this, they achieve some remarkable things and are called successful, brilliant, lucky, and so on.

Luck • I personally do not believe in luck. Luck is when preparedness and opportunity get together. If you are prepared, you become lucky. A close friend of mine, who is a well-known and respected business consultant, studied a particular company and bought shares of stock while it was still in its infancy. These shares have now grown tremendously in value and have made him a very wealthy man. There are those who would scoff and say, "I should be so lucky." It wasn't just luck. He was prepared. When he and his wife were first married, they had scrimped and saved and lived in a modest apartment. They even sold their car and rode the bus to work so they could save a nest egg. It was this nest egg, which they had so painfully saved, that was used to make their "lucky" investment.

Had they not prepared, they would not have had the means by which to avail themselves of all this "luck."

Expectations • The successful people with whom I have visited seem to find their accomplishments not too difficult and many times surprisingly easy, simply because it seems so few are really trying—really believe in themselves.

I have found throughout life that successful people come in all shapes and sizes. They have widely different backgrounds, intelligence, and education. But I have found the one thing they have in common is that they expect more good out of life than bad and that they expect to succeed more often than fail—and they do!

Money • Rid yourself of an old myth, if such has been plaguing you, that money is not important. It is important, vitally important! It is just as important as the food it buys, the shelter it provides, the doctor bills it pays, and the education it helps to procure. Money is important to you as you live in a civilized society. To split hairs and say that it is not as important as other things is just arguing for the sake of the exercise. Nothing will take the place of money in areas in which money works.

"What is money?" Money is the harvest of your production. The amount of money you will receive will always be in direct ratio to the need for what you do, your ability to do it and the difficulty of replacing you.

I'm amazed at the number of people who tell me they want money but don't want to take the time and trouble to qualify for it. Until they qualify for it, there's no way they can earn it.

All you need is a plan—a road map—and the courage to arrive at your destination, knowing in advance that there will be problems and setbacks, but knowing also that nothing can stand in the way of your completing your plan if it is backed by persistence and determination.

Keep money in its proper place. It is a servant, nothing more. It is a tool with which you can live better and see more of the world around you.

Money is necessary in your modern life. But you need only so much of it to live comfortably, securely, and well. Too much emphasis on money can reverse your whole picture and make you the servant and your money your master.

You do want to have money and the things it can buy, but you also must check up continually to make sure that you haven't lost the things that money cannot buy.

My dear investor, the world can be your oyster. Approach it with enthusiasm, intelligence, and gusto. The ultimate in satisfaction can be yours!

Glossary
of
Investing

ACCRUED INTEREST · Interest accrued on a bond since the last interest payment was made. The buyer of the bond pays the market price plus accrued interest.

AMORTIZATION · Accounting for expenses or charges as applicable rather than as paid. Includes such practices as depreciation, depletion, write-off of intangibles, prepaid expenses, and deferred charges.

ANNUAL REPORT · The formal financial statement issued yearly by a corporation. The annual report shows assets, liabilities, earnings, how the company stood at the close of the business year, how it fared profit-wise during the year, and other information of interest to shareowners.

ASSETS · Everything a corporation owns or is due to it: cash, investments, money due it, materials, and inventories, which are called current assets; buildings and machinery, which are known as fixed assets; and patents and goodwill, called intangible assets.

AVERAGES · Various ways of measuring the trend of stocks listed on exchanges. Formulas—some very elaborate—have been devised to compensate for stock splits and stock dividends and thus give continuity to the average. In the case of the Dow-Jones industrial average, the prices of the 30 stocks are totaled and then divided by a figure that is intended to compensate for past stock splits and stock dividends and that is changed from time to time.

BALANCE SHEET · A condensed financial statement showing the nature and amount of a company's assets, liabilities, and capital on a given date. In dollar amounts the balance sheet shows what the company owned, what it owed, and the ownership interest in the company of its stockholders.

BEAR · Someone who believes the stock market will decline.

BEAR MARKET · A declining stock market.

BEARER BOND · A bond that does not have the owner's name registered on the books of the issuing company and that is payable to the holder. Has coupons attached.

BID AND ASKED · Often referred to as a quotation or quote. The bid is the highest price anyone has declared that he wants to pay for a security at a given time; the asked is the lowest price anyone will take at the same time.

BIG BOARD · A popular term for the New York Stock Exchange, Inc.

BLOCK · A large holding or transaction of stock, popularly considered to be 10,000 shares or more.

BLUE CHIP · A company known nationally for the quality and wide acceptance of its products or services, and for its ability to make money and pay dividends.

BLUE SKY LAWS · A popular name for laws various states have enacted to protect the public against securities frauds. The term is believed to have originated when a judge ruled that a particular stock had about the same value as a patch of blue sky.

BOND · Basically an IOU or promissory note of a corporation, usually issued in multiples of $1,000. A bond is evidence of a debt on which the issuing company usually promises to pay the bondholders a specified amount of interest for a specified length of time and to repay the loan on the expiration date. In every case a bond represents debt—its holder is a creditor of the corporation and not a part owner as is the shareholder.

BOOK VALUE · An accounting term. Book value of a stock is determined from a company's records by adding all assets and then deducting all debts and other liabilities, plus the liquidation price of any preferred issues. The sum arrived at is divided by the number of common shares outstanding, and the result is book value per common share. Book value of the assets of a company or a security may have little or no significant relationship to market value.

BROKER · An agent who handles the public's orders to buy and sell securities, commodities, or other property. For this service a commission is charged.

BULL · One who believes the stock market will rise.

BULL MARKET · An advancing stock market.

CALLABLE · A bond issue, all or part of which may be redeemed by the issuing corporation under definite conditions before maturity. The term also applies to preferred shares, which may be redeemed by the issuing corporation.

CAPITAL GAIN OR CAPITAL LOSS · Profit or loss from the sale of a capital asset. A capital gain, under current federal income tax laws, may be either short term (six months or less) or long term (more than six months). A short-term capital gain is taxed at the reporting individual's full income tax rate. A long-term capital gain is subject to a lower tax.

CAPITAL STOCK · All shares representing ownership of a business, including preferred and common.

CAPITALIZATION · Total amount of the various securities issued by a corporation. Capitalization may include bonds, debentures, preferred and common stock, and surplus.

CERTIFICATE · The actual piece of paper that is evidence of ownership of stock in a corporation. Loss of a certificate may cause at least, a great deal of inconvenience, at worst, financial loss.

COLLATERAI · Securities or other property pledged by a borrower to secure repayment of a loan.

COMMISSION · The broker's basic fee for purchasing or selling securities or property as an agent.

Common Stock · Securities that represent an ownership interest in a corporation. If the company has also issued preferred stock, both common and preferred have ownership rights. Claims of both common and preferred stockholders are junior to claims of bondholders or other creditors of the company. Common stock are in turn junior to preferred. Common stockholders assume the greater risk, but generally they exercise the greater control and may gain the greater reward in the form of dividends and capital appreciation.

Conglomerate · A corporation that has diversified its operations, usually by acquiring enterprises in widely varied industries.

Convertible · A bond, debenture, or preferred share that may be exchanged by the owner for common stock or another security, usually of the same company, in accordance with the terms of the issue.

Coupon Bond · Bond with interest coupons attached. The coupons are clipped as they come due and are presented by the holder for payment of interest.

Cumulative Preferred · A stock having a provision that if one or more dividends are omitted, the omitted dividends must be paid before dividends may be paid on the company's common stock.

Current Assets · Those assets of a company that are reasonably expected to be realized in cash, or sold, or consumed during the normal operating cycle of the business.

Current Liabilities · Money owed and payable by a company, usually within one year.

Dealer · An individual or firm in the securities business acting as a principal rather than as an agent. Typically, a dealer buys for his own account and sells to a customer from his own inventory. The dealer's profit or loss is the difference between the price he pays and the price he receives for the same security. The dealer's confirmation must disclose to his customer that he has acted as principal. The same individual or firm may function, at different times, as either a broker or dealer.

Debenture · A promissory note backed by the general credit of a company and usually not secured by a mortgage or lien on any specific property.

Depletion · Natural resources, such as metals, oils and gas, and timber that conceivably can be reduced to zero over the years, present a special problem in capital management. Depletion is an accounting practice consisting of charges against earnings based upon the amount of the asset taken out of the total reserves in the period for which accounting is made. A bookkeeping entry, it does not represent any cash outlay, nor are any funds earmarked for the purpose.

DEPRECIATION · Normally, charges against earnings to write off the cost, less salvage value, of an asset over its estimated useful life. It is a bookkeeping entry and does not represent any cash outlay, nor are any funds earmarked for the purpose.

DIRECTOR · Person elected by shareholders to establish company policies. The directors elect the president, vice president, and all other operating officers. Directors decide, among other matters, if and when dividends shall be paid.

DISCOUNT · The amount by which a preferred stock or bond may sell below its par value.

DISCRETIONARY ACCOUNT · An account in which the customer gives the broker or someone else discretion, which may be complete or within specific limits, as to the purchase and sale of securities or commodities including selection, timing, amount and price to be paid or received.

DIVERSIFICATION · Spreading investments among different companies in different fields. Another type of diversification is also offered by the securities of many individual companies because of the wide range of their activities.

DIVIDEND · The payment designated by the board of directors to be distributed pro rata among the shares outstanding. On preferred shares, it is generally a fixed amount. On common shares, the dividend varies with the fortunes of the company and the amount of cash on hand, and it may be omitted if business is poor or the directors determine to withhold earnings to invest in plant and equipment. Sometimes a company will pay a dividend out of past earnings even if it is not currently operating at a profit.

DOLLAR-COST-AVERAGING · A system of buying securities at regular intervals with a fixed dollar amount. Under this system the investor buys by the dollars' worth rather than by the number of shares. If each investment is of the same number of dollars, payments buy more when the price is low and fewer when it rises. Thus temporary downswings in price benefit the investor if he continues periodic purchases in both good times and bad, and the price at which the shares are sold is more than their average cost.

DOUBLE TAXATION · The federal government taxes corporate profits once as corporate income; any part of the remaining profits distributed as dividends to stockholders may be taxed again as income to the recipient stockholder.

DOW THEORY · A theory of market analysis based upon the performance of the Dow-Jones industrial and transportation stock price averages. The theory says that the market is in a basic upward trend if one of these averages advances above a previous important high, accompanied or followed by a similar advance in the other. When the averages both dip below previous important lows, this is regarded as confirmation of a basic downward trend. The theory does not attempt to predict how long either trend will continue, although it is widely misinterpreted as a method of forecasting future action.

EQUITY · The ownership interest of common and preferred stockholders in a company. Also refers to excess of value of securities over the debit balance in a margin account.

EX-DIVIDEND · A synonym for "without dividend." The buyer of a stock selling ex-dividend does not receive the recently declared dividend. Every dividend is payable on a fixed date to all shareholders recorded on the books of the company as of a previous date of record. For example, a dividend may be declared as payable to holders of record on the books of the company on a given Friday. Since five business days are allowed for delivery of stock in a "regular way" transaction on the stock exchange, the exchange would declare the stock "ex-dividend" as of the opening of the market on the preceding Monday. That means anyone who bought it on and after Monday would not be entitled to that dividend. When stocks go ex-dividend, the stock tables include the symbol "x" following the name.

EX-RIGHTS · Without the rights. Corporations raising additional money may do so by offering their stockholders the right to subscribe to new or additional stock, usually at a discount from the prevailing market price. The buyer of a stock selling ex-rights is not entitled to the rights.

EXTRA · The short-form of "extra dividend." A dividend in the form of stock or cash in addition to the regular or usual dividend the company has been paying.

FACE VALUE · The value of a bond that appears on the face of the bond, unless the value is otherwise specified by the issuing company. Face value is ordinarily the amount the issuing company promises to pay at maturity. Face value is not an indication of market value. Sometimes referred to as par value.

FLOOR · The huge trading area where stocks and bonds are bought and sold.

FLOOR BROKER · A member of the stock exchange who executes orders on the floor of the exchange to buy or sell any listed securities.

GILT-EDGED · High-grade bond issued by a company that has demonstrated its ability to earn a comfortable profit over a period of years and pay its bondholders their interest without interruption.

GOOD DELIVERY · Certain basic qualifications must be met before a security sold on the exchange may be delivered. The security must be in proper form to comply with the contract of sale and to transfer title to the purchaser.

GOOD 'TIL CANCELLED ORDER (GTC) OR OPEN ORDER · An order to buy or sell that remains in effect until it is either executed or cancelled.

GOVERNMENT BONDS · Obligations of the U.S. government, regarded as the highest grade issues in existence.

GROWTH STOCK · Stock of a company with a record of growth in earnings at a relatively rapid rate.

HOLDING COMPANY · A corporation that owns the securities of another, in most cases with voting control.

INDENTURE · A written agreement under which bonds and debentures are issued, setting forth maturity date, interest rate, and other terms.

INSTITUTION · An organization holding substantial investing assets, often for others. Includes banks, insurance companies, investment companies, and pension funds.

INTEREST · Payments a borrower pays a lender for the use of his money. A corporation pays interest on its bonds to its bondholders.

INVESTMENT · The use of money for the purpose of making more money, to gain income or increase capital or both.

INVESTMENT BANKER · Also known as an underwriter. He is the middleman between the corporation issuing new securities and the public. The usual practice is for one or more investment bankers to buy outright from a corporation a new issue of stocks or bonds. The group forms a syndicate to sell the securities to individuals and institutions. Investment bankers also distribute very large blocks of stocks or bonds (perhaps held by an estate).

INVESTMENT COMPANY · A company or trust that uses its capital to invest in other companies. There are two principal types: the closed-end and the open-end, or mutual fund. Shares in closed-end investment companies are readily transferable in the open market and are bought and sold like other shares. Capitalization of these companies remains the same unless action is taken to change, which is seldom. Open-end funds sell their own new shares to investors, stand ready to buy back their old shares, and are not listed. Open-end funds are so called because their capitalization is not fixed; they issue more shares as people want them.

INVESTMENT COUNSEL · One whose principal business consists of acting as investment adviser, and a substantial part of his business consists of rendering investment supervisory services.

INVESTOR · An individual whose principal concerns in the purchase of a security are regular dividend income, safety of the original investment and, if possible, capital appreciation.

ISSUE · Any of a company's securities, or the act of distributing such securities.

LEGAL LIST · A list of investments selected by various states in which certain institutions and fiduciaries, such as insurance companies and banks, may invest. Legal lists are often restricted to high-quality securities meeting certain specifications.

LEVERAGE · The effect on the per-share earnings of the common stock of a company when large sums must be paid for bond interest or preferred stock dividends, or both, before the common stock is entitled to share in earnings. Leverage may be advantageous for the common when earnings are good but may work against the common stock when earnings decline.

LIABILITIES · All the claims against a corporation. Liabilities include accounts and wages and salaries payable, dividends declared payable, accrued taxes payable, fixed or long-term liabilities such as mortgage bonds, debentures, and bank loans.

LIEN · A claim against property that has been pledged or mortgaged to secure the performance of an obligation. A bond may be secured by a lien against specified property of a company.

LIMITED ORDER · An order to buy or sell a stated amount of a security at a specified price, or at a better price.

LIQUIDATION · The process of converting securities or other property into cash. The dissolution of a company, with cash remaining after sale of its assets and payment of all indebtedness being distributed to the shareholders.

LIQUIDITY · The ability of the market in a particular security to absorb a reasonable amount of buying or selling at reasonable price changes. Liquidity is one of the most important characteristics of a good market.

LISTED STOCK · The stock of a company that is traded on a securities exchange.

LOCKED IN · An investor is said to be locked in when he has a profit on a security he owns, but does not sell because his profit would immediately become subject to the capital gains tax.

MANAGEMENT · The Board of Directors, elected by the stockholders, and the officers of the corporation, appointed by the Board of Directors.

MANIPULATION · An illegal operation. Buying or selling a security for the purpose of creating false or misleading appearance of active trading or for the purpose of raising or depressing the price to induce purchase or sale by others.

MARGIN · The amount paid by the customer when he uses his broker's credit to buy a security.

MARGIN CALL · A demand upon a customer to put up money or securities with the broker. The call is made when a purchase is made; also if a customer's equity in a margin account declines below a minimum standard set by the exchange or by the firm.

MARKET ORDER · An order to buy or sell a stated amount of a security at the most advantageous price obtainable.

MARKET PRICE · In the case of a security, market price is usually considered the last reported price at which the stock or bond sold.

MATURITY · The date on which a loan or a bond or a debenture comes due and is to be paid off.

MEMBER FIRM · A securities brokerage firm organized as a partnership or corporation and owning at least one seat on the exchange.

MORTGAGE BOND · A bond secured by a mortgage on a property. The value of the property may or may not equal the value of the so-called mortgage bonds issued against it.

MUNICIPAL BOND · A bond issued by a state or a political subdivision, such as county, city, town, or village. The term also designates bonds issued by state agencies and authorities. In general, interest paid on municipal bonds is exempt from federal income taxes and from state and local income taxes within the state of issue.

NASD · The National Association of Securities Dealers, Inc. An association of brokers and dealers in the over-the-counter securities business. The Association has the power to expel members who have been declared guilty of unethical practices. NASD is dedicated to, among other objectives, "adopt, administer and enforce rules of fair practice and rules to prevent fraudulent and manipulative acts and practices, and in general to promote just and equitable principles of trade for the protection of investors."

NASDAQ · An automated information network that provides brokers and dealers with price quotations on securities traded over the counter. NASDAQ is an acronym for National Association of Securities Dealers Automated Quotations.

NEGOTIABLE · Refers to a security, title to which is transferable by delivery.

NET ASSET VALUE · A term usually used in connection with investment companies, meaning net asset value per share. It is common practice for an investment company to compute its assets daily by totaling the market value of all securities owned. All liabilities are deducted, and the balance divided by the number of shares outstanding. The resulting figure is the net asset value per share.

NET CHANGE · The change in the price of a security from the closing price on one day to the closing price on the following day on which the stock is traded. The net change is ordinarily the last figure on the stock price list. The mark $+2\frac{1}{8}$ means up $2.125 a share from the last sale on the previous day the stock traded.

NEW ISSUE · A stock or bond sold by a corporation for the first time. Proceeds may be issued to retire outstanding securities of the company, for new plant or equipment, or for additional working capital.

NONCUMULATIVE · A preferred stock on which unpaid dividends do not accrue. Omitted dividends are, as a rule, gone forever.

NYSE COMMON STOCK INDEX · A composite index covering price movements of all common stocks listed on the "Big Board." It is based on the close of the market December 31, 1965, as 50.00 and is weighted according to the number of shares listed for each issue. The index is computed continuously and printed on the ticker tape each half hour. Point changes in the index are converted to dollars and cents so as to provide a meaningful measure of changes in the average price of listed stocks.

ODD LOT · An amount of stock less than the established 100-share unit or 10-share unit of trading: from 1 to 99 shares for the great majority of issues, 1 to 9 for so-called inactive stocks. Odd-lot prices are geared to the auction market. On an odd-lot market order, the odd-lot dealer's price is based on the first round-lot transaction that occurs on the floor following receipt at the trading post of the odd-lot order. The differential between the odd-lot price and the "effective" round-lot price is 12½ cents a share. For example: You decide to buy 20 shares of ABC common at the market. Your order is transmitted by your commission broker to the representative of an odd-lot dealer at the post where ABC is traded. A few minutes later there is a 100-share transaction in ABC at $10 a share. The odd-lot price at which your order is immediately filled by the odd-lot dealer is $10.125 a share. If you had sold 20 shares of ABC, you would have received $9.875 a share.

OFFER · The price at which a person is ready to sell. Opposed to bid, the price at which one is ready to buy.

OPTION · A right to buy or sell specific securities or properties at a specified price within a specified time.

OVERBOUGHT · An opinion as to price levels. May refer to a security that has had a sharp rise or to the market as a whole after a period of vigorous buying which, it may be argued, has left prices "too high".

OVERSOLD · An opinion, the reverse of overbought. A single security or a market that, it is believed, has declined to an unreasonable level.

OVER-THE-COUNTER · A market for securities made up of securities dealers who may or may not be members of a securities exchange. Over-the-counter is mainly a market made over the telephone. Thousands of companies have insufficient shares outstanding, stockholders, or earnings to warrant application for listing on an exchange. Securities of these companies are traded in the over-the-counter market between dealers who act either as principals or as brokers for customers.

PAPER PROFIT · An unrealized profit on a security still held. Paper profits become realized profits only when the security is sold.

PAR · In the case of a common share, par means a dollar amount assigned to the share by the company's charter. Par value may also be used to compute the dollar amount of the common shares on the balance sheet. Par value has little significance so far as market value of common stock is concerned.

PENNY STOCKS · Low-priced issues, often highly speculative, selling at less than $1 a share. Frequently used as a term of disparagement, although a few penny stocks have developed into investment-caliber issues.

POINT · In the case of shares of stock, a point means $1. If ABC shares rise 3 points, each share has risen $3. In the case of bonds, a point means $10, since a bond is quoted as a percentage of $1,000. A bond that rises three points gains 3 percent of $1,000, or $30 in value. An advance from 87 to 90 would mean an advance in dollar value from $870 to $900 for each $1,000 bond. In the case of market averages, the word point means merely that and no more. If, for example, the Dow-Jones Industrial Average rises from 870.25 to 871.25, it has risen a point. A point in this average, however, is not equivalent to $1.

PORTFOLIO · Holdings of securities by an individual or institution. A portfolio may contain bonds, preferred stocks, and common stocks of various types of enterprises.

PREFERRED STOCK · A class of stock with a claim on the company's earnings before payment may be made on the common stock and usually entitled to priority over common stock if company liquidates. Usually entitled to dividends at a specified rate, when declared by the board of directors and before payment of a dividend on the common stock, depending upon the terms of the issue.

PREMIUM · The amount by which a preferred stock or bond may sell above its par value. In the case of a new issue of bonds or stocks, premium is the amount the market price rises over the original selling price.

PRICE–EARNINGS RATIO · The price of a share of stock divided by earnings per share for a 12-month period. For example, a stock selling for $100 a share and earning $5 a share is said to be selling at a price–earnings ratio of 20 to 1.

PRIMARY DISTRIBUTION · Also called primary offering. The original sale of a company's securities.

PRINCIPAL · The person for whom a broker executes an order, or a dealer buying or selling for his own account. The term "principal" may also refer to a person's capital or to the face amount of a bond.

PROFIT-TAKING · Selling stock that has appreciated in value since purchase to realize the profit that has been made possible. The term is often used to explain a downturn in the market following a period of rising prices.

PROXY · Written authorization given by a shareholder to someone else to represent him and vote his shares at a shareholders' meeting.

PROXY STATEMENT · Information required by the SEC to be given stockholders as a prerequisite to solicitation of proxies for a security subject to the requirements of Securities Exchange Act.

PRUDENT MAN RULE · An investment standard. In some states, the law requires that a fiduciary, such as a trustee, may invest the fund's money only in a list of securities designated by the state—the so-called legal list. In other states, the trustee may invest in a security if it is one that a prudent man of discretion and intelligence, who is seeking a reasonable income and preservation of capital, would buy.

QUOTATION · Often shortened to "quote." The highest bid to buy and the lowest offer to sell a security in a given market at a given time. If you ask your broker for a "quote" on a stock, he may come back with something like "45¼ to 45½". This means that $45.25 is the highest price any buyer wanted to pay at the time the quote was given on the floor of the exchange and that $45.50 was the lowest price any seller would take at the same time.

RALLY · A brisk rise following a decline in the general price level of the market, or in an individual stock.

RECORD DATE · The date on which you must be registered as a shareholder on the stock book of a company to receive a declared dividend or, among other things, to vote on company affairs.

REDEMPTION PRICE · The price at which a bond may be redeemed before maturity, at the option of the issuing company. Redemption value also applies to the price the company must pay to call in certain types of preferred stock.

REIT · Real estate investment trust, an organization similar to an investment company in some respects but concentrating its holdings in real estate investments. The yield is generally liberal since REITs are required to distribute as much as 90 percent of their income.

REGISTERED BOND · A bond that is registered on the books of the issuing company in the name of the owner. It can be transferred only when endorsed by the registered owner.

REGISTERED REPRESENTATIVE · A registered representative is a full-time employee who has met the requirements of an exchange as to background and knowledge of the securities business. Also known as an account executive or customer's broker.

REGISTRAR · Usually a trust company or bank charged with the responsibility of preventing the issuance of more stock than authorized by a company.

REGISTRATION · Before a public offering may be made of new securities by a company, or of outstanding securities by controlling stockholders—through the mails or in interstate commerce—the securities must be registered under the Securities Act of 1933. Registration statement is filed with the SEC by the issuer. It must disclose pertinent information relating to the company's operations, securities, management, and purpose of the public offering. On security offerings involving less than $300,000, less information is required.

Before a security may be admitted to dealings on a national securities exchange, it must be registered under the Securities Exchange Act of 1934. The application for registration must be filed with the exchange and the SEC by the company issuing the securities. It must disclose pertinent information relating to the company's operations, securities and management.

REGULATION T · The federal regulation governing the amount of credit that may be advanced by brokers and dealers to customers for the purchase of securities.

REGULATION U · The federal regulation governing the amount of credit that may be advanced by a bank to its customers for the purchase of listed stocks.

RIGHTS · When a company wants to raise more funds by issuing additional securities, it may give its stockholders the opportunity, ahead of others, to buy the new securities in proportion to the number of shares each owns. The piece of paper evidencing this privilege is called a right. Because the additional stock is usually offered to stockholders below the current market price, rights ordinarily have a market value of their own and are actively traded. In most cases they must be exercised within a relatively short period. Failure to exercise or sell rights may result in actual loss to the holder.

ROUND LOT · A unit of trading or a multiple thereof. On most exchanges the unit of trading is generally 100 shares in stocks and $1,000 par value in the case of bonds. In some inactive stocks, the unit of trading is 10 shares.

SEAT · A traditional figure-of-speech for a membership on an exchange. Price and admission requirements vary.

SEC · Securities and Exchange Commission, established by Congress to help protect investors. The SEC administers the Securities Act of 1933, the Securities Exchange Act of 1934, the Trust Indenture Act, the Investment Company Act, the Investment Advisers Act, and the Public Utility Holding Company Act.

SECONDARY DISTRIBUTION · Also known as a secondary offering. The redistribution of a block of stock some time after it has been sold by the issuing company. The sale is handled off the exchange by a securities firm or group of firms, and the shares are usually offered at a fixed price that is related to the current market price of the stock. Usually the block is a large one, such as might be involved in the settlement of an estate. The security may be listed or unlisted.

SINKING FUND · Money regularly set aside by a company to redeem its bonds, debentures, or preferred stock from time to time as specified in the indenture or charter.

SPECIAL OFFERING · Occasionally a large block of stock becomes available for sale that, due to its size and the market in that particular issue, calls for special handling. A notice is printed on the ticker tape announcing that the stock will be offered for sale on the floor of the exchange at a fixed price. Member firms may buy this stock for customers directly from the seller's broker during trading hours. The price is usually based on the last transaction in the regular auction market. If there are more buyers than stock, allotments are made. Only the seller pays a commission on a special offering.

SPECIALIST · A member of an exchange who has two functions: First, to maintain an orderly market, insofar as reasonably practicable, in the stocks in which he is registered as a specialist. The exchange expects the specialist to buy or sell for his own account, to a reasonable degree, when there is a temporary disparity between supply and demand. The specialist also acts as a broker's broker. When a commission broker on the exchange floor receives a limit order, say, to buy at $50 a stock then selling at $60, he cannot wait at the post where the stock is traded to see if the price reaches the specified level. So he leaves the order with the specialist who will try to execute it in the market if and when the stock declines to the specified price. At all times the specialist must put his customers' interests above his own.

SPECULATOR · One who is willing to assume a relatively large risk in the hope of gain. His principal concern is to increase his capital rather than his dividend income. The speculator may buy and sell the same day or speculate in an enterprise he does not expect to be profitable for years.

SPLIT · The division of the outstanding shares of a corporation into a larger number of shares. A 3-for-1 split by a company with 1 million shares outstanding results in 3 million shares outstanding. Each holder of 100 shares before the 3-to-1 split would have 300 shares, although his proportionate equity in the company would remain the same; 100 parts of 1 million are the equivalent of 300 parts of 3 million.

STOCK DIVIDEND · A dividend paid in securities rather than cash. The dividend may be additional shares of the issuing company or shares of another company (usually a subsidiary) held by the company.

STOCKHOLDER OF RECORD · A stockholder whose name is registered on the books of the issuing corporation.

STOP ORDER · An order to buy at a price above or to sell below the current market. Stop buy orders are generally used to limit loss or protect unrealized profits on a short sale. Stop sell orders are generally used to protect unrealized profits or limit loss on a holding.

STREET NAME · Securities held in the name of a broker instead of his customer's name are said to be carried in a "street name." This occurs when the securities have been bought on margin or when the customer wishes the security to be held by the broker.

TIPS · Supposedly "inside" information on corporation affairs.

TRADER · One who buys and sells for his own account for short-term profit.

TRANSFER · This term may refer to two different operations. For one, the delivery of a stock certificate from the seller's broker to the buyer's broker and legal change of ownership, normally accomplished within a few days. For another, to record the change of ownership on the books of the corporation by the transfer agent. When the purchaser's name is recorded on the books of the company, dividends, notices of meetings, proxies, financial reports, and all pertinent literature sent by the issuer to its securities holders are mailed direct to the new owner.

TRANSFER AGENT · A transfer agent keeps a record of the name of each registered shareowner, his or her address, and the number of shares owned, and sees that certificates presented to his office for transfer are properly cancelled and new certificates issued in the name of the transferee.

TREASURY STOCK · Stock issued by a company but later reacquired. It may be held in the company's treasury indefinitely, reissued to the public, or retired. Treasury stock receives no dividends and has no vote while held by the company.

UNLISTED · A security not listed on a stock exchange.

VOTING RIGHT · The stockholder's right to vote his stock in the affairs of his company. Most common shares have one vote each. Preferred stock usually has the right to vote when preferred dividends are in default for a specified period. The right to vote may be delegated by the stockholder to another person.

WARRANT · A certificate giving the holder the right to purchase securities at a stipulated price within a specified time limit or perpetually. Sometimes a warrant is offered with securities as an inducement to buy.

WHEN ISSUED · A short form of "when, as, and if issued." The term indicates a conditional transaction in a security authorized for issuance but not as yet actually issued. All "when issued" transactions are on an "if" basis, to be settled if and when the actual security is issued and the exchange or National Association of Securities Dealers rules the transactions are to be settled.

WORKING CONTROL · Theoretically ownership of 51 percent of a company's voting stock is necessary to exercise control. In practice—and this is particularly true in the case of a large corporation—effective control sometimes can be exerted through ownership, individually or by a group acting in concert, of less than 50 percent.

YIELD · Also known as return. The dividends or interest paid by a company expressed as a percentage of the current price. A stock with a current market value of $20 a share that has paid $1 in dividends in the preceding 12 months is said to return 5 percent ($1.00/$20.00). The current return on a bond is figured the same way.

DIVIDEND RECORD

Company _____

Date Dividend Paid	Number of Shares	Rate per Share	Total Amount of Dividend

348

STOCKS

Company _____

Date Bought	No. of Shares	Price Per Share	Total Cost	Date Sold	No. of Shares	Price Per Share	Total Net Proceeds

Index